Praise for Jeffrey Greene and *French Spirits*

"An affectionate memoir."   —*Boston Globe*

"If you have ever dreamed of owning and restoring a country home in France (and who has not?), Jeffrey Greene's charming and hilarious book will surely convince you to think again, while impressing you with his courage, patience, optimism, and total love of France and the French, even at their most exasperating!"
—Michael Korda

"Extremely well written. . . . Lyrical. . . . Recommended for all arm-chair travelers, especially Francophiles."   —*Library Journal*

"An engaging account."   —*France* magazine

"*French Spirits* reads like an eloquently recalled dream in which the lives and events of both the distant past and the immediate present constantly speak to one another, cross paths, inhabit the same space. A strangely beautiful, haunting work."   —Charles Siebert, author of *Wickerby: An Urban Pastoral* and *Angus*

"Pleasing. . . . Greene has real respect and empathy for the people he describes, and he doesn't use them as merely amusing background, which makes his book refreshingly different from some other recent American-abroad memoirs."   —*Publishers Weekly*

"Whether Greene and his wife are discovering their first legless lizard, planning a wedding on a construction site, buying a donkey, resurrecting a stone angel, or sorrowing over a dying fruit tree, *French Spirits* is a love story that is gentle, witty, affectionate—and in the hands of a poet who understands that the transitory nature of happiness holds transformative power in any language, as graceful as it is ghost-haunted."   —Laura Hendrie, prize-winning author of *Remember Me* and *Stygo*

© 2000 by Mary Weiss

About the Author

JEFFREY GREENE received his MFA from the University of Iowa and his Ph.D. from the University of Houston. He is the author of *To the Left of the Worshiper* and *American Spirituals*, which won the 1998 Samuel French Morse Prize. He was also the winner of the Randall Jarrell Prize and the Discovery/The Nation Award. His work has appeared in *The New Yorker, The Nation,* and many other journals and anthologies. He lives in Paris.

Perennial

An Imprint of HarperCollins*Publishers*

French Spirits

A House, a Village, and a Love Affair in Burgundy

JEFFREY GREENE

Grateful acknowledgment is made to the following publishers for permission to
reprint previously published material:

Excerpt from *My Mother's House and Sido* by Colette, translated by Una Vincenzo Troubridge
and Enid McLeod. Translation copyright © 1953 by Farrar, Straus & Young,
translation copyright renewed 1981 by Farrar, Straus and Giroux, LLC.
Excerpt from *La Maison de Claudine* by Colette copyright © Librairie Hachette, 1960.
Excerpt from "The Mower" from *Collected Poems* by Philip Larkin.
Copyright © 1988, 1989 by the Estate of Philip Larkin.
Excerpt from *Memoirs of Hadrian* by Marguerite Yourcenar, translated by Grace Frick.
Copyright © 1954, renewed 1982 by Marguerite Yourcenar.
Excerpt from *Madame Bovary* by Gustave Flaubert, translated by Gerard Hopkins. Copyright
© 1999 by Oxford University Press (Oxford World's Classics).
Excerpt from "Burnt Norton" in *Four Quartets* by T. S. Eliot: in the United States:
copyright © 1936 by Harcourt, Inc., and renewed 1964 by T. S. Eliot, reprinted by
permission of Harcourt, Brace & World, Inc.; in the U.K.: copyright © 1936 and
renewed 1964 by T. S. Eliot, reprinted by permission of Faber and Faber Ltd.

For specific historical material about Rogny-les-Sept-Écluses and the
presbytery, I relied on *Rogny & Saint-Eusoge: Depuis les Origines jusqu'à Nos Jours*
(Auxerre: Imprimerie de la Constitution, 1897), by Gaston Gauthier.

A hardcover edition of this book was published in 2002 by William Morrow,
an imprint of HarperCollins Publishers.

HarperCollins books may be purchased for educational, business, or
sales promotional use. For information please write: Special Markets Department,
HarperCollins Publishers Inc., 10 East 53rd Street, New York, NY 10022.

First Perennial edition published 2003.

Designed by Gretchen Achilles

The Library of Congress has catalogued the hardcover edition as follows:
Greene, Jeffrey.
    French spirits / Jeffrey Greene.
      p. cm.
    ISBN 0-06-018820-0
    1. Burgundy (France)—Social life and customs—20th century.
2. Country life—France—Burgundy. 3. Greene, Jeffrey, 1952—Homes
and haunts—France—Burgundy. I. Title.
DC611.B7742 G74 2002
944'.41083'092—dc21   2001031695

ISBN 0-06-093410-7 (pbk.)

03 04 05 06 07 ❖/RRD 10 9 8 7 6 5 4 3 2 1

For Mary,

and for Susan Prospere

In memory of André Krakowska (1936–1999)

$\mathcal{T}$he word "presbytery" had chanced that year to drop into my sensitive ears and had wrought havoc.

"It's undoubtedly the most cheerful presbytery that I know of . . ." someone had said in my hearing.

Far from me the idea of asking one of my relations: "What kind of a thing is a presbytery?" I had absorbed the mysterious word with its harsh and spiky beginning and the brisk trot of its final syllables. Enriched by a secret and a doubt, I slept on the word and bore it off to my wall. "Presbytery!" I would shout over the roof of the hen-house and Miton's garden, towards the perpetually misty horizon of Moutiers. From the summit of my wall, the word rang out as a malediction: "Begone! You are all presbyteries!" I shouted to invisible outlaws.

Later on the word lost some of its venom and I began to suspect that "presbytery" might very possibly be the scientific term for a certain little yellow-and-black striped snail. A chance remark was to be my undoing, in one of those moments wherein a child, however solemn or fanciful she may be, fleetingly resembles the picture made of her by grown-up people.

"Mother! Look what a lovely little presbytery I've found."

COLETTE

Contents

Contents

Acknowledgments

My deepest thanks to Carolyn Marino at HarperCollins for editing this book and seeing it through the many steps to publication. Thanks also to Andrée Abecassis and Lettie Lee at the Ann Elmo Literary Agency for their belief in my work and for their wisdom and good advice.

I am very grateful to Richard Farrell and Claudine Phillips for their editorial help and their insights into French culture. I thank Véronique Arnaud for her valuable research into the former inhabitants of the presbytery. I am deeply indebted to the following friends for years of support and their help with this book: Charles Siebert, Rebecca Brian, Frédéric Plan, Lena and Jacques Jami, and Jean-Louis and Ariane Roussat. Much love and thanks to my mother, Gretchen Van Blaricom, who has a large role in these pages. Finally, I am grateful to the University of New Haven for a research grant supporting my work.

A Note Concerning Names

The swiftness of change is a major part of this story, and since I started writing the book five years ago, we have lost friends, family, and neighbors, people we can't replace. They are people who have moved away, died, or suffered illnesses. For the sake of privacy, I've changed the names of people who are very ill or who have disappeared. I've also changed the names of people who are incidental to the story. To all, thank you for contributing to our good life in Rogny-les-Sept-Écluses and to this book.

French Spirits

Place de l'Église

*W*hen the earth's axis tilts away from the sun and we slide down into the narrow pit of gray winter months, Madame Savin moves from Châtillon-Coligny to Rogny and parks her gray Renault 21 in front of our presbytery on the place de l'Église. She opens the hood and puts a blanket and a layer of cardboard over the engine. Then she covers the car in a gray tarp, anchoring the edges with bricks and boards that she stores in a niche along the mossy side of the church. She carefully wedges stones under the tires, just in case her Renault decides, without warning, to roll stealthily off on its own. She has become the village's high priestess of precaution.

After she takes off the tarp and uncovers the engine in the 8:00 A.M. semidark, then folds the tarp away behind a neat pile of bricks, boards, and stones, she turns on the ignition and for ten minutes punches the accelerator down to the floorboard, filling the place de l'Église with a deafening engine roar. Madame Savin, late fifties, gray as the winter itself, is determined to warm the engine with rage, sending Coco, our closest neighbor, out of his two-room house, shaking his head and shouting in defense of the *pauvre voiture*. Finally, she pulls away from the stone curb that rings a young chestnut tree, a replacement for the huge Liberty Tree whose roots once networked through the foundations of the church and every home on the *place*. It was cut down to save our section of the village, called the Haut-Bourg, the high town, from slow underground destruction by a single tree.

Madame Savin visits the cemetery several times a day. Her second husband is buried there with three bullets in his heart. Usually she commutes the ten kilometers from nearby Châtillon-Coligny, but she winters in Rogny because she's afraid the snow might keep her from the cemetery, and the cemetery is just three-tenths of a kilometer to the east of the place de l'Église. You can practically see it from our kitchen window down the rue du Haut-Bois. The cemetery is where the town ends and the fields begin, furrowed into great clods of stiff winter mud, which in the summer nurtures rape, corn, wheat, oats, soybeans, and sunflowers. Beyond are pastures with cement-colored cows we call ghosts, and there are stands of managed trees and woods that on Sundays in autumn are scoured by platoons of hunters.

The cemetery has a tall concrete perimeter. The monuments inside are mostly drab granite boxes rising out of the gravel, no grass, just a mixture of artificial and real flowers and dozens of little funeral plaques that look like polished bookends, inscribed with names and appropriate sentiments—"Memories," "Regrets," and "Sorrows." The largest chained-off area is occupied by the *famille* d'Harmelle, one of France's noble families. The Harmelles still own most of the property in the area and at one time owned our presbytery by virtue of paying the taxes on it for thirty years. Since the Harmelles are relatively recent landowners here, the markers list only the titles of their turn-of-the-century generations—a world of marquises, barons, and princesses. The Harmelles also contributed more than their share of sons, as artillery and cavalry lieutenants, to the abyss of the Great War. Down the first row, in the southwestern corner, Madame Savin, when she isn't haunting the Haut-Bourg, haunts her husband, beating her chest or praying for him, now ensconced in the neutral stratum of Purgatory.

The story is that her husband, Claude, developed cancer and one day, three years ago, shot himself three times in the heart. He shot himself out in the courtyard so as not to bloody the house. One has to wonder how a sixty-year-old man could shoot himself three times in the heart. The whole thing must have gone horribly wrong, as so often suicides do. Still, he managed to keep pulling the trigger. It's hardly surprising that Madame Savin sees treachery everywhere: in her car, in her home, and in the sky over her head. When in the deep of winter we get a day in the seventies, the warmth of the sun teasing the garden, Madame Savin will explain that a great wind is coming, and she carefully puts extra boards on her car.

There are no real impediments to Madame Savin's visits to her husband's grave, even if she didn't winter here. After all, it's not as if the ten kilometers between Châtillon-Coligny and Rogny wind through a mountain pass. The road follows the Loing River Valley, a mostly gentle slope with the river and the Briare Canal on one side and copses and rolling fields on the other. Contrary to what Madame Savin believes, it almost never snows in Rogny. But sometimes a deep freezing fog descends, to frost everything with white breath. The effect is that the air fills with parts of walls and village corners. Rime-covered branches reach out of nowhere; spots of fields appear like tunnel vision. The rest slips in and out of consciousness. At worst, the air becomes meat-locker cold, and Rogny seems as dead as Madame Savin's husband.

One might imagine winter depressing here, and I suppose it is for many. But then I see the Burgundy that I pictured before I really knew anything about it: the quiet, smoky landscape; wild pigs and deer edging out of the gloom; old châteaux, half-obscured by trees, apparitions of a former world peering into this one. In winter, epochs, and people, are suspended and mixed.

In another age, Madame Savin's husband would have been buried in the churchyard, the cemetery for the ancient town. From her own house, in a row of small ones that bank around the south side of the church, she could have gazed the whole day on her Claude's grave. If she visited him, she would walk out on a large slope of grass encircled by thick plane trees, limbs amputated, in early February, back to their stubby shoulders. And if she paused for a moment in her prayers among the panels of shadows, she could turn and look over the steep slope at the town below, barges on the canal stacked with timber or filled with grain. In the nineteenth century, barges rose on a massive stone staircase of seven locks and disappeared over the horizon formed by the far slope of the valley on their way to the Loire River, or they appeared out of the sky and descended, then passed below the slope toward the Seine and Paris.

A historic engineering feat ordered by Henry IV, the construction of the locks began in 1604. Originally named Canal de Loire-en-Seine, the Briare Canal was the first major canal in Europe and the first in the world to link two major rivers. A century before it was built, ancient forges, fired by charcoal, produced metalwork in the valley, and a century earlier still, the wheels of large mills already turned in the steady flow of the Loing River. The feudal châteaux of Cottard, La Broutière, or La Brénellerie, alive with the comings and goings of *chevaliers* and esquires, stood at the heart of their fiefdoms.

In the eleventh century, the church itself was constructed and christened Saint-Martin-de-Rogny, the name later changed to Saint-Loup. Even nearly a millennium ago it must have looked as if a six-year-old had designed it—blocky square steeple, oversized nave, and stubby choir. Before the church, there was a ninth-century chapel and ancient fortifications; before those, Roman defenses, and back and back.

But in 1828, the Council of Rogny decreed that the old cemetery was too close for the comfort, or welfare, of the inhabitants of the place de l'Église, and a field outside town was designated as a new cemetery. The plan was to move the cemetery after a five-year waiting period, but the council feared that the newly buried would give off "exhalations pernicious to the health of the inhabitants"; therefore, the graves would have to be opened immediately and the dead evicted from the *place,* left on their own in the fields beyond the town wall. It's not clear where the dead are now. Only graves from late in the nineteenth century are marked.

It would be unfair to portray Madame Savin as simply the widow of the *place,* a caricature or "case," fussing on a separate plane informed only by losses, prayers, and damaging winds. In fact, Madame Savin is very much a part of the network on the *place,* tethered as if by the roots of the old Liberty Tree, our twofold symbol of connectedness and destruction.

When her front left tire went flat, Monsieur Marteau, who lives on the opposite side of the *place,* helped her change it. I'd often imagined letting the air out of her tires myself to give us a quiet morning, just one of my cruel musings.

My wife, Mary, just sleeps through it all. On the weekends, she's beat. Besides running a research lab, she's been yoked with an obligatory three-year stint as chairman of her department. "All headaches and no clout," she complains.

Madame Savin could drive through the wall; Mary wasn't going to be roused. But I get up early to write, and it takes me a half hour to recover any artistic sensibilities after the engine roar. The window of my study looks out on Madame Savin's Renault hiding under the tarp by the chestnut tree. After Monsieur Marteau put on a spare and jacked the car down, he warned Madame Savin, *"C'est la dernière fois que je vous aide. C'est ridicule, les briques, les pierres, les planches. De la merde partout!"* He swore he'd never help her again if she covered her car on the *place* or left her bricks, stones, and boards piled up against the church. I rejoiced, thinking the problem solved; I should have known better. As soon as Monsieur Marteau left to visit relatives, the car reappeared, a lump under its tarp.

Madame Savin makes soup for Coco and, at the edge of evening light, around 4:30 in the afternoon, brings it across the *place* and bangs on his door. She also stops and talks to the Bougés, whose property borders ours to the north. They share the town news and opinions about the weather, which for Madame Savin means preparing for the coming storm or great wind. Often she slips into Ariane and Jean-Louis's garden and weeps out her many complaints against life, which drives Ariane to tears of desperation, since she also has Monsieur Marteau's crazy wife ambushing her in her own kitchen and Madame Briançon, in the next house down, making cakes and sending herself regularly into diabetic shock. Madame Savin's weeping in the yard is more, Ariane thinks, than she should have to bear. *"C'est in-sup-por-table!"* Every day it is like this. Every day! Madame Marteau arrives from another planet. *Vous voyez?* And then Madame Savin, *mon Dieu, la pauvre femme*, is weeping at the bird feeder. How do I ask her to leave?"

Then, of course, comes the freak winter storm that Madame Savin has been predicting all along, with blasts of wind in the night, crackling of hail at the windows. Lightning rips out of the sky and charges through the houses of the *place*, burning out the televisions in each one.

The next day, after the Renault has been thoroughly tortured and Madame Savin has gone off to see what's left of her husband's grave, our neighbors share news of downed trees that had stood so reliably from the time of their great-grandparents. They count snapped lines, broken roof tiles, and torn-off shutters. During the last big storm, one of our trees fell into Monsieur Bougé's sheep pasture. Being neighbors, we share such trespasses. One spring a couple of his sheep had found a hole in his fence and walked through our orchard, then up the stone staircase past the dovecote, to munch contentedly, side by side, on Mary's tree roses. So our tree crashed into his pasture to settle accounts for the time being. After Monsieur Bougé saw me feebly trying to cut the tree up by hand, he brought his chain saw, with a can of gas and chain oil, and together we went to work, amid the sputter, wail, and sawdust. After we finished by flinging the logs back over the fence, we walked up to his woodshed and talked.

Monsieur Bougé is a short, square man in his seventies, but he looks sixty. Like many country Frenchmen, he is supernaturally strong. When you shake his hand, you feel as if you are holding a facsimile of his body—hard and round, so stubby you can hardly get your hand to fit it. He is reserved, though not unfriendly, and is quite serious about proprieties—there's always the right way to do things and, therefore, much to criticize, a pastime irresistible for the French. One propriety he shares with all his neighbors is wine. He holds up a bottle of wine and says, "After the work, the recompense!" It is ten in the morning.

He had been born in the house that neighbors ours, and now in back he raises sheep and rabbits and in the shed cuts his firewood for the winter. When his mother died, he had the house gutted and insulated, and now he comes every day to work on the grounds and light fires in the fireplace, warming rooms for the comfort of his childhood memories. At the woodshed he picks up a tattered green army coat, partly stiffened into the shape of his body, partly deflated in the straw.

"*Vous voyez ça*. It was Americans who gave me this coat in forty-four. I wore it crossing the German border with the American army." He invited me into his mother's house, where a sideboard and several tables each displayed a bayonet—French, German, American, and probably British. I assumed that this wasn't his mother's choice in decor, but who knows? Bougé was clearly proud to have fought with the Americans in their uniform, which pleases me, since we are the only Americans in the area and it's hard to know where one stands as a foreigner in a region at the center of rural France and with a strong undercurrent of Le Pen's National Front movement. In fact, a Le Pen sticker has been fading for years where it was stuck on a lamppost in front of the presbytery. Most important, we are foreigners inhabiting a French historical monument, a building connected to the struggles of the peasants with the nobility and the clergy.

Every French village has a church, often centuries old, and with it on the church square a presbytery, the official home of the local curé, or priest. Depending on official and personal resources, the priest lived comfortably or on the brink of poverty, growing his own fruits and vegetables or accepting charity from his parishioners. Often church social events were held at presbyteries, sometimes after mass or on holidays. Even at the end of the twentieth century, it remained an important setting in the story of the townspeople's lives, a story which so recently Mary and I, complete outsiders, blundered into. Because of the sharp decline in church attendance and so few young men entering the clergy, there were more presbyteries than curés to inhabit them, so many became private homes or fell into disrepair.

It's hard enough to know what people think of you in any situation, hard indeed for Americans who have moved into a Burgundian village. It's not that Americans are a mystery to the villagers. They watch Americans gun each other down from cars that can talk and helicopters that can think—all the flimsiest television shows. They listen to rap while they dig up floors and pour cement, and they wear American-brand sneakers made in Indonesia. All of the larger towns nearby have American-style malls and business strips. The difference is that Americans themselves rarely live in these villages.

For at least a year, people in the town decided that we were English, no matter what they were told. This is because the English are often seen in Rogny, touring by car, staying in bed-and-breakfast places called *chambres d'hôtes,* or passing through on pleasure barges. Slowly the villagers have accepted the fact that they have two Americans living among them, and they try very hard to think of where we might find other Americans, as if that were part of our goal. In general, it has helped us that Mary has lived in France for twenty-five years and speaks almost flawless French, but the French know that Mary's French is neither village French nor

French French. When they learn that she works at the Pasteur Institute, they are ready to claim that she is more French than American. Of Pasteur they are very proud.

If forced to guess, I'd say we were, and still are, mostly regarded as innocents or eccentrics, certainly damned fools for trying to tackle the reconstruction of the presbytery. Yet, from the very first days that we lived in the presbytery, gifts began to appear on the stone sill of our kitchen window. All were riches from the countryside—pheasants, partridges, a pail full of perch and *poissons-chats,* whole branches laden with bigarreau cherries almost the size of plums. Then leeks would appear and Italian tomatoes that looked like human hearts. Carrots, potatoes, and salad greens, freshly pulled from the earth. Then cooked apples and pears, and on and on. We didn't know whom to thank next. The entire place de l'Église was quietly delivering gifts—Coco, Marteau, Ariane and Jean-Louis, Bougé. Then came cakes from Madame Briançon and Madame Savin. Other gifts came from Monsieur Delapierre and later from the adopted daughters of Madame Bourgeois, Jo and Véronique. Still others came in a folktale fashion—from whom, we don't know.

One winter night, back when the kitchen fireplace supplied our only heating, we received a telephone call. We had installed the phone right away as a precaution—we had to consider the dangers of heavy construction. The call came from Madame Dureuil to thank us for saving the presbytery.

"Monsieur, everyone is saying what good luck. Someone is going to restore our old presbytery!"

She told us how she remembered her confirmation, with the other town girls down on the curé's prayer path, more than half of a century ago, how they wove *couronnes* of wildflowers to wear in their hair for the ceremony and afterward paraded over to the cemetery to leave them on the graves of family members. Over the years all the families had gathered in the orchard after mass for wine, picnics, and games.

This was just the first in a trail of memories, anecdotes, and scraps of information that would bring us to a vision of the building, compellingly alien from our own dream of owning a country house. The presbytery had always suffered from a lack of funds, yet it stood at the center of community life. How could it be left unlived in, uncared for; overrun by spiders, centipedes, mice, swallows, and bats; exposed by great shafts of light coming through gaps in the tile roof? Rainwater, penetrating the floor of the attic, damaged the oak beams, and ceiling plaster fell, blackened with mold, to the ancient redbrick floor tiles.

The last curé, Père Jo, lived in the presbytery fifteen years ago. He is legendary among the inhabitants of the Haut-Bourg and to almost anyone who knows the town of Rogny. He was controversial; both deeply loved and disliked; the tutelary spirit of the homeless, the poor, the village drunks. When Mary and I began the reconstruction of the presbytery, we found a sea of Père Jo's wine bottles in the *cave,* the stables, and the *grenier,* or attic. The village people who strongly disapproved of Père Jo would say diplomatically, *"Il était trop moderne pour moi."* He was too modern, and they would describe him wearing his soccer jersey both at town meetings and in bars. We knew nothing of the life of a country curé, and coming from America, where priests, rabbis, and ministers may be held up as fonts of moral guidance, we were, to say the least, astonished and enraptured by the stories about and the evidence of the last curé's life. Above all, Père Jo was a rarity, a charismatic. He has left an afterglow in the expressions of those who remember him. If you ask anyone on the place de l'Église about him, they shake their heads in bemused disbelief or begin to scold him in retrospect. Père Jo was transferred with the reorganization of the local churches and retired shortly thereafter. The present curé works on a rotating basis, a different village each week, trying to keep the small congregations alive.

Mary and I talked about looking up and meeting Père Jo to find out more about his life and the story of the presbytery itself, but we waited too long. A few years after we moved in, he died. L'Église de Saint-Loup overflowed with friends and parishioners who came to pay a last tribute at his funeral and to attend his burial at the cemetery down the rue du Haut-Bois. Our great chance to speak to the presbytery's last occupant and learn more intimately the building's history had gone.

The Harmelles shut up the presbytery after Père Jo's retirement, and the church fell increasingly into disuse and disrepair. The funeral was one of its few recent functions. Mass is held only once a month, and funerals, baptisms, and weddings are sporadic. Town statistics show there is a ratio of one wedding to every three deaths and one-and-a-half births. Funerals seem to come at the end of winter, like spring cleaning, and the sparse weddings in late spring. Despite these statistics, the population of Rogny has remained roughly the same as it was two hundred years ago: in 1801, there were 860 inhabitants; now there are 740, not including the summer residents. The population reached its highest level—1,595 in 1881, in spite of several cholera epidemics, which took as many as 68 lives in just one two-month period. After the 1880s, the population declined rapidly as railroads replaced canals as an important mode of transporting goods and coal replaced wood for heating in the cities.

As in most towns and villages in France, every building on the place de l'Église is historically *classé*, which means that if you plan to make any changes to the exterior of your building you must submit a dossier carefully documenting them to the *mairie*, the mayor's office. The *mairie* has to recommend your proposed changes before the request is sent to the regional administration for final approval. You must provide photographs, architect's drawings, and written descriptions for adding a dormer or Velux window. You must also pay administration fees. Of course, chances are that, in the end, your request will be denied. In theory, "classing" buildings is a very good way to preserve the architectural integrity and the atmosphere of old villages. However, if neglected roofs and walls come crashing down, who is the administration going to fine? Besides, classing the church and the place de l'Église as historical monuments doesn't protect us from cars buried in bricks, stones, and boards.

In fact, disrepair, neglect, and decay are agents in the natural process of village metamorphosis. Though churches, châteaux, and hovels disappeared, their stones and bricks remained to become locks for the canal, *auberges*, schools, new houses, new châteaux, and even reconstructed presbyteries. In 1818, the Harmelles built a comfortable new château out of the ruins of an earlier one that stood on grounds they acquired. A building may be constructed from the ground up, but parts of it may have stood before.

The metamorphosis may be subtler if the process of disrepair, neglect, and decay has been reversed on a regular basis. If you look at the Église de Saint-Loup, you will see that doorways and windows kept changing places. You will see ghostly outlines, some in stone and some in brick, some arched and some square. Depending on the century, during almost a millennium, parishioners may have entered through different parts of the church, and the light may have fallen on them from different windows as they took Communion or sang their hymns.

The decayed state of the presbytery was part of the natural cycle of Rogny and the place de l'Église. Before the presbytery stood reconstructed in 1756, there was a ruined presbytery near the same site. Materials from it were integrated into the new incarnation. In fact, you cannot dig anywhere on the grounds without uncovering fragments of the past—pieces of brick or pottery, a child's toy, a rusted tool, a spent cartridge. You can't dig a new bed for a garden without hitting the walls of ancient fortifications.

One could extend the point to the Republic itself. Each time the Republic was restored, Rogny planted a Liberty Tree. The first was planted at midday, November 10, 1793. The village people gathered to consecrate the tree by burning the titles of the deposed feudal ranks. In 1848, another tree was planted on the place de l'Église after the abdication of Louis-Philippe to celebrate the third riddance of the Bourbons and royal rule. The tree for the Third Republic stands next to the canal. So it goes.

There's an annual turning point in the process of disrepair, neglect, and decay. It comes in the month of February, when the light comes back. Some days the sun gains as much as four minutes between rising and setting. Wheat and rape begin to sprout. Daffodils and tulips knife their way out of the soil. Even lilacs begin to leaf. February is the month when neighbors have piles of sand delivered in front of their houses. They cart out their orange cement mixers to pour new floors or reface crumbling walls. They fix the gaping cracks called *lézardes,* where in fact lizards hide, or they cut out new windows to brighten gloomy rooms. February is the time for big projects.

One day toward the end of February, Madame Savin vanishes with her Renault. The tarp, the boards, and the stones all disappear. Only two bricks remain against the wall of the church, just under the outline of a door that had been cemented over. Probably the famous widows of Rogny walked through that door. Isabeau de Courtenay was widowed twice, first in 1380 with the death of Guillaume, the first known Sire of Rogny. She remarried, only to be widowed again when her jealous son murdered his stepfather. Jehanne Garrault, widowed in 1566, was accused of false faith by the lord of Franchise in his attempt to seize her estate, the Fief of La Claverie. Anne le Marteau was also twice widowed, first in 1600 and then in 1630. Still she had twelve children baptized in Saint-Loup of Rogny. When Madame Savin returns to Châtillon-Coligny, a spell of widows seems to lift.

On a warm February afternoon, the presbytery appears as we saw it for the first time when we drove up the very steep slope from the low town, the road winding past small houses and tiny pastures. The house lies directly in front of you as you climb the last rise and the place de l'Église opens. The presbytery is long and low, with five tall, shuttered windows facing directly east. Its facade is apparent round stone called silex, with larger blocks of cut stone around the doors and windows. The four chimneys rise over the moss-covered roof. When we pulled into the *place* and stopped the car between the Liberty Tree and the public well, Mary and I knew that we would buy and live in the presbytery. Everything we saw beyond that first moment would only confirm our conviction. At first Mary wouldn't even get out of the car—a premonition, a sense of wonder, a moment of relief.

The Presbytery

*H*ow is it that real estate agents know even before they look at you, as they shout on the phone to a colleague, that you are a waste of their time? They must develop a sixth sense to spot dreamers, like us, who know nothing about owning a house. The agents spend their days taxiing people around a particular region, fumbling with keys and feeling about for light switches, each house a disaster, a trap, a mystery, an answered prayer. They wipe spiderwebs out of their eyes, confuse the facts, answer each question with "I'll find out for you," knowing that they'll never have to. Meanwhile their clients see themselves sleeping, eating, listening to music, bringing up children, getting drunk, making love in rooms that strangers have forsaken because of a job change or moving up, or in some cases divorce or death.

Mary and I, with our little white Maltese, Christabel, waited patiently to be noticed by a middle-aged man wearing a green checked jacket with an ocher shirt and dark green pants, a kind of uniform of the French salesman. Seizing the chance to impose herself before his next phone call, Mary announced, *"Monsieur, nous cherchons un moulin ou une petite maison, pas trop cher, pour restaurer, quelque chose sur le Cousin ou la Cure.*" We wanted a cheap house or old mill to restore, maybe on the Cousin or Cure rivers. We had lived long enough in France to know that all such negotiations begin with *"C'est impossible à trouver."* This conversation began with an equivalent: *"Quelle surprise, madame. Tout le monde cherche la même chose."* Everyone is looking for the same thing.

Mary responded, "You've listed a mill in Mélusien, and we're interested in learning more about it." Touring nearby, we had seen the mill and noted the distinctive Day-Glo–orange poster proclaiming *à vendre*. We wrote down Jean Rousselet, rue de Paris, a small real estate office in Avallon. Undeniably, a picture of the mill was taped to his window, and it became all too clear to Monsieur Rousselet that his afternoon was as good as shot.

Before the summer of 1992, Mary and I had never seriously considered owning a house together, so there must be a mental condition that could be called house buyer's psychosis. No one can be rational about such a huge commitment or expense as buying a country house. That summer, we had both become stricken while staying in a relatively unknown region of northwestern Burgundy. Once the condition takes over, you begin to hallucinate. Maybe you see an ivy-covered house in the Burgundian rural landscape, the reality of a photo in a nerve-worn magazine stacked in your dentist's waiting room. Maybe you see your life set in the restorative pastoral calm and solitude of nineteenth-century painting and literature. You see a chance to live a second life, to reinvent yourself in another country. Or you see your rural childhood home, if you had one, your childhood river, a place to slip back to in middle age, into the reassurances of a remembered world. Unfortunately, your childhood home is long gone, and as you age you become ever more tangled in the person you happen to be, no matter how many houses you acquire. Still, when looking at houses, you see many things that aren't there.

For years, Mary and I had visited French friends in their country houses along the Loire, in Normandy, or in Burgundy. Our friends invariably bad-mouthed their places shamelessly—*Quel boulot! Ça coûte une fortune! Ce n'est jamais fini! Quel esclavage!* In turn, we'd answer the requisite and sincerely felt *Quel paradis!* as we sat in gardens, listened to songbirds in young fruit trees, or inspected the freshly finished rooms. We assumed that complaining in a state of happy slavery is one of the delights.

The idea of Mary's and my owning a country house together was even more preposterous because we spent most of the year living on separate continents. When we got together, we lived in an unreal world of driving off to Italy on a whim or indulging in three Paris films on a given Sunday. One owns a country house to get away from the confines of the city and one's place of work. One can let the kids go nuts.

The summer of 1992 Mary and I exhausted ourselves driving from Paris to Szeged in Hungary. We took up a long-standing invitation from Mary's colleagues Erika and Péter to vacation there. As early as the seventies, Mary had worked with Hungarian scientists, who, in spite of severely limited resources in materials and the influx of techniques mainly from the outside, managed to maintain their strong scientific tradition. Mary had great respect for their commitment, and in turn they hung her picture in the cafeteria of the Hungarian Academy of Sciences Institute. I had read and loved the poetry of Attila József and Miklós Radnóti, whose tragic lives are legendary, and I was interested in the glories of Hungarian intellectual life that produced the likes of Leo Szilard and Edward

Teller, the former known for his work on the Manhattan Project and the latter for the hydrogen bomb.

In 1992, the Russians had already pulled out of Hungary, leaving behind their unwanted statues and dismal barracks scrawled with graffiti. The government was desperately trying to privatize state holdings while at the same time larger European companies were buying small Hungarian industries and terminating their operations to avoid competition from low-wage workers. The massacre in the Balkans was well under way, with refugees filtering over the border. Péter warned, "Stay on Rósza Ferenc under the lights while crossing Népliget Park." The whole town seemed to be out strolling the paths, making love on the riverbank, or watching the outdoor movie theater, the projection filling the trees with huge figures and flickering scenes. We kept looking for refugees.

In spite of their difficulties, the Hungarians couldn't have been more generous. The institute in Szeged housed us near the Tisza, which curved through the city in its deep riverbed toward Serbia, the border of which was obscured by trees downriver. On the Buda side of Budapest, we had a room provided by the Hungarian Academy of Sciences near the Fisherman's Bastion, where we could look down at the Parliament Building with its urchinlike spires high over the Danube or gaze over the hot sprawl of industrial Pest. Finally, we headed southwest to the academy's vacation facility, a nineteenth-century estate on the shore of Balaton, central Europe's largest lake.

Balaton was Erika and Péter's childhood dreamworld, the vacation sanctuary that glimmers with youthful parents, and brothers, sisters, and cousins back in their child bodies. They could swim in waters that would rinse from their minds the war rubble and the strictures of life in the Communist bloc. And each summer, years later, they brought their own child to sail, fish, or play tennis until the balls disappeared into dusk. For them, Balaton has the infinite buoyancy to float the past and the present, while Mary and I, on our walks, were looking at all the wrong things. For one thing, Balaton that summer suffered algae problems, and large suffocated eels were drifting one after the other into shore. Then, to our amazement, we began to see among the rocks at the water's edge green and brown snakes. We saw them everywhere, the small males knotted around females, two or three weaving into the crevices, coils of others motionless together. In some places every rock had a snake warming itself in the sun. Because Mary loves the French expression for *crawling* or *writhing with,* she declared, *"Ça grouille de serpents!"*

"Are there always so many snakes here, Péter?" she asked.

"Where? In Hungary?"

"Here, of course, around the lake. You can see them from the esplanade. They cover the rocks. And there are eels washing up too."

"I hadn't noticed." Péter was a little annoyed. This was the wide lake he'd swum across in his athletic glory days.

"They're brown and green. They're mating. You can't miss them." Mary can accept that people see what they want to see, but snakes and eels fit a special category. Furthermore, Péter was a biologist. Like Péter, the rest of the Hungarians hadn't noticed the snakes and eels either; they went about their hard-core and undoubtedly hard-earned vacationing, setting lines and tossing balls of meal into the opaque water to attract carp, a Hungarian favorite in soup, with paprika.

Mary's nature is to fixate, and I've often thought that this was the quality that made her gifted in science. One of her favorite lines, a quote from a pretentious teacher she had in high school, is "It's intuitively obvious to the most casual observer." However, when she said it, rarely did anyone know what she was referring to. In any event, she couldn't recruit Erika and Péter to go snake watching.

We stayed at Balaton for a couple of days, strolling the esplanade counting snakes before driving back to Austria. Then the rains came, as if to wash us out of central Europe. We held on for two nights in Baden, a town of healing baths and rose gardens on the outskirts of Vienna, but after the second night we drove in a cloud of truck spray the grueling six hundred kilometers through Austria and Germany. We had decided to reward ourselves with a quick visit to Alsace.

At eight in the evening, we pulled up at Chez Klein in Beblenheim, one of our favorite *chambres d'hôtes,* with its half-timbered buildings that mix together a wine bar, a workshop for antiques, and guest rooms. The rooms are furnished with restored antiques, all painted in traditional Alsatian style and all with price tags, so the rooms tend to change if you go there a few times. That evening we crossed a stretch of tall full-leafed vineyards down to Ostheim, a village with a huge stork's nest on top of a bombed-out wall that was left as a war memorial. Ostheim has a great little family restaurant that practically no one knows about and is only open on weekends. That night, in the middle of our *poulet au Riesling,* lightning crashed into town, turning the rest of the evening into a candlelit affair, with reverent murmuring, guarded laughter, and a child crying in the background. We walked out to find Christabel wide-eyed on the dashboard as if she'd seen the destruction of the world.

Our final destination was Chagny in Burgundy's Saône-et-

Loire, a region that Mary taught me to love. Its gentle hills slope south and east with the world's most precious vineyards of Pinot Noir and Chardonnay grapes. Among the manicured rows of vines, small stone villages appear, each with a simple Romanesque tower.

Mary and I had been coming to Burgundy since we met in 1986, and at least once a year we recklessly spend two nights at Lameloise, a three-star restaurant with a hotel. Mary knew the family from the time that they ran a small one-star restaurant that had a twenty-five-franc menu—*escargots, coq au vin à la bourguignonne,* and a dessert that promised to be just as light as the preceding dishes. She and Boris Ephrussi, Mary's former mate, would spend evenings indulging in the traditional Burgundian cooking and walking through Chagny's long evenings frenetic with swallows.

I've seen pictures of Boris, tall, almost condorlike, receiving medals from the French Academy of Sciences or young and serious—his intensity an anomaly in the drawer full of our vacation photographs. Because he spent the late part of World War II planning air raids on bridges for the RAF, two other scientists followed up on some of his findings on the "one gene and one enzyme" theory to claim what Boris considered his Nobel Prize. Boris died from a mysterious ailment reminiscent of Tolstoy's Ivan Ilyich's. I can't help but think in awe of them—Boris, the old-world intellectual and charmer, the surviving relic of one of Europe's grimmest centuries, embittered in the end, and Mary, a fresh, energetic American, decades younger, held under his spell, her love a mixture of forces. The pleasures of Burgundy were theirs. Mary introduced me to them.

Lameloise is not just a three-star restaurant and luxury hotel; it's a conspiracy. You might imagine pretensions, airs of extravagance, hints of aristocratic elegance, but instead you are invited to notice perfections as if they just naturally occur there, from the flower arrangements to a light, brilliant Volnay, from the *escargots* in ravioli speckled with truffles to the meticulously selected and cured *fromages de chèvre* of the region, from the *foie gras* surprise in a cabbage leaf beside the *pigeonneau rôti* to the *charlotte aux poires*. Meanwhile, Monsieur Daniel, the *maître d'hôtel* who over the years has personally assumed responsibility for our culinary education, passes on names and addresses of small *viticulteurs,* as if we were involved in espionage.

On Mary's request for the latest intelligence, Monsieur Daniel responded without hesitation, "Maurice Écard's Savigny-les-Beaune, Jean Boillot's Volnay, or René Gras-Boisson's Saint-Roman or Meursault. These might interest you this year, madame." On his next pass by the table, he left a card with the information written out. It was also Monsieur Daniel who said, *"Tout en étant cher, c'est bon marché."* While a meal at Lameloise is expensive, it is at the same time a bargain. Just our kind of logic. At some point Jacques Lameloise will appear to explain the dishes we have eaten, as if their essence were simply a matter of chemistry; the experiment can never be verified at home.

Before we go up to our room, the *patronne,* Madame Lameloise, fills us in on the family dramas and triumphs that have transpired over the year. After such an evening we can't help feeling that we belong to the place. No one is more contented with the Lameloise conspiracy than Christabel, who has a special fondness for large beds and rooms with couches and cushy rugs, particularly after days grilling on the hot, dusty roads in Hungary and being rattled by storms in Alsace.

We spent our one full day in the Côte de Beaune weighing

down our Peugeot with cases of Savigny and Chassagne-Montra-chet and then touring churches and monasteries. When we left for Paris, we started out on "green roads," those scenic routes indicated on Michelin maps. We drove through the wine villages of Meursault and Pommard before heading northwest into hills along the Bois de la Chaume, where we came to Lusigny-sur-Ouche, a small, irresistible village near the source of the Ouche River. There couldn't be more than twenty stone houses built on the hill. The river, so near to its source, runs limpid through the town, trout darting among the shadows. In spite of the varnished wood boxes with floppy white and pink petunias mixed with snapdragons, the town didn't seem touristic. It was couched next to a tall forest of pine, hornbeam, and chestnut trees. Meanwhile below, the Ouche forms a valley that eventually leads to the Canal de Bourgogne.

It's no surprise that Lusigny would be exactly the sort of village that Mary and I would like to buy a small house in, and, as if we had willed it, a ruined mill appeared in the center of town, its front door posted *à vendre*. Mary and I walked back and forth inspecting the little ruined mill. We looked over the stone wall into its enclosed garden that had grown wild around several arthritic fruit trees and a deserted blue swing set. We stood on one of the stone bridges and watched the river rush along the side of the building. We even tried to peek in through one window where "1830" had been chiseled, and could see nothing through the locked shutters. Finally, we found a phone booth and called the number copied from the For Sale sign. A woman informed us, somewhat apologetically, that the building was gutted and the price was 450,000 francs.

We walked down to the crossroads of the town where the mill-race joined a larger stream, and then we strolled back up into the cool, shaded forest. Over lunch in Lusigny's one restaurant, we discussed the pros and the cons of the mill. Mary, getting a little concerned, declared, "It's *too* far . . . it's *too* expensive . . . and it's *too* ruined!" She knew that in my head I was already engineering floors and rooms. In spite of my unruly dreaming, I had to agree with Mary—buying the mill was out of the question. There were too many cons.

That August, some friends offered us use of their house in the Saussois, not far from Auxerre. The building was originally a school and retained a square, institutional look. It stood behind a large iron gate under a series of looming limestone cliffs gnawed out by the Yonne River. The river ran placidly on the other side of the road in front, and on the far bank there was a small sandy beach used by campers who crammed their caravans and tents into grounds of postage-stamp size. The Saussois is renowned for rock climbing. All across the face of the cliffs you could see brightly colored cords attached to youthful climbers puzzling their way along routes of varying degrees of difficulty while swallows swooped around their heads and crowlike black *choucas* scolded them for overreaching their element.

Mary and I looked forward to a week's stay in a place where, mornings, we both could work and, afternoons, picnic with our little dog at the edge of the Yonne or one of the other two rivers in the area, the Cure and the Cousin. Augusts mattered specially to us because we separated every autumn while I taught at the University of New Haven in the States and Mary ran her lab in Paris. That August, alone together in rural France in a house beside a beautiful river, we knew we'd found something we'd want again every year. We wandered along the rivers, looked for *à VENDRE* signs, and suddenly found that we couldn't stop ourselves, pulling up to each little town, awaiting the *coup de foudre*, the blow of lightning, the perfect place destined just for us.

We focused on the Cure and the Cousin, clear, fast-moving rivers that run past two medieval towns, Vézelay and Avallon. Vézelay, often likened to the perched towns of Tuscany, has one of the most famous Romanesque churches in France, the Basilique Sainte-Madeleine, a major destination of medieval religious pilgrimages and the site where Saint Bernard inspired the fanatical Second Crusade and where Richard the Lion-Hearted, King of England, and Philippe Auguste, King of France, combined forces to stage the disastrous Third. Avallon is an old fortified town that has been habitually crushed since Celtic times—the Saracens, the Normans, and the English, all taking turns; yet above the ramparts the old town center remains, with its impressive clock tower.

This area of Burgundy is on the edge of the Morvan, wild and infertile, now mostly parkland. The region is only two hours from Paris, which we agreed was a manageable distance should we find the right place. We drove to the source of each river and then down to its confluence, dreaming our lives into many homes that were not for sale and that, even if they had been, were certainly beyond our means.

On one of our excursions we came to the village of Mélusien, where we found another mill for sale. It was larger than the one in Lusigny, and the Cousin rushed through a neighboring cow pasture, then pooled beside the garden in back before passing under the house itself. Sunlight came down through leaves and branches of tall trees growing along the bank, light and water in constant happy motion. From the mill itself there were views up or down the river. A tall hedge enclosed the garden, which had a terrace and a well-kept lawn bordered with flowers and flowering bushes. There was a shed for tools and garden furniture. The village of Mélusien was hardly more than a crossroads, three kilometers from Avallon.

The property was everything I had dreamed of. A major highway, A6, came straight down from Paris to Avallon, in a region rich with natural and cultural resources. We could go on endless excursions deep into the Morvan, and we'd be only an hour from the Côte d'Or, our favorite region for dining and buying wine.

But the old mill itself was ugly. Nothing could change that. It was a big, two-story box, with white stucco etched to look like large stones glued with gray concrete and a modern molded tile roof. As if for deliberately comical ugliness, large green pipe railings were built in around a second-floor balcony. Even if the whole building were stripped down and refaced, we would still be left with a box.

"It's hideous!" Mary insisted, and yet we went straight to Monsieur Rousselet's real estate agency in Avallon.

The mill became a fixation for me. During my first ten years, my family had lived in Wilton, a small town in western Connecticut. Our house was the last, at the end of a country road where it turned to dirt. The house, hardly more than a shack, sat on top of a hill, with two stone walkways under oak trees. On the property below, a river cut through the meadow. Because the river ran rapidly between rocks and over little falls, the sound of rushing water was the background music of my childhood.

My mother, a teenager with one child already, and my father, a young sculptor, managed a down payment on the house and its seven acres of woods bordering a vast protected area of Pound Ridge Water Company land. The idea of moving to the country was one of my mother's fantasy scenarios, which, by sheer will, she forced into reality, no matter the cost to everyone involved. She dragged my father, ordinarily very practical, into her scheme, her head dizzy with notions of raising our own food and living off the land, all inspired by M. G. Kains's *Five Acres and Independence,* published in 1935. She read the practical guide on small farming when she was fourteen but must have skipped the chapter "Tried and True Ways to Fail," which lists the pitfalls—"too little capital," "uncongenial soil," "too many pets or wild animals," "inexperience," "city hours," and "laziness."

So my parents moved out of New York City and bought goats that immediately got sick on mountain laurel, so that my father had to shove pills the size of Salvo laundry soap rounds down their throats to save their lives. When the goats were well, they were far too amusing to eat, so we used only their milk. Dogs and foxes ran off with our ducks, and when we butchered one chicken we ate it like morose cannibals. My father tried to skin a rabbit once but became too dizzy to finish the job, leaving the mess to my less queasy mother. Meanwhile, as if by magic, our lettuce, carrots, and corn vanished as soon as they came up.

My father worked off and on, leaving early in the morning, as a surveyor or a milkman. Later he was a draftsman and a machine designer, using skills he learned in college. Mostly he hated work, as almost any artist does, collecting unemployment compensation when he could. My mother always worked steadily, taking a job first as a dental assistant and then as a technician.

I was proud of my unconventional parents, and I didn't know then that all they had in common were lousy childhoods. My father was shuffled around Brooklyn among his Jewish uncles and cousins, even sleeping at times in the same bed with his little sister and the neighborhood doctor while his mother received shock therapy at a sanitarium. He was shipped off to college to learn textile design for the family business down on Orchard Street but began to sculpt instead. Toward the end of the war, he enlisted in the Merchant Marine Academy and ended up, among many other voyages, transporting Jewish refugees out of China to South America during the Maoist Revolution.

My mother comes of English and Dutch aristocratic wealth, deflated by the Depression. Her father died of a botched operation for appendicitis when my mother was four. Soon after her father's death, a squirrel gnawed through wiring in the attic of her childhood home, setting it on fire. Creamy, a light-haired retriever, woke the family, barking at the smoke, and my grandmother tied sheets together so that she and her two small daughters could climb out from an upper window. Creamy died heroically and the house was lost, but the family continued. Over time, my grandmother became too embittered and busy to care much for her children. My mother was unruly, so she sent her off to an Episcopal boarding school in upstate New York, where for a year my mother refused to speak. Finally, at fifteen she fled the school to work as a model and later as a department store representative, selling a hair product called Cream of Life. She met my father through mutual artist friends when she lived in the Village.

My brother and I spent a great deal of time alone in the country. Our nearest childhood pal lived a mile away, up the winding road past frog ponds, pastures, and modest red barns. Often only the fireplace heated our house; at times we had little to eat besides popcorn. Despite the hardships of those years, my mother suffering most from loneliness and financial responsibility, the Connecticut house was my personal Eden. My father's scratchy Dixieland records dinked away, the river rushed in the background, and my parents talked into the night. That's all there was. The house was shaded by dense summer greenery or surrounded by the dead stillness of tree shadows and starlit snow. Charles Lamb says in *Essays of Elia* that "the solitude of childhood is not so much the mother of thought as it is the feeder of love, silence, and admiration." Those positive forces inform all my memories of that seemingly brief but powerful period of my life.

My mother took a new job as a research scientist at the Yale medical school. After falling asleep at the wheel one too many times while commuting, the car wandering off the shoulder and stalling harmlessly in a snowbank, she announced that we were all moving to New Haven. My parents' separation followed shortly. In fact, we all separated—my brother, who was older, dumped me as one of the rituals of puberty; my mother vanished into survival schemes and multiple jobs, not to mention neurosis; and my father went back to New York.

I have what I'm sure is a distorted memory of my childhood home and the sense of family unity. Yet for none of the houses and apartments I have lived in since, in all of the places—Connecticut, Vermont, Iowa, California, Texas, and Paris—have I developed the same attachment or affection as I had for that house in the woods.

We began actually to destroy the soul of the place when my father, my brother, and I drove down from New Haven to put in new cabinets, paint and panel the rooms, and clear the land for the real estate market. This was my earliest experience in home improvement or restoration, and after all our efforts an architect bought the place and incorporated the house in a section of a monstrous boxy gray structure, a triumph of that studied gracelessness one acquires in architecture school.

When Mary and I found the mill, I saw in the stream, countryside, and solitude an opportunity to re-create the nuances of the Connecticut house. We pushed Monsieur Rousselet, reluctant still, to discuss the mill and other properties that might fit our requirements.

As it turned out, he had a number of houses to show us, one more depressing than the next, but the mill topped the list. It would cost almost twice as much as our outside limit for a country place. Every room reeked of mold, and the striped or flowery wallpaper peeled above bulging wooden floors. There was a central wall that seemed to be sucking water out of the whole region and infusing the house with it. The floor on the deck upstairs was shot, too, so water leaked into a kitchen that Mary declared "had not a single thing to recommend it." The house was clearly a sinking ship, but mesmerized by the river flashing with sunlight and damselflies, I was ready to sink with it.

Out of obligation, we visited the other houses. One was a converted *lavoir*, a washhouse, that stood near a stagnant mosquito pond and had a muddy trench in back that the agent said was a *"vrai ruisseau à truites,"* a genuine trout stream. Another house, near a bend in the Cousin, was lost in some bushes and had obviously been deserted for years. It was characterless, and the land was dark, the river clogged with logs and branches. At the day's end, we saw a house in Mélusien that had clearly defeated its owners. It stood half-reconstructed, materials and silent tools strewn about, a testament to the crushing costs and labor involved in restoration.

That night in the Saussois, neither of us could sleep; the river ran too brightly through my head while Mary could see only a house of horrors. She knew that I could talk us into buying the place, spending ridiculous sums we didn't have. In her mind, the only solution was to keep looking and so save us from my worst impulses, but as a week passed nothing better showed up.

To the west of the Saussois is a town called Mailly-le-Château, where a statue of a weeping wolf was erected to commemorate the systematic eradication of the European wolf in the region. The statue is ironically pitiful, the wolf crossing one paw over its eyes, its head bowed in a deep sob. For us, it marked the border of a region we had yet to explore. We passed the weeping wolf and went into Auxerre, where we were bound to find a number of real estate agencies, in a last-ditch effort before leaving Burgundy or succumbing to the horrid mill.

That day we must have visited a half-dozen agencies, setting up several appointments, before we came to l'Immobilière Continentale, an agency organized unlike any of the others. They had assembled notebooks based on price ranges, with photographs of properties and lists of vital information. The properties ranged from apartments to châteaux, but all shared one characteristic— they were *belles demeures*, beautiful residences. We were assigned an attractive, handsomely dressed agent named Madame Brissot. Unlike the others, she could read our hearts, probably because her sensibilities were not so different from ours. She had several attractive mills available and was quite happy to show them to us. We followed her little red Renault into the bright summer countryside and saw a mill with the medieval look of half-timbered construction, low-beamed ceilings, and small windows, warm though dark interiors of rooms that center on the hearth. The owners had tastefully restored it, but apparently the husband had developed cancer, his wife nursing him through a horrible decline. She could no longer manage the place, physically or spiritually.

For us, the countryside was too bleak and remote, just large cultivated fields spreading in every direction. The house, dark to begin with, was at the bottom of a valley, and the river itself was minimal. All along, Madame Brissot had urged us to look at an old presbytery that she knew of in a different region. "It isn't a mill, of course, but the village has a river and a canal, and the building and the grounds are unique." She had clearly fallen in love with the place herself. That day she couldn't come with us, nor were keys immediately available, but she ran her finger along departmental roads on the map deep into the Puisaye.

We never considered the possibility of living in a presbytery. After all, presbyteries were for priests. Yet we found ourselves driving farther and farther into a part of Burgundy unfamiliar to us, dense forests opening suddenly to gentle farmland. At the same time the landscape was filled with rivers, lakes, and ponds. We reached Rogny in late afternoon and crossed its bridges in total delight before ascending the steep slope to the high town and entering the open square with its young Liberty Tree in full leaf, the church towering into blue afternoon sky, the presbytery crossing the length of the place de l'Église in front of us. I got out of the car immediately, but Mary didn't move.

"What's the matter?"

"You go. I need a minute."

Tears came to Mary's eyes because she knew at once that the sour, rotting mill of Mélusien had been exorcised.

What we found was a château in miniature, as if a witch had cast a spell on some noble house and profoundly shrunk it. Only the tall windows that faced east in front and west in back had kept their great size. A high wall of cemented stone extended to the north along the rue de Dammarie, where there was a large gate that opened to the terrace and the stables. The stables had half-beam construction and a slate roof that made them look considerably older than the house itself. Another wall extended westward connecting the house to a square dovecote with a pointed tiled roof covered in deep green moss and topped by a zinc spike. This wall formed a passage between the house and the church.

The terrace just behind the house stood about ten feet above the orchard, with a broad stone wall and a large lichen- and stonecrop-covered staircase. The expanse of terrace gave a view over the property, and lifting your gaze higher, you could see across the whole river valley. Climbing roses, clematis, and honeysuckle grew along the terrace wall, and the orchard had peach, pear, cherry, plum, apple, and walnut trees, along with four pines, two of which towered at the brink of the slope. At the end of the orchard was the priest's meditation path, lined by parallel rows of ancient hornbeam trees. We had never seen such a place.

Mary and I took pictures of each other standing next to the dovecote, the terrace and the house in the background. Christabel was held up in the middle of each shot, black nose, black eyes, as in all of our photographs, depressing even our most ardently dog-loving friends. Within fifteen minutes the three of us squeezed into a phone booth next to the canal, calling Madame Brissot to arrange to see the house as soon as possible.

When we returned to the Saussois, Mary said, "Let's look around for something about the Puisaye." Our friends had a small collection of books, mainly field guides, but they did have some books on Burgundy that described the Puisaye as "secretive," "unknown," "watery," and "forested." It's a region of woodcutters, potters, and legends. The word "puisaye" is most likely a combination of Celtic words meaning "pond" and "forest."

That night, everything was calm, except, of course, for us. The cliffs were totally visible, bathed in lunar white. We walked with Christabel along the Yonne River, which seemed hardly to be flowing yet was filled with gentle surface break—the fish were attracted to the moon. We were probably glowing ourselves, sensing that we were on the verge of a great change.

In spite of the bright day before and a clear night, the next morning was warm and cloudy, the air growing heavy with nearing rain. We sped past the weeping wolf to meet the prim but cheerful Madame Brissot at 10:00 A.M. on the place de l'Église. Having seen so many awful places, we had a deep trepidation about the interior of the house. But as we came in the central double-door entry, bracing ourselves for disappointment, a whole new enthusiasm took over.

Madame Brissot led us down the large entry hall that bisected the building and opened up the back door to the terrace, then in each room and hallway opened the shutters to several windows that reached to the ceiling. All the walls had been painted white, and within a few moments we knew that the presbytery was built for light and air. To the left of the main entry, Madame Brissot showed us the hallway and the large living room and two bedrooms; to the right she led us to a room that we now call the library because it has elaborate wood paneling on the walls and a niche perfect for a large desk. Proceeding along the garden side, we came to another large hallway, with an old garden door all in glass panes, a built-in closet and storage area, and a doorway to the largest bedroom. To get to the kitchen, we passed through an odd narrow corridor that ran diagonally from the hall. The kitchen had a tall beamed ceiling, a six-foot-high fireplace, and another garden door. All the floors were covered with either square or hexagonal tiles of fired brick called *tomette*, giving the house a unifying rusticity.

Madame Brissot took us up a central staircase that spiraled to the *grenier*, or attic, a majestic space transected by the four chimneys. The centuries-old oak framework, called *ferme à entrait relevé*, formed striking starlike structures at the two ends of the house. In between, elaborate oak structures like bridges came down to the crossbeams in the floor.

Even before finishing the tour, we were discussing money and procedures with Madame Brissot. Clearly the house had been deserted for years, but someone had looked after the grounds, planting young trees and tending the roses and clematis. Great tangles of blackberries had claimed much of the dovecote, part of the stables, and almost the entire statue of Christ at the end of the *charmille*, or prayer path. The *charmille* had become a kingdom of rabbits.

I saw that the walls needed taping and plastering, as did the ceilings, and that all the shutters and windows needed reconditioning. There was serious water damage from two holes in the roof. Still, restoration seemed manageable. The price was high for us, but Madame Brissot said that the owner, Madame Malaud, would accept a good deal less because a previous offer had been accepted but the deal had fallen through. We probably would have paid far more than the asking price and destroyed ourselves financially. However, we took Madame Brissot's word and made the verbal offer down on the prayer path, surrounded by a half-dozen wide-eyed rabbits.

As Madame Brissot had predicted, the offer was accepted. In one preposterous week, we had found and bound ourselves to a presbytery in a town and a region we had never heard of before. We sent a bottle of champagne from Paris to Madame Brissot and made reservations at a hotel in the neighboring town of Saint-Fargeau. It was my last weekend before returning to the States, and we had two major goals in mind: to get estimates for repairing the two large holes in the roof and to enjoy a picnic on the terrace.

The light in late August changes dramatically. In the evening, it no longer lingers past ten, and the sun rises later and later each morning. On our last weekend, the swallows were already gathering for their migration. More than fifty of them lined up on the gutters and wires outside our hotel-room window in the intermittent rain. When the swallows go, the season is over. It's that simple. The air empties of all their chatter and mesmerizing aerial displays.

Before we arrived, Mary and I agreed that we should hire only local plumbers, electricians, and roofers to work on the house. We felt it our duty to invest in the economy of our immediate area; besides, we would benefit from having reliable experts nearby to whom we could turn. They would know us, and they would know the house. They would join in on the reconstruction.

The first priority was to fix the holes in the roof. We arranged for three different roofers to come and make estimates. The first was Monsieur Petri, a dark-haired man in his thirties who lives in one of the new *pavillons,* modern houses that stand blockishly on the treeless northwestern slope of the hill. He looked more like a man who'd smoke a pipe while mowing the lawn than someone who earned a hard living by pouring cement and roofing.

He went up to the *grenier* with clipboard in hand and probed with his fingertips some of the sagging *liteaux* (the term is derived from *lit,* bed). They are thin strips of wood forming a lattice and are supported by heavier pieces of wood called *charpente.* The old roof tiles hook to the *liteaux* and are held in place by the weight of the tiles that overlap them above. Light, wind, and some snow can actually pass between the tiles, while the rain, normally, will run off. During the day the roof from the inside looks like a well-ordered universe of stars.

When Monsieur Petri pushed the roof with his fingertips, the "bed" easily lifted and fell. The bed was more like a hammock. We immediately understood the bad news. Monsieur Petri said, *"Vous voyez ça!"* His gaze traveled the firmament of little spots of light between the tiles and then he pointed up and said, "The *liteaux* and at least three-quarters of the *charpente* have to be replaced. Each tile has to come down and be scraped by hand. Then there is the antimoss treatment." He ended with the familiar *"Vous avez du pain sur la planche."* You have some bread to cut.

The moss we thought so beautiful actually holds in moisture, which in turn rots the *liteaux* and *charpente*. Some major beams also needed replacing. Monsieur Petri took measurements and left with his pleasant smile. So much for patching a few holes and so much for the real estate listing claiming the roof was in *bon état,* good condition. Monsieur Petri assessed us more carefully than he did the roof. He concluded that anyone who would buy the ancient deserted presbytery had money to waste on a wreck and sent a *devis,* an estimate, for almost half the cost of the house.

The second *devis* came from Monsieur Macquet, another mason and roofer, who, though we didn't know it at the time, was actually the assistant mayor. He was a small, mustached man who walked about somewhat grumpily, trying to offer ways to keep his price down. He said, "If you paid more than three hundred and fifty thousand francs for the place, you got rolled!"

At the time, his use of the expression *roulé* didn't endear him to us. Where was his reverence for the place? Why wouldn't he want to contribute to the loveliness of the place de l'Église and the village? Though his estimate came to less than half of Monsieur Petri's, we couldn't have someone work on the presbytery who didn't respect it.

Finally, Monsieur LeMaître showed up, younger, good-looking, an animated sort of guy with a mischievous smirk. His strongest recommendation was that he had just restored the large roof on the church in nearby Saint-Privé. Not only did he want to restore the roof, but he would also put in the electricity, heating, and plumbing: a package deal.

LeMaître stood in the kitchen, looking it over bemusedly. He put out his hands as if hallucinating the edges of a table, then pointed to where someone might be sitting.

"I spent the night before my wedding in this kitchen, and Père Jo was seated here. When the sun rose, we emptied the last bottle."

They couldn't have been more hungover for his wedding. It's called a *gueule de bois,* a "wooden throat," probably referring to the aftereffects of smoking and drinking. We asked about the sea of bottles. Were they the curé's? *"Ça, c'était au Père Jo."* He shook his head in amusement. This was the first we heard of notorious Père Jo.

We had our picnic on the stairs that led from the terrace to the orchard. Wildflowers, moss, and grass grew in every crevice of the large stones. Mary made the comment "Wouldn't it be fun to have a wedding here? We could get married under the pear tree."

The tree had a profusion of large, mealy pears, and many had already fallen, to the delight of dizzy rabbits and drunken yellow jackets. The late-summer air was itself slightly sick with fermenta-tion. I thought about LeMaître's delirious night with Père Jo and the festivities the following day. I tried to picture our wedding out among the old neglected fruit trees. In that moment, the past and the future seemed to mix.

Two Curés

*H*ouses tend to inhabit us as much as we inhabit them. They are housed in our consciousness and in our sleep. Their happiness adds to our pleasure, just as our worries cast shadows through them. They explain to our neighbors what we think of them and ourselves; they show our obsessions with the past and gossip about our failures. So when for years no one lived in the presbytery, it had nothing to say beyond what its history stood for and the persistent disinterest of its owners. It was closed up in its tall louvered shutters, faded gray, the plaster ceilings slowly cracking apart in the dark, moisture condensing or leaking in, beams rotting. The health of a house, even a solid house with meter-thick walls, depends on a resident. Without one, the presbytery quickly became a heavy presence on the place de l'Église, and people imagined spirits where there were hallways, doors, and spaces meant for living bodies.

After we bought the house and piled up *devis* for a roof, plumbing, and electricity, we immediately wanted to know more of its history. Neither Mary nor I had ever been in a presbytery until we were about to buy one. We knew only that such buildings housed curés, and if there were spirits wandering about, they'd likely be of a religious sort. Mary suggested that we talk to our neighbors Jean-Louis and Ariane to learn more about the house and the village. Madame Brissot had already introduced us to them because they had been friends of Madame Malaud, the former owner, and kept a set of keys to the property.

Sunday was my last day in the country before I had to leave for Paris and then the States. In late August, the air becomes cool and dry in the mornings, the village gilded in sunlight, the fields vivid with their monolithic rolls of straw. Mary and I crossed the place de l'Église to a weathered gate between Monsieur Marteau's house and Madame Briançon's. The gate opened to a short driveway and several restored farm buildings. Along the driveway were a few struggling roses and recently planted dahlias. Our mission was to become better acquainted with our new neighbors and interrogate them about the presbytery.

We found Jean-Louis outfitted in overalls, a tape measure in his pocket, ready for a full day of *bricolage*, do-it-yourself home renovation. He was sitting in a corner of his yard, just staring at the sunlight that filed through the low branches. Was he musing so profoundly about *bricolage*? Once stirred from his reverie, he seemed delighted to see us. *"Entrez! Entrez!"*

Ariane must have heard us, and so she rushed out of their half-restored house to greet us. Her hair had been recently dyed a familiar blond, but it was not as unnatural-looking as other women's in the village. She was wearing a tight, pink, short-sleeved sweater and thick glasses, tinted enough to shade the world in sepia. In fact, she could have come straight from Queens, except for her accent. It was as if she'd known us for years.

"*Mary, Jeffrey, bienvenue! Voudriez-vous quelque chose, un apéritif?*"

"We have to drive back to Paris," Mary said, refusing for both of us, knowing well we'd pass into a torpor before noon. "We came over to say good-bye, and ask if you'd continue to keep the keys to the presbytery."

An hour later Jean-Louis was opening a bottle of Chablis, a wine from the region just northeast of the Puisaye. He was particularly proud of its address because of its *rapport qualité-prix*, its quality-to-price ratio. Such addresses are highly valued and are passed on to others as great favors.

As it turned out, Jean-Louis indulged in talking about old houses as much as he indulged in musing about working on them. He admitted readily, "*Je suis paresseux*. Lay-zee!" Ariane confirmed this confession, as if Jean-Louis's laziness were his primary infamy. "*Vingt-cinq années de travail sur cette maison et je me douche toujours avec un tuyau d'arrosage!*" After twenty-five years of working on this house, I still shower with a garden hose.

Jean-Louis was a very good-looking man in his late fifties, hair thinning, wire-rimmed glasses. While he was full of warmth and enthusiasm, he also seemed shadowed by melancholy, or was it just pensiveness? He had been a proofreader for *Le Point*, the French version of *Time* magazine, and thus had far more formal education than most of the inhabitants of the Haut-Bourg. He was only "lay-zee" when it came to *bricolage*. But neither "lazy" nor *paresseux* is the right word. Perhaps "ritualistic" is. One studies each demanding project in fullest detail, discussing with neighbors its execution, learning the techniques, and comparing the prices of materials. And then the years pass, and one must study the project all over

again. We'd learned later that, like many Frenchmen of his generation, Jean-Louis indulged in smoking and alcohol, and he reveled
in the least healthy sorts of *charcuterie*. He was paying the price
with heart trouble and had to practice restraint, albeit reluctantly.
The day before, we'd seen him strolling slowly around the Haut-
Bourg. He'd paused in front of the church's eleventh-century
Romanesque portal, just to stare, as perhaps he had as a young man
trying to picture himself in the future.

When I asked about the history of the presbytery, Jean-Louis
responded, "The presbytery has always depended on charity,
which means that its history can be described by a single word—
poverty." He told us that over the last fifteen years only Madame
Hervé and her two daughters had camped in the empty rooms for a
month at a time over several summers. The Marquis Jacques
d'Harmelle had rented the old building to them. They stayed in the
presbytery to be near Madame Hervé's mother, a lifelong resident
of Rogny. Jean-Louis and Ariane's kids would play with the
daughters in the deserted stables or the *charmille*. They'd climb
into the hot, secretive dark of the *grenier*. Madame Hervé yearned
to buy the house from the Harmelle family, most of whom are
bankers in the sixteenth *arrondissement* in Paris. The property was
passed down over the decades to sons and daughters and to some of
their sons and daughters. We'd notice later on the *acte de vente*, the
deed, that nine members of the Harmelle family were former owners of the presbytery. Clearly they would have to call a small con-
vention to decide anything, which they finally did, selling the
house to Madame Malaud. She had intended to put in twice
the value of the house to renovate it, but her plans changed, and the
house would sit for another five years.

Ariane said, *"C'est fou!"* Then in English, " 'Tis cray-zee!" It was as if "crazy" and "lazy" were the same thing. "Madame Hervé wanted to buy the presbytery, but she depended on her mother to pay for it. Her mother refused. Her daughter wasn't going to own such a house. Her mother said, "It's out of the question. Too many old spirits live there."

According to Jean-Louis, the house had suffered almost two hundred and fifty years of poverty, and the villagers believed that it was filled with spirits. I couldn't help being reminded of Oscar Wilde's short story "The Canterville Ghost," which wonderfully mocks American callousness to European superstitions and to the long miserable histories of feudal manors. In the story, an American minister buys the Canterville Chase and moves his family in, even though he has been clearly warned that he is buying a house haunted by Sir Simon de Canterville, who murdered his own wife, Lady Eleanore, in 1575. The ancient, aristocratic ghost has been, over the years, particularly smug about the efficacy of his haunting. But instead of being horrified when confronted by the ghost, the minister urges him to use Tammany Rising Sun Lubricator to oil his noisy chains and manacles, and the minister's wife tries to give him Dr. Dobell's Tincture because she mistakes the ghost's subsequent rage for illness. The twins pelt the ghost with peashooters and set buckets of water over doors as booby traps for him.

Jean-Louis got up from his chair and said, *"Attendez, j'ai quelque chose d'intéressant pour vous."* He returned with a stack of pages held together with a rubber band. It was a photocopy of an entire book on the history of Rogny. Gaston Gauthier, who had been a primary-school teacher in the school just below the Haut-Bourg, wrote it in the late nineteenth century. *"C'est un cadeau."* Jean-Louis insisted that we accept the book as a gift.

Our neighbors walked us out to the *place,* where we had a full view of the presbytery closed up in its gray shutters. It would remain a house of spirits for one more autumn, since the sale of a house in France takes months to finalize. After our good-byes, I walked the grounds with Mary to collect impressions before leaving. The presbytery may have been a heavy presence for the villagers, but for us it seemed ennobled by the decay, as if its materials could so naturally reunite with the land. If the house had been built within the last fifty years, it would have looked shabby and depressing.

I didn't have to ask Mary what she thought of the accusation "There are too many old spirits." If a ghost appeared, Mary would argue rigorously, "What are you doing here? You're implausible!" For her, the spirit goes with the body, and that's all there is to it. I'm not quite as literal-minded about such things. We had those piles of empty wine bottles in the *grenier* and the stables, and I imagined a spirit drinking dust for fifteen years.

That autumn semester at the University of New Haven, I was assigned an upper-level course in one of my specializations, English Romantic writers. The themes in the course seemed so integral in one way or another to our new adventure in the Puisaye: the coalescence of man and nature, the intimations of the child-self, the revolutionary spirit of France, and the disastrous, overachieving exploits of Napoleon, eventually leading him to his glorious doom. The English majors loved enthusiasm, wherever it came from.

For my honors class in composition, I chose for discussion James Baldwin's essay "The Discovery of What It Means to Be an American." There was no class discussion. Only two students read the assignment. I tried to explain that, like Baldwin, I lived in

France, so I knew that to truly understand what it is to be an American, you must live outside oppressive social strictures and consider other cultural perspectives and freedoms. They had that familiar look—*whatever*. How could I compare myself to Baldwin, an African-American writer concerned with identity in two contentious countries in the fifties? My life in France was merely circumstantial. Mary lived there. I should have said there are a million ways to know yourself as an outsider, American or not.

I also had two developmental courses that combined modern history and reading. While working on chapters covering 1939–1945, I said the word "Nazi," and my student Cedric, who wore CEDRIC in gold just under his throat, shouted out, "Nazi, that's racist. I'm Jewish. I bet you didn't know that. You don't believe me, do you, Docta Greene. I'm studying everything about the Holocaust." Eyes rolled, but I believed him.

"Docta Greene, you're Irish, right?"

"No, my father is Eastern European Jewish, and my mother is English and Dutch."

"Dutch?"

I almost never discuss my personal life with my students; they need too much help for me to use up time with anecdotes. Still, they knew that I lived in France, and they thought that made me different from the rest of their professors. Cedric continued, with some snickering in the class, "Your wife is French, right?"

"No, the woman I live with is from New Orleans, but she lives in France. She's a molecular biologist."

I could see that the students were disappointed, so I tried to impress them. "She is highly esteemed in her field. She lectured at Yale when she was twenty-four." To them, Yale was just New

Haven. They could forgive Mary for being a molecular biologist but not for being American.

"I thought she was French," Gabriella said accusingly. She was still wearing her ValuRite uniform. With kids and car troubles, she was three absences over the limit. "Is she here with you?"

"Let's work."

"You mean she's there in France."

"What you doing here?" Jennifer jumped in.

"I'm coming to see you in Paris, France. You don't believe me, do you, Docta Greene?" Cedric said.

"You're in trouble in this class."

"You've changed, Docta Greene." Cedric repeated this each time I came around to help with an assignment.

When I had a break from preparations, editing, and committee work, I would slip back into my other self, the one who had a personal life in France. I would read Gauthier's history of Rogny and Saint-Eusoge. I imagined the children of the village coming to school in their *sabots* and the *instituteur* Gauthier carefully checking their hands for dirt before they'd work on their lessons, huddled around the woodburning stove that took several hours to put a dent in the cold radiated by the walls that surrounded them. I couldn't image Gauthier's students teasing him the way mine teased me, but who knows? If anything can be deduced about Gauthier from his text, it's that he was a stickler for detail and documentation; his notes and appendix equal the length of his book's main text and are often much more interesting. Gauthier included in his appendix two documents written by Polluche, the first curé to live in the presbytery. One document was a statement listing the possessions of the rectory, and the other was his memoir on the presbytery's reconstruction in 1754. From these documents, a shadowy portrait emerges of the first curé and the existing building, a building that he dreamed of and fought for doggedly.

In Polluche's time, two types of curés served in the church. The first consisted of second sons of landowners who, by becoming officers in the military or by entering the clergy, could secure comfortable futures without a large inheritance. The second type of curé was a villager who, with an ecclesiastical education, could hope to elevate himself to a higher station in society. Judging from the problems he encountered, Polluche was a true country curé who sought to construct a presbytery of some extravagance to buttress his social ambitions.

When Polluche received his *bénéfice* in Rogny—his stipend, housing, and benefits—he found the original presbytery in near ruins. One gable leaned dangerously against a grange, and the chimneys, as he put it, "teetered two feet out of line." The house stood in its precarious state between a shed on one side and the stables on the other, where there was also a *vinée*, a room where grapes were pressed and their juice stored in fermenting vats before the wine was bottled. Polluche diplomatically occupied the crumbling presbytery for three years in order to establish himself among the parishioners and earn their goodwill. But then he sent a request to Monsieur l'Intendant d'Orléans for the total reconstruction of the building. The *intendant* was the highest official in the provinces and directly represented the king's authority. The *intendant* ordered experts to assess the state of the presbytery, and they affirmed the need for reconstruction and gave an estimate of the costs.

When some of the villagers learned that the bill would amount to 3,600 francs, they sent their own request to the *intendant* for a simple renovation of the original presbytery and charged, undoubtedly with good reason, that Polluche had influenced the experts to endorse his own interests. The *intendant* ordered a second assessment by a different group of experts, who obediently confirmed the convictions of the first. This decision further antagonized some of the parishioners, whom Polluche called *mutins*, mutineers, in his memoir.

The *intendant*, having little interest in involving himself in such petty village disputes, passed the problem on to the subdelegate of Montargis, who, to Polluche's humiliation, would dispense only 1,800 francs, believing that a new building with "a kitchen, a bedroom, and an office would suffice the village curé" of Rogny. However, in the old presbytery, Polluche already had a kitchen, two bedrooms, two offices, and a wine cellar, so he felt that the subdelegate's decision was not only a considerable slap in the face but also a demotion. In response, Polluche offered to raise on his own an additional 1,800 francs on the condition that the original plans ordered by the *intendant* be executed. The inhabitants, of course, saw that they would be taxed and gave Polluche "a thousand miseries."

Then, in a weird turn of events and in the only place in his recorded documents where he uses the word *Dieu*, Polluche becomes darkly triumphant: "God permitted that they [certain inhabitants] would no longer be a nuisance, since He called them to Him most suddenly."

After Polluche's adversaries were so fortuitously called to God, the old presbytery was demolished, and the new presbytery was constructed in the upper garden of the rectory. Polluche concludes his memoir in understated victory: "No one opposed."

I couldn't help but picture Polluche, with his remarkable

wheeling and dealing, as a formidable survivor and at the same time a pest. He left a document in which he lists a number of protests regarding properties and privileges held by the rectory. He had several disputes with the "messieurs of the canal," the transporters of charcoal and floated wood. The rectory controlled several acres of land along the canal and in the field of Jacquier, an important part of the island in the center of town. Rent was charged on storage property for charcoal, and taxes were levied on floated wood that waited to be loaded on barges.

Polluche was a country priest who seemed to operate profitably in all spheres of society, but no doubt at greatest cost to the peasants. It's no surprise that, following the Revolution, the Constitutional Assembly confiscated the property of the church, which owned an enormous percentage of the land in France and also had a right to a huge percentage of harvested crops. Much of the church's landholdings were quickly sold to the bourgeois, rich peasants, and remaining nobles to help pay off a huge national debt that had accrued after the war with England and the exorbitant cost of supporting the American Revolution.

On November 26, 1791, the public prosecutor sold the confiscated presbytery to Monsieur Delaboire for 1,900 francs. Beginning in 1832, the curés lived mostly in a much smaller building called the new presbytery. Still, with the exception of an addition on the north end of the house and some interior remodeling, we live in the building that Polluche had dreamed of and constructed.

Coincidentally, Polluche and I were the same age, forty, when we first stood before our respective ruins. Polluche, however, had a very clear notion of his duties to the community he served and of how to achieve his personal goals, while I acquired the ancient presbytery on pure quixotic impulse, completely ignorant of the true nature or condition of the building. My knowledge of French history was, at best, sketchy, and I had had no exposure to the workings of the French Catholic Church, or any church for that matter. My most serious deficit was that I had no experience living in or working on a building whose main structural elements were stone, mortar, plaster, tiles, beams, and wattle.

One can pass a whole winter without snow in New Haven, but sometimes a storm will come and erase the city. I rented a third-floor apartment with a view of sycamores that in the heavy snow was canceled along with all the self-help meetings, ball games, and evening classes. I was planning to take revenge on my honors students. I had complained about their use of clichés. One student said defiantly, "You're old, and we're young. If we don't know a cliché is a cliché, is it still a cliché?"

"Yes!" I was preparing a list of clichés when the snow came, and with it WAVZ began to list the closures and cancellations. The traffic grew muffled and the city darkened. Even now, I love when a snowstorm brings life to a halt.

That same day Mary had signed the *acte de vente*, in the presence of two *notaires*, who earned 3 percent for an hour of their ceremonious presence. Madame Brissot and Madame Malaud were also there, everyone looking for his or her cut. Mary and I could only celebrate with a phone call on a late November night for her and a snowy afternoon for me. "The Bank of France may collapse!" "The Bank of France" is Mary's pet name for our finances. "But now we officially own a ruin."

We had lived four years working on separate continents, celebrating or commiserating on the phone. I could have supported a small family on what we spent on phone bills. Now we owned a presbytery with an ocean between us. While it seemed New Haven itself was being canceled by a snowstorm, I wrote my request for a leave of absence, telling the provost I planned to get married in France.

Mary visited the presbytery only two times that autumn. She was very busy with her lab and the new administrative responsibilities. It gets dark early, so the drive from Paris and back is arduous. Also, the house was a shared folly, so as it stood closed up and silent, it only added to a sense of separation. On one of her trips down, Mary had lunch with Jean-Louis and Ariane, who told her more about the notorious and well-loved Père Jo. With LeMaître's description and the mass of wine bottles, we had become increasingly curious about him.

Mary called me to tell all she'd learned about Père Jo, how he was seen at night dancing on the kitchen table, how he often invited homeless people to sleep in the presbytery, and how on weekends families and their dogs would pile into trucks and drive in from the surrounding farms and fields, where they lived and worked, for games and festivities in the orchard of the presbytery. In the stables, we found evidence of these games. Père Jo had constructed one for the children—a large sheet of wood carefully painted as a school with windows cut to the size of faces. The game was labeled *JEU DE MASSACRE*. One can only imagine a game of toss-and-duck where mostly Père Jo was the willing target and the children the assassins. Among these children were the poor and underprivileged who would live during the summer in a large bourgeois house in the Bas-Bourg, Lower Town, that once belonged to a wood merchant. Now it is the house of les Demoiselles Ducroix. While Père Jo supported the homeless and programs for poor children, he was also the chum of the town drunks, being one himself, sleeping in the trunk of his car when he'd lost the house keys. In the end, he lived and slept among the broken tiles in the kitchen, the northernmost part of the house. With its huge fireplace, the kitchen is easy to heat, and the rest of the building was falling into disrepair. Père Jo was already living in the kitchen when he drank all night with the young LeMaître before his wedding.

Since I had read Polluche's memoir on the construction of the presbytery, I was struck by differences between the dissipated but good-hearted Père Jo and the petty operator Polluche, who fought with the inhabitants of the village. But it wouldn't be until after Père Jo's death three years later that I'd actually see a photograph of him and learn more about his life. This chance came when Mary and I visited les Demoiselles Ducroix.

Demoiselles is an odd expression, particularly when applied to those two kindhearted, elderly women who, by their own initiative, look after some remaining records of the parish. Over tea, they brought out a number of photographs of the presbytery's last curé. Some were from news clippings and others personal shots; Père Jo is the shortest man in any of the photos, whether he is standing among a group of priests at their ordination or among a group of pilgrims in front of the church tower at Lourdes. Nothing in the photos betrays the mischief or the goodness that he had become known for in our village—one just sees a pleasant-looking man, black hair combed straight back, largish nose, straight, short eyebrows, and rather sympathetic eyes. He looked more interesting as he grew older, wearing half-wire-rimmed glasses like Malcolm X's.

It occurs to me, in retrospect, that we could have invited Père

Jo to our wedding at the presbytery. At the time he was sixty-nine, and I'm sure that seeing the decayed presbytery come to life again, the gardens filled with wedding guests, wineglasses in hand, would have amused him. Certainly, he wouldn't be shocked that foreigners were living in the former religious building, and he would probably be at ease among us on grounds he had known since 1959.

My request for a leave was granted in less than a week, with hearty congratulations from the provost. My leave was unpaid, of course, and the administration didn't seem to mind having one semester's worth of my salary to boost some new applied program. Meanwhile, I was looking forward to joining the old spirits of the presbytery, which I believed were good even if Mary refused to acknowledge their existence. For me, they materialize in the house's afternoon light or speak as the mind's voice speaks; the walls, the rooms, and the grounds are so infused with centuries of Frenchmen, partly coloring, now, the moments of our own lives.

If Americans have little respect for European ghosts, it's because, to the offspring of immigrants, always racing ahead, history is an impediment. Still, I remember from my childhood a television program called *A Meeting of Minds*. It was a mock talk show where, in place of interviews with current entertainment celebrities, figures such as Aristotle, Attila the Hun, and Saint Thomas Aquinas would come back from the dead in the costumes of their time. They were interviewed and incited into debates across the ages by comedian Steve Allen, who acted, in the realm of suspended disbelief, as our interlocutor with greatness. In my musings, I sometimes conjure up a similar debate in our library, between the ghosts of Polluche and Père Jo, the first and the last curés, emblematic respectively of the primacy of French Catholic power at the end of the ancient regime and of the drinking-pal camaraderie with socialist farmers. Polluche built the presbytery two decades before the birth of the United States, while Père Jo saw a ten-year agricultural revolution that brought late mechanization to once hand-sown fields. Polluche is the spirit of entitlement, while Père Jo is that of solidarity.

The Provincial of an Earthly Order

Charcoal making was a life of choked fire and smoke, piled wood smoldering under a blanket of earth. It was a life in an eternal forest of controlled nature; the cutting was selective, the wood an ancient, ongoing crop. The hovel of the *charbonnier,* his wife, and eight children was made of the same nineteen-year-old trees that were selected for making charcoal. The older trees were used for lumber and firewood. Thin logs were bound together to construct a frame. Roof and walls were so many layers of branches and leaves woven together. The family slept in a house of trees among the trees. By the slow burning of wood to make charcoal, they could earn enough to buy bread, potatoes, and bacon.

By the late thirties, the profession was already dying. No one in the village at that time could truly foresee the coming of the Second World War. Future deportees were earning a living, or they were still residing with their families and among neighbors. No one knew that Jean LeClerc and Marcel Bizot, who survived the

Great War, would be shot on the roadside as hostages. There was no way for the old men to predict this. They walked past the very spot countless times. It was a time when ice was delivered in cold, translucent blocks covered in straw, a horse or donkey pulling the cart up the steep rue de la Montagne to the place de l'Église; charcoal was brought likewise to the stove bin. The stove was used for both heating and cooking. This was the world of Coco's childhood.

"Put your hand here." Coco grabs my wrist, holding my hand against the left side of his face. "Feel that? The cold?" He places my hand against the warm right side. *"Vous sentez la différence?"*

We are standing together in a crater that was once our kitchen floor. Coco has been loosening the packed earth with a power tool that resembles a small jackhammer while I shovel the debris out of the way. All the floor tiles, cracked from centuries of splitting wood in the kitchen, have become landfill somewhere at the edge of the village.

The left side of Coco's face is icy because he lost the bone in that region of his jaw. A portion of his tongue was also removed. Now there's not enough circulation there. The nerves in the scar tissue are sensitive to raw air and a chilly wind. By the intensity of pain in his mouth, he can predict the weather. He goes through the winter wearing a black knit hood, holding the side of his face as if he had been in a brawl. The other side of his face is warm with work and red wine that he waters down so that it doesn't "prick" his tongue.

He has been ordering me around all day in my own house; his drooling is ungovernable. He is frustrated because I can hardly understand his French; he sounds like an impetuous child talking with his mouth full. He wants a pail; I bring him a shovel. His pain is obvious; the room is near freezing. Yet he works because he insists on it. It's not the money.

Of the *charbonnier*'s eight children, four are still alive, including Coco, who had radical surgery for mouth and throat cancer—the deadly synergy of *pastis* and cigarettes—and his brother, who has just had his larynx removed. The brothers are the beneficiaries of socialized medicine. When the war began and Rogny became a part of occupied France, Coco's family was forced out of the woods. They lived in the two-room house just outside our kitchen window on the north side of the place de l'Église. Coco still lives there.

Coco is a true child of nature, half wild. Monsieur Bougé calls him *un pochard et un braconnier,* a drunk and a poacher. Gilbert, our mason, thinks he is a worthless fool and refuses to work with him. Jean-Louis and Ariane say he is a *soulasson,* a comical drunk. The summer Parisians consider him *l'idiot du village.* Yet he has secured a whole underworld of connections and loyal friends. Madame Briançon and Madame Savin depend on him. He is the caretaker of the church and us. He is the self-appointed provincial of an order. We can't imagine Rogny without him.

I had returned to France after the fall semester, and by January, Mary and I had already begun work on restoring the presbytery. Our first project was to remove the peeling wallpaper, an arduous job as it turned out. In January, the dark comes early, so it seemed as if we'd work well into the night. One evening, a loud rapping at the window startled Mary and me. Anyone passing on the place de l'Église could see us inside in our winter coats scraping off wallpaper in the gaping white living room. We had only one halogen lamp and a Japanese kerosene heater, its concave reflector giving off an orange glow over the floor tiles.

When we moved to the window and could see beyond the glare, we found an elfish spirit who might have jumped out of the book *Legends of the Puisaye*. We thought he was anywhere between forty and seventy years old—we couldn't tell. He was pointing emphatically to the right, meaning for us to let him in the front door. When we passed through dark, web-filled halls and unlatched the door, the little man shouted *"Bonsoir!"* and marched through the rooms as if he had haunted the presbytery all of his life.

"I am an old friend of Père Jo," he announced; then, in mock worship, he took off his black worn-out cowboy hat, knelt in the direction of the church, and genuflected. Grinning brightly, he wiped away a flow of drool from the side of his mouth with an ancient handkerchief and finished by blowing his nose. A sudden stranger had occupied our house, filling it with vapors of *pastis*. In the wan light, we could see that his face was deformed; we thought that he had forgotten to put in his false teeth.

Clearly, he had a rapport with the house, which we did not. He led us to the next room, pointing. *"C'était le bureau de Père Jo. Son lit était là, et là on prenait un verre ensemble."* Père Jo worked, slept, and drank in the same room. Coco was half sitting in the air. We thought he was asking for a drink. At the time we had nothing to offer, not even a chair. A mixture of repulsion, pity, and amazement paralyzed Mary and me.

He showed us a set of photographs that he had in his pocket, glossy black-and-whites from decades ago. He was in uniform, with patrol dogs. *"C'est l'Algérie."* It was the same small man, a flyweight, no more than a hundred and thirty pounds, but unusually handsome. The difference now couldn't have been more jarring.

That was the first time we met Coco. His name is André

Krakowska; his family was Polish. His closest friends call him André or Dédé. Everyone else calls him Coco after the consonance in Krakowska. In the army he was a dog trainer, and since then he has held several jobs in local factories and for the department of roads and highways. Still, he knows logging best. He has trademarks—his dirty cowboy hat; his German shepherd, Dan; and his dark jokes about his own death.

"You are leaving?" he shouts out from his front door as we load the car on a Sunday afternoon.

"*Oui,*" Mary responds.

"I am leaving too, *par le ciel*!"

"But one day we all must leave through the air," said Mary.

"It's not obligatory," intrudes another neighbor from the far side of the *place*. If Coco is not leaving through the air, he pretends to be hanging himself from the bell tower or collapsing from a heart attack in the garden.

Coco elected himself the overseer for the reconstruction of the presbytery. He opened and closed the house and gates for the workers, organized the deliveries of materials, let the workers use his sink and facilities, and invited them all in for drinks, not just the workers but also the truckers and deliverymen. He was a natural manager of workers. The more we learned about Coco, the more he began to appear to us as one of the most capable and shrewd men in the village. He had connections everywhere, and these connections were reinforced through neighbors helping neighbors and the ritual of communing over the hallucinogenic combination of *pastis* and *gros rouge*.

Coco's friends would begin stopping on the *place* at seven in the morning for *un verre*, a glass, usually sterilized by alcohol. He would then cross the *place* and open up the church, one of his duties as caretaker. Then around nine, Coco would hop on his moped and go sputtering off, Dan barking in the fumes all the way down the hill. He'd go just to buy a *baguette* and then a *verre* of *rouge* at the Saint-Mathurin Bar. He always managed to work somewhere: cutting wood, clearing land, or digging trenches for drainage pipes. At 12:30, he'd return to eat lunch with Madame Briançon or Madame Savin, and from 1:30 to 3:00 he'd close his shutters and nap. Then, as if he lived two days in one, he'd get up again for another round of drinking and work: stacking and cutting wood or going off on another mysterious job. In the evening, one of the women on the *place* would bring him soup. His church and his shutters were closed by eight.

In the winter of 1993, temperatures plunged to −17 Celsius, cold for our area of Burgundy. Without heating in an empty stone house, there is no way to escape the cold. Fires warm only the fire side of your body; everywhere else seems like the frozen depths of the universe.

We had already started the heavy work of making the presbytery habitable. Monsieur Deluche, who had been strongly recommended to us by our friend Jean-Louis, was completely restoring the roof. Tiles were piled on the terrace, and the skeleton of the roof emerged as if the skin of a rotting animal had finally peeled away. Deluche encouraged us to hire Monsieur Nottin and his brother to install the plumbing, heating, and electricity.

It's hard not to type the personalities of the workers. Melville categorized the temperaments of sailors according to where they worked on ships, ranging from the moody cooks belowdecks to the lighthearted furlers singing among the ropes and yardarms. In the French countryside, temperament seems based on levels of technical skill.

Roofing is hell work. It's the bottom of the boat turned upside down. It's dangerous, thankless, and grueling. There's no shelter from the cold, the heat, the rain, or the wind. The air around you hums with wasps and hornets, and the *greniers* are crawling with spiders and filled with bat shit and the encapsulated skin and bones of mice and voles deposited by owls. Deluche fit the part of the moody worker—black hair; deep tan; thick, strong arms; a brooding look. Still, he had a cunning sense of humor.

Nottin, on the other hand, looked like a French flying ace from the Great War in his well-fitting green overalls. He was older and much slimmer than Deluche and had pale skin and thin blond hair. His gray eyes and air of studied reflection gave him a certain dignity. Aside from working as an electrician and plumber, Nottin was a heating expert, which required him to keep abreast of the innovations and techniques of insulation and effective heating units.

That winter, I would leave Paris early on Friday mornings, cruising against the current of inbound commuters. I'd pick up supplies from one of the large home-building suppliers, Zerflou or Dacier, and work the whole day plastering, taping, scraping down windows and glazing them. In the late afternoon or early evening, I'd pick up Mary at the train station in Montargis, thirty minutes away, and we would work together all weekend, steaming the walls and chipping at wallpaper. For only one hundred and sixty francs a night, we rented a *gîte;* the term literally means "shelter" but is used to refer to rental apartments or cottages. In this case, the *gîte* was a restored farmhouse that had been divided into two living quarters. Our side was very small, simply a bedroom, kitchen, and bath. The interior had recently been redone, so you had the odd experience of entering an old, rough-looking shell of a building but living and sleeping in a generic modern house. On the other side of a dividing wall, there was a tenant farmer's family, and they unfortunately had control of the central heating.

Utterly exhausted each night, every pore filled with plaster or cement or some dirt fallen on us from a long-ago pestilent age, our hair stiff with it, we would return to the *gîte*, bathe, cook dinner on the two electric burners, share a bottle of wine, and collapse. Christabel, accustomed to the pillows and stuffed chairs of Paris, thought she had become trapped in a siege. She had to endure the piles of rubble, the yard ramparted with building materials, and the grass booby-trapped with briers and nettles. The cold, broken floor tiles were absolutely unacceptable. The construction-site commotion sent her into a rage of barking or reduced her to a quivering nuisance, so she spent many of her days sleeping in the solar warmth of our Peugeot.

What we thought were our grimmest days in the house turned out, in fact, to be our rite of passage. We would return to Paris after a weekend of work, our joints stiff and muscles sore until midweek when we'd recover enough to imagine another spirited foray against the ruins. On every level we confronted obstacles and difficulties. There were additional beams to be replaced, and reinforcements had to be made in the roof. The damp north wall of the bathroom required insulation. Then, because of the great shifts in temperature that winter, the walls inside the house would literally weep with condensation, tears trailing down the woodwork. Other times, the rooms radiated an unbearable chill. Nottin convinced us to insulate the outer walls of the entire house, a job I'd do myself. On top of all this, Malaud, the former owner, had hired painters to spray the whole interior of the house white, making it almost impossible now to get the old wallpaper off and wounding our pride as we thought how clean the inside had initially appeared. Costs were rapidly rising.

In spite of how hard we worked or how discouraged we became, those winter days were filled with wonder. The house, the village, and the region began to open up to us, to feel familiar. At night we'd close the house and descend into the village, where each chimney was smoking in the moonlight and the canal and the river were filled with ice. We'd pass over the bridges and locks and drive out of the valley. Above the town again, we'd have a view of the stables and pastures of the Haras de Cottard, where world-class Arabian horses were raised. Later we'd stand in the square of the farmyard, surrounded by ruined buildings and looming farm machinery, the fields and edge of the forest under the stars. By morning, we were transported to an entirely different landscape, the air solid with a freezing fog and the copses and old cornstalks covered in rime. The Arabian horses, already unearthly in their beauty and grace, were out exercising in the clouds.

One evening, Coco appeared at a window. *"Non, non! On ne fait pas un feu comme ça."* He shook his deformed head with disapproval. The fire wasn't centered. Coco, accompanied by Dan, came through the garden gate and then through the kitchen door, determined to rescue us from our ignorance. Christabel was sent into a fury, snapping and barking alternately at Coco and Dan, Coco shouting out, *"Ce n'est pas mignon!"*—This is not cute!—and Dan, being a gentleman, stood stoically before the storm of ill temper. Our quiet evening would turn into a scramble until Christabel's anger abated to an occasional ugly growl. I tried to console Dan by rubbing him behind the ear, but Coco, whose face was flushed, making him appear ten years older than his ordinarily indeterminate age, said, *"Non, ne caressez jamais comme ça."* He patted Dan briskly three times on his back to demonstrate how I was to caress the dog from now on. Then he tried to make friends with Christabel, who tended to act more like the monster in the film *Alien* than a six-pound lapdog. Whatever Coco knew from training dogs in Algeria wasn't going to help here.

I tried to imagine this small woodsman from a simple village transported to North Africa, maybe to a town like Ghardaïa, about which I had read, a village of blue buildings rising out of the red desert. The French army was defending gas pipelines twenty kilometers away, while the Americans had oil wells on the other side of the town. We'd learn later that many of the young men in the village during the fifties and sixties had served in Algeria. So much of that atrocious war remains a mystery, the French being so adept at evading culpability. Even within some French families, it is forbidden to discuss the war. God knows what Coco trained the dogs to do or what he thought of Muslims, their Casbahs, cafés, and mosques. Here Coco was in his element—the misty winter, the woods, the mosses, the smoky village.

Mary and I were about to give up work for the night and head for our *gîte,* but Coco insisted on trimming up our fire. This time we had wine to offer in exchange for his tutelary gestures. Satisfied with his work, he asked for water in his wine and then he stood with his glass by the gaping fireplace as he once did when Père Jo slept in the kitchen, and claimed with much drool and fury that the *gendarmes* had been placing traps for him. He'd been caught twice for driving his moped while drunk. It was a conspiracy.

"*C'est Madame Dubois.* She saw me pass in front of her house, and then she makes a quick phone call to the *gendarmerie. Et voilà.* The *gendarmes* were waiting."

The *gendarmes* would wait for Coco when he returned from the Saint-Mathurin. He wiped his face and grinned, turning his cowboy hat Napoleon-like. "*J'ai changé de route.*"

The *gendarmes* quickly tired of Madame Dubois's calls and cold nights staring down the rue de la Montagne or rue des Colombes waiting for Coco to sputter around the corner. On another evening, Coco showed up covered with scratches, having varied his route into blackberry brambles.

"*Ça ne fait rien,*" he insisted. It's nothing.

We had rented our *gîte* from Monsieur Fougère, a rough and rather evil-looking man who might have been the miller in *The Canterbury Tales*. But his appearance was a false gauge of his character. His wife had oddly come to resemble the hens she raised: small head, round body, perky and pleasant. We often bought roasting chickens and fresh eggs from her. Fougère had restored several *gîtes* in the area and with his wife ran a *chambre d'hôte,* the French version of the bed-and-breakfast. These were ancillary sources of income to supplement his main occupation, large-scale agricultural farming. We were amazed to learn that Fougère was himself a tenant farmer, that the land he lived and worked on belonged to the Harmelle family. Though Fougère managed other tenant farmers and developed side businesses, it was as if on some basic level the old regime still existed—the aristocratic family holding a monopoly on land, the peasants paying tribute. But on another and more fundamental level, we were discovering that in our part of France a whole new subculture had developed, one of initiative, one that balanced self-reliance and the social and economic realities of an agricultural community. The French economy had long forsaken villages like Rogny. But the village people have confidence in hard work, in their own skills, and in imagination.

Fougère owned nothing himself, but he had negotiated a special deal with the Harmelles. He would be reimbursed for the renovations he made on the old farm buildings while he also had the right to rent the property to vacationers. In a sense, Fougère was subletting. He'd register the buildings with the *Guide Officiel de la Fédération Nationale des Gîtes de France,* an association that publishes and distributes a national listing of *gîtes* and *chambres d'hôtes* and ranks their comfort levels and the beauty of their surroundings. The rankings are represented by so many *épis,* stems of wheat, instead of the stars usually associated with hotels and restaurants. Fougère's *gîtes* merited two stems of wheat, losing a third because of a large fertilizer tank that stood functionally next to the driveway. It was considered an eyesore.

In spite of being a modern-day serf, Fougère was prosperous; however, he did not have a high opinion of his aristocratic landlords. "*Les Harmelles, quels cons! Le marquis* is crazy, but his uncle, *le comte,* is the worst. It's the count who put that barrier up, the one on the route past the family château. It's a communal road. It's public, for no matter whom. But *le comte* thinks the opposite. He thinks the world is his. He threatens everyone with his gun, hunters and lawyers alike. He shoots at them. *Ça, ce sont les Harmelles.*"

We thought perhaps Fougère was fomenting another revolution, but as soon as the subject shifted, so did his humor. We were not only interested in Fougère's *gîtes* as inexpensive places to stay while working on our uninhabitable house; we also needed a place for visitors who were not up for sleeping amid debris. In addition, we were soliciting from neighbors advice on renovation, and Fougère had done plenty. Nothing brightens French spirits more than explaining the right way to do something.

Deluche and his crew worked from right to left across the roof. To us, in our inflated pride, the process matched the renovation of the Sistine Chapel. On one end, the tiles emerged a bright reddish orange, the zinc gleamed around the chimneys, and white *ciment de fixation* gave a new finished look to the corners and peaks. The presbytery began to display a revivified nobility, its original aspect. On the church side, the roof retained its mossy, forsaken look, beautiful in another region of the heart, a building infused with nature.

Because the south end of the house remained in the shadow of the church throughout the winter, the walls retained humidity, and after almost two hundred and fifty years the two oak beams at the corners of the roof and a major structural beam in the ceiling of the two bedrooms had to be replaced. Deluche arranged to have the special *entreprise de charpente* of Monsieur Millot do the work, an impressively large crane looming over the house and effortlessly drawing out one great beam through the back wall and replacing it with a new one slipped through the same hole. The two corner beams were lowered and fixed in place with oak pegs, just as had been done centuries before.

The damage, however, didn't end with the beams. I had decided to insulate all of the exterior walls with *polyplaque*, Styrofoam-backed Sheetrock. We ordered a huge shipment of the insulating material from Zerflou, who filled our front hall with panels and adhesive. Each panel was rather large—two meters by one—and heavy; still it was easy enough to cut and fit. Once the adhesive had been applied and the panels banged into place, the walls retained the pleasing irregularities of their original form. I had quickly completed three rooms when I realized that the walls were buckling. Something had gone terribly wrong. When I pulled out some of the panels, parts of the wall came off with the mortar adhesive. The plaster had turned to flour, and the mortar had become sand. In a rage, I tore down all my work, panel by panel. The house seemed rotted and pestilent to the core. Mary stood in shock as I stacked up over a dozen panels of ruined *polyplaque*. I could hardly talk during the two hours back to Paris.

Nottin called Deluche the next day to ask what had gone on in the house, and Deluche went down immediately to gawk at the pile of panels and the crumbling walls. Both men were horrified. Deluche called: "Madame, what happened to the house?"

"The walls didn't stick," Mary explained.

"The walls didn't stick?" Deluche repeated after her.

"I meant nothing is sticking together."

Deluche sensed Mary's confused panic. He didn't know much about *polyplaque* himself or how it might be anchored to crumbling walls, but he promised to contact some masons to find out what to do.

Getting professional advice takes a certain amount of diplomacy. Skilled workers know that if you give out too much free advice, you undermine your own business. Deluche managed to learn the technique for restoring such deteriorated walls, and he offered to spend a Saturday morning passing on the precious knowledge.

The amount of work was to be more than quadrupled. Deluche took a small pick and began hacking at the plaster and loose mortar until he reached stone. After shoveling out the resultant rubble, he laid down a piece of plywood and mixed a wheelbarrowful of cement while pouring in *hydrofuge* to make the cement water-resistant when it dried. Mary, like a war correspondent, was carefully penciling down the formulas. Deluche wet the stones and the old mortar to solidify the flourlike dust that the cement would never stick to. Then he began the tricky part—actually throwing cement. He used a flick of the wrist, and the cement flew off the end of his trowel, smacked into crevices, then fell to the plywood. Enough stuck so that when he scraped up the rest and threw it again, a much larger percentage would hold. Slinging cement is not easy; skill comes with feel, the wristy motion more like hitting in racquetball than swinging in tennis. Once enough cement had covered a designated area, he smoothed it with his mortarboard. By the end of the morning, one-sixth of one wall had been dug out and resurfaced. The new surface would provide a solid anchor for cementing the *polyplaque*.

To hire a mason to do the work would have been absurdly expensive. Hammering walls and slinging cement was just too labor-intensive for skilled workers. I knew that I would have to come down during the week as well as on weekends to finish insulating all of the outer walls. Fortunately, Coco couldn't have been more pleased. He and Dan arrived through the garden with a shovel and a wheelbarrow, and the little red-faced man and I began removing the rubble that had once been the curé's walls. Each half hour or so, Coco abruptly halted his determined work to march back to his little house and reignite himself with *gros rouge*.

The day of Deluche's lesson, I dug out a good portion of the wall that he had started. I mixed a wheelbarrowful of cement with *hydrofuge*, but before wetting down the walls, I got a camera and set it up with its remote timer to take a shot of Christabel, Mary, and me covered in dust and squatting in the rubble, our spirits restored. This picture would be on our wedding invitation.

True to our reverie, Mary and I began planning our country wedding. We had entered a new intimacy, one far outside any realm we had known before—it was a place where we could get lost together. The terrace, the garden, and the orchard that Polluche had designed seemed the most natural place for a wedding like ours, an informal ceremony in a warm gathering of our families and old friends, a glorified picnic with the people who had stuck with us through all the eccentric choices and turns in our lives.

We were not a young couple getting married and starting out. Mary had already been through a divorce with one partner and the death of another while I had always maintained a deep skepticism about the prospects of marriage, discouraged from the start by my parents' divorce. Yet we had worked on different continents, crossing oceans of solitude, and still remained committed. We even tried scientific sorcery to have a child, appearing dutifully at fertility clinics at Yale and the University of Paris, until the technical remoteness of the procedures outstripped even our prodigious imaginative capacities. Certainly, I could list reasons both practical and heartfelt for our getting married, but the most important one was that we were having loads of fun.

Shortly after the polyplaquing catastrophe, our longtime friends Steve and Tobé Malawista came to visit us, wanting to tour the building about which they had heard so much. We were totally unprepared for guests, but fortunately Fougère had a *chambre d'hôte* available. The Malawistas drove down from Paris with a friend from England who was related in some way to the royal family. In the middle of February and with all the construction, our visitors had to use their generously speculative imaginations to see the charm in what we were doing. But if anyone could see the charm, it would be Steve and Tobé, who adore France. Still, they were a bit shocked.

"Oh, Mary! My God, look at you!"

When the Malawistas arrived, Mary was wearing an old gray down-filled jacket and was holding a pick. She was covered in plaster dust.

"Mary, what have you been doing?"

"Well," Mary responded, "there's been a disaster. The insulation refuses to cooperate, and the walls are falling apart. So now we're banging plaster and throwing cement."

Steve and Tobé couldn't believe that this was their Mary, the one who played the cello and loved opera, the one who traveled with them to fine restaurants and hotels, the one who was a distinguished scientist.

Tobé said, "How interesting, Mary. But the house is gorgeous, and Jeffrey, it's so exciting, isn't it?" We put down our tools and gave big hugs despite our being covered in dust.

It was Steve and Tobé who, on a trip to Tuscany, originally brought Mary and me together. My mother had worked in Steve's lab at Yale for over twenty years, and so I had known the Malawistas since I was a teenager. Mary had met Steve years before, when, for his sabbatical year, he came to Gif-sur-Yvette to work in Boris's lab. After Boris's death, Mary took a leave to work in Boston as a visiting Harvard professor before taking over the lab at the Pasteur Institute. While in the States, she would often drive off in her little orange VW to spend weekends in New Haven with the Malawistas. Before we met, Mary had invited Steve and my mother to spend a sabbatical in her lab. To celebrate the beginning of a glorious year in Paris, Tobé organized a gathering of friends, Mary among them, to stay at the Gargonza, a restored medieval *castello*, and a nearby farmhouse near Monte San Savino. My mother had already arrived in Paris and I came over to visit her after finishing my doctorate. Tobé had invited my mother and me to Tuscany. At this point, the number of guests had swelled, and Mary refused to spend her vacation with so many strangers. I happened to be just one more unexpected stranger. Tobé assured Mary, "You have to come. You'll see. You'll like Jeffrey."

I wasn't the only objectionable guest. My mother was bringing her golden retriever, Angel, and practically all the guests were dog haters. In the morning, I'd walk the three miles between the Gargonza, where I was staying, and the farmhouse to join the main group, and within two days Mary and I would be taking suspiciously long walks with Angel among the broom, cypresses, and tall grass of the Tuscan hills or lingering, Angel still with us, in a rented Fiat, looking out over the Arezzo Valley to the far spill of lights which was Cortona. Very soon Steve and Tobé were willing to take full credit for our romance, and all the dog haters fell in love with this one exceptional dog, Angel. When Mary and I came back, the dog haters were competing with one another to walk her.

Before we took our friends on an awkward tour through the construction site, Christabel, "the horrible little dog!" was banished to the Peugeot. No one would confuse Christabel with the likes of Angel. It wasn't likely that she'd bite Steve or Tobé, but we didn't want to take chances with a relative of the royal family. The tour was filled with many How extraordinary!'s while our guests looked at stripped walls and dilapidated doorways. We had told the Malawistas about our wedding plans—just an informal picnic on the terrace—and we were hoping not only that they'd come but also that Tobé could somehow sing for us. Tobé's career as a concert singer was blooming; she had recently given performances in New York, Paris, and London. We couldn't have been more pleased when she said that she'd be delighted to perform for us and our guests, all of whom were yet to be invited.

Mary surveyed the terrace and grew perplexed. "Where could we put a piano?" Then she announced with a sudden rush of pessimism, "A piano in the garden is only going to invite rain, and where are we going to find a piano anyhow?"

We all began musing about the piano and where the best place for a concert would be. The living room? The *salle de fête*? The church? In the middle of piano contemplations, Coco appeared in the yard with a hedge clipper and a long electrical cord. He was smiling through his saliva, clearly drunk, calling out his one word of English, "Ho-kay!"

Mary introduced him to our astonished friends. "This is Coco, *notre bon voisin*."

Coco, our good neighbor, shook each friend's hand and gave a hardy, though indecipherable, *"Bonjour!"* He then went through the garden gate to the church to plug his extension cord into the church electricity in order to cut our hedges.

Tobé said, "Maybe we could have the concert at the Château de Prunoy." Prunoy, only a few villages away, was an appealing little château that had been converted into a hotel with a restaurant.

Over the next month the idea evolved into a soiree hosted by Steve and Tobé with a private concert and dinner party at nearby Prunoy. The whole château could be reserved for an evening. Then my mother called and insisted that she should make the dinner for the wedding. My mother loves nothing more than cooking and decorating for holidays and gatherings, and so she appropriated responsibility for all planning and execution of the garden ceremony and feast. Our original notion of a modest *fête* mushroomed into plans for a two-day celebration on the twenty-eighth and the twenty-ninth of May. From the outset, we didn't expect a large group, since we were inviting people who had to travel far and at great expense to a village none of them had ever heard of. But to our amazement, almost everyone accepted. I was reminded of Flaubert's *Madame Bovary*: "Emma, for her part, would have liked a marriage at midnight by the light of torches, but her father thought such an idea nonsensical." Of course, it wasn't my father or anyone else for that matter dictating our plans really; it was just circumstances getting out of hand.

Making the house habitable took on a new urgency. When I wasn't slinging cement and polyplaquing the walls, I was reconditioning the shutters in the yard where the sun would give warmth by midafternoon, hinting at the coming spring. I sanded and repaired each gray shutter, finishing with a semigloss, mold-resistant white paint. After Coco and I hoisted them back into place, we stood back between the well and the Liberty Tree, Coco spreading his arms, feigning pride: *"Ah, ma belle maison!"* The entire place de l'Église was transformed by the white shutters; the house looked brilliant.

Coco's interest quickly shifted to the well, where he told me to watch as he dropped a small stone. I thought of what an unusual relationship we were forming. It wasn't friendship exactly, and yet he was becoming an important part of our lives. He was "our good neighbor," as Mary called him, but her appellation *notre bon voisin* didn't exactly fit someone so mischievous. After all, it was Coco who had shot all the holes in the church's weather vane, a cock with three holes in the tail, one in the breast, and one in the neck. So he wasn't a guardian or caretaker. Most of the time he was bossing me around. I was his *élève*, his pupil. He was right. What did I know about life in his mossy village? We must have been an odd sight, two men, a middle-aged American and a small, disfigured Frenchman, with their heads stuck inside a covered well. It never occurred to me how deep a well on the top of a hill would have to be dug. I could see the smallest coin of light. When Coco dropped the pebble, it seemed to fall all the way to the waters of the Bas-Bourg itself; the tiny coin shimmered with a slight ripple.

Le Serpent

The Bas-Bourg has five bridges. The Pont de Sully is the largest. It spans the canal where it meets the Loing River. This is also the point where the Loing reconverges with itself after passing on either side of a central island. The canal, which continues to the northwest, is lined with rows of massive sycamores. In the summer on the right bank, there are always several large *péniches*, or barges, tied up to the Quai Sully across from the Auberge de la Vieille Colombe. These are usually tour or restaurant barges—*Joie de Vivre*, *Chanterelle*, and *Henri IV*—or infrequent working barges. One barge is actually called *Indifférence Profounde*, which leads us to imagine that some manifestation of despondency had docked in our village. The smaller family boats use the *centre nautique*, a port just up the river. The post office and the festival hall are on one side of the Pont de Sully, and on the other is a park with weeping willows, the monument for the dead, and the river, leaving the canal to commune again with copses and fields. The village kids meet in the park to practice making out or looking disenfranchised.

The Quai Sully provides space for many of the village's *animations* and vagabond activities, most of which come from the social think tank of the Friendship Club. It organizes dances, dinner soirees, and knitting and painting expositions. The Quai Sully is used for the bonfire of Saint Jean, itinerant circuses, and *vides-greniers*. A *vide-grenier*—literally, an attic emptying—is a sale of tools rusted beyond redemption, bald tires, greasy jars, broken cameras, moldy lace, and table after table of lamps, glasses, plates, souvenirs, and gifts no one ever wanted. The *quai* attracts "gypsy" vendors who work out of *poids lourds*, large trucks, and sell industrially made Persian rugs, tools and aluminum ladders, and poor-quality furniture. They are not to be confused with the Romany people who camp a number of times during the year across the river from the Moulin de Cottard, where they do laundry, fish, and sell baskets. Their goats are tied to a convenient tree; their chickens peck around between caravans.

On a miserable day in early February, earnestly gray and penetratingly cold, a vendor had set up a dozen mattresses on the Quai Sully next to his truck. His arrival had been announced in pink Day-Glo advertisements posted around town for two weeks. And there he was with a dozen mattresses on display, covered in plastic, as if ready to serve a village full of narcoleptics. The town, in fact, was dead, everyone indoors against the cold. We happened to be driving by, and Mary insisted that we try the beds.

Testing mattresses is a passion for Mary. If she spends a night in a soft bed, her back goes into a spasm, and she is sick for days. In France, it seems impossible to find a hard bed. Five years after Mary moved to France, she broke her back jumping a horse. She had always loved horses and is still a fanatic about them. Growing up in New Orleans, she worked in local stables just to earn the privilege of riding its horses. When she came to France, she'd ride three times a week early in the morning before going to the laboratory. One morning, her horse stopped abruptly just after jumping a gate, and Mary fell bottom first in the indoor training ring. Because of endorphins, shock, or force of habit, she got back on the horse and finished her ride. Then the pain set in; her number twelve dorsal vertebra was crushed. This is the one just above where her back sways at her waistline and below her shoulder blades.

She spent a month immobilized in the hospital. If she had made a wrong move, she might never have walked again. Once she was out of the hospital, she had to spend three months lying on a board. She could stand briefly but never sit. She spent her days reading by a picture window in the house where she lived with Boris in Gif-sur-Yvette, a suburb of Paris. The window had a prospect over the garden, and she identified all the different birds that visited. Her check marks from those long, still days can be found in our *Guide to the Birds of England and Northern Europe*.

Mary felt each of the vendor's mattresses for firmness and then lay down on a few, staring into the winter sky. They seemed poorly made and expensive, but Mary found one she had to have, the only mattress in France firm enough to truly please her. On Mary's insistence, I climbed on the mattress with her. "It's perfect, isn't it?"

I couldn't tell much in my winter coat. "Of course it's great." I didn't know how long I'd be required to lie there in the middle of the village, the vendor assuring us, *"Il est d'une qualité exceptionnelle. Regardez la couture. C'est extra."* It looked, on the contrary, to be of rather low quality and the sewing slipshod. But I could sleep on anything. Mary, still staring at the sky, asked, *"Ça coûte combien?"* We were soon sliding the mattress on top of the Peugeot and, holding it with our arms out the window, creeping up the hill to the presbytery.

We set the mattress down, still wrapped in plastic, in the room that Coco identified as Père Jo's office. It is the room next to the kitchen, where Père Jo had slept. Then Mary playfully provoked our first housewarming, unbuttoning and pulling down her jeans, her legs covered with goose bumps, her skin shocked by the icy air. We kept our coats on, but still Mary had her bare bottom against the cold, dusty plastic.

Père Jo's old office was palely lit through chinks in the louvered shutters and by the windows of the garden doors, in the steady dimness of winter. Above us were leaves of peeling paint and paint-covered spiderwebs, with black mold spots on the walls. The fireplace had a broad semicircle of fallen carbon knocked down by strong winds, hanging bats, or the flutter of nesting birds. Completely alien to the character of the building, the iron hot plate in the fireplace had been cast with the image of a nude woman.

The grayness of the place, by contrast, made our happiness and physical passion all the more brightly colored. No setback could wholly keep our good spirits in check. It seems odd to enjoy such pleasures in a house of celibacy, that unfathomable ecclesiastical law created at the Council of Trent. The rumors that we heard of Père Jo's lovers had a natural, sad truth to them; his love would have transpired here in this gray stillness.

With each week that passed, we made major gains in our occupation of the presbytery. Electricity and plumbing were installed in the north side of the house, and Nottin was finishing up on the church side. Deluche and his helpers were finally at the stage of installing the new zinc gutters and drains. He was also patching the roofs on the stables and the dovecote until we could recover enough financially to have them restored properly.

While I was digging out the old plaster and mortar, I was rewarded with a number of wonderful discoveries. I uncovered old beams in walls and ceilings, old flat bricks of buried ovens and hidden chimneys, and cut stone blocks constructed around the front windows. We found closets and doorways that had been papered over, and we opened them with no small trepidation, not knowing what might lie behind them. We expected to find a body or objects steeped in great mystery, and such discoveries are not unheard of. When Jean-Louis and Ariane were remodeling their bedroom, they uncovered an old brick oven in the wall next to the headboard. When they broke through the brick, they found a large World War I artillery shell nesting in the dark, along with a small brass statue of a one-armed saint. If the shell had gone off, it would have taken half of the place de l'Église with it. A bomb disposal unit was dispatched from Paris to pull the shell out of the oven. How many shells are still lurking in the walls? And who knows how many other secrets they keep?

Our French friends with country houses generously improved our quality of life through hand-me-downs. They considered us poor, struggling siblings, and we were welcome to appliances and furniture waiting for bulk trash disposal in April. We were given a fine bottled gas stove, rusted through in a few places, and temperamental, but completely operational. We woke up a small refrigerator from its long sleep in a friend's Paris basement. A Harvard frame and sheet of pressboard suited Mary's mattress nicely. Plates and chairs began to appear. An old red card table served for our dinners in front of the kitchen fire.

As the weather grew warmer, more and more of our activities shifted to the grounds. Our first priority was to liberate the dovecote, the stables, and the statue of Christ from blackberry brambles, called *ronces*. The brambles defend themselves like dense coils of living barbed wire. In spite of our donning thick rubber gloves and arming ourselves with hand sickles and pruning shears, the brambles resisted fiercely, leaving forearms, ankles, and cheeks punctuated with blood. The battle wounds only raised our fury and determination, particularly so for Mary, who saw the brambles standing between her and her dream of a border garden on the terrace. She clipped the stalks at the base and flung long whips of *ronces* into the yard. Slowly we reached the doors of the dovecote, achieving our first major victory. Having refined our tactics and heady with success, we moved our theater of operations to the stables and the former pigsties, the major strongholds of the brambles.

The more we worked, the more we felt the vital force of the living things around the presbytery. The black soil was woven through with worms and powerful roots—*ronces*, roses, lilacs, Judas trees, nettles, wisteria. The *ronces* would smother whole apple and plum trees, which were already covered in lichen and moss. Tall trees were caught in massive constrictions of ivy, and balls of airy mistletoe grew below the denser crows' nests. Hordes of *limaces*, slugs, appeared overnight to chew the shoots of lupine and delphinium to the ground. One morning we saw a whole field covered in gleaming spun glass, the new wheat bewitched by tiny black spiders.

Then the larger animals began to make their appearances, often at first as mysteries. Each night I'd hear a strange whirring sound above the roof or past the chimney. I couldn't guess the source until I found myself on the prayer path under the stern gaze of three tawny owls. Now I see them flashing in the garden or announcing their reentry into the bell tower of the church where they nest. Once we discovered a large scattering of walnut shells under the pear trees and then understood the bizarre displacement of fruit when we saw a fiery red squirrel leap high up the branches of the hornbeam trees. Wild cats prowled after baby rabbits. Voles shuffled in leaves. Large buzzards kept sentry on the fence posts; kestrels hung in the air like divine messengers. In the middle of town, otters patrolled the island or swam past the Moulin de Cottard and the encampment of the Romany people. Once I found a struggling deer, its antlers hooked in a fence. I was caught in that strange predicament that often occurs in confrontations with wildlife: am I going to help, or will I turn frenzy into a nightmare? Fortunately, the terror that I caused when I tried to grab an antler helped the deer to shake free.

I have a difficult time reconciling in my own mind the vast cultivation of the land and the preponderance of human history with the astonishing amount of wildlife and the persistence of nature. Numerous Paleolithic settlements have been uncovered. Just a few villages away, a second-century Roman amphitheater stands in the woods. It held four thousand people where now the grassy seats are encircled by a crumbling stone wall and look down on a small pit. It's hard to picture such a crowd in those woods or imagine what people may have observed in the pit. Even on our own property a pot of 110 Roman coins was found in 1854. They are on display in a museum in Auxerre. Each village has at least one château, some dating back to the ninth century. The area has had a considerable population through the ages and yet the wildlife thrives.

The woods and ponds are filled with game—wild pigs, deer, partridges, pheasants, rabbits, geese, and ducks. This is understandable. Some animals are stocked. The farmers often guarantee so many birds released on the grounds and then invite businessmen from Montargis to hunt on their land. The farmers provide rooms and meals, another ancillary industry to assure survival of their land. But there are also fox, badgers, skunks, and weasels; grebes, herons, egrets, and cormorants; and turtles, snakes, salamanders, and frogs. I can jog a circuit of three villages in an hour—that's how close together the villages are. Yet, at any moment, wild animals can and do appear. What the scholar Nicole Eizner says about French rural life, that "nature is a form of culture, and the village is a part of nature," seems to fit Rogny. The inhabitants cherish their coexistence with the natural world.

After conquering the brambles nearest the presbytery, we began to clear the prayer path, which is essentially a tunnel of branches reaching out to each other. At the far end, the brambles had overtaken the statue of Christ, who has his right index finger pointed toward the highest branches of the hornbeam as he gazes serenely down the alley. His finger is actually broken; he holds up only a loop of rusted wire that supported the plaster appendage. The brambles seemed a long continuation of his robe. Just as the Liberty Tree had sent its roots into our houses, making a part of nature our village foundations, Christ wore the robes of nature. Once we cut away the brambles, the foot of the statue revealed the message *LE MONDE LÀ-HAUT EST MEILLEUR*. The world above is the better one.

Madame Hervé brought the statue to the prayer path during one of her summers camping in the presbytery. It came originally from Père-Lachaise, the cemetery in Paris, where "there is a great density of famous dead," as a friend once described it. After Madame Hervé had the statue mounted, she saw tears well up in its plaster eyes. At the time she had been trying desperately to buy the presbytery. She took the crying statue as another bad sign along with the reluctance of the Harmelles to sell and her mother's conviction that the house was haunted. Having heard the story, we couldn't think of removing the statue.

Besides cutting back the *ronces,* we clipped the hedges that form a wall from the well down to the *charmille* and border one of Bougé's sheep pastures. We recently learned of a village ordinance for *bon voisinage,* or being good neighbors: hedges can be a maximum of only two meters high. Ours were at least two and a half. I'm sure we have violated scores of ordinances, but our neighbors are too circumspect to bring such offenses to our attention.

We finished the hedges, and a day or two later, while piling up the clippings, I uncovered a copper-colored snake, less than a foot long. There are only two types of snakes in our part of France— the *couleuvre,* largish but harmless, and the *vipère,* much smaller, with a telltale *V* on the flat of its head, although this is not a reliable identification. I have seen *couleuvres* swimming in ponds, slipping into walls, or flattened on the road. This was not one. I called Mary to come identify it. Because she had heard somewhere that vipers have stubby tails, she declared, "It's a viper. It's our civic duty to kill it."

"Hell, no!" I was shocked, hearing this from Mary, a biologist and lover of animals. Besides, having never killed a snake before, I imagined many writhing pieces after my botching the job.

Mary insisted, "By law we're supposed to kill it, report it, or something."

"Just wait. I'll get a can or a box. It should have a proper trial before we execute it." As it turned out, the snake was surprisingly timid. It froze in the grass, making it easy to trap.

We had to find someone who could identify a viper, but it was early afternoon, and the whole place de l'Église seemed to be sleeping. We were walking from house to house with our viper in a garbage can. We called out to Ariane and Jean-Louis that we had a viper. Coco seemed to have disappeared, and Marteau was definitely napping. The viper would get a stay of execution until someone appeared. Mary and I went back to our yard work.

A few moments later Coco came through the garden gate, drunker than usual, with a loaded shotgun. Madame Briançon had told him that the foreigners were carrying a viper in a garbage can from house to house on the *place*. When we came to greet him, Coco was already aiming his shotgun. He was going to blow the bottom out of a perfectly good garbage can. But then he pulled back the barrel of his shotgun and reached down, half inside the can, the gun swinging around toward Bougé's place. He came up with the little creature that wove itself around his rough fingers. *"Ah, non, non, c'est un ami. Les orvets sont bons pour le jardin."* Coco convinced us that the *orvet* was our garden's friend.

I had never seen an *orvet* before, a legless lizard, pure copper with fine black racing lines down its sides, a gentle little face. Occasionally, a large green lizard will wander into the house, causing mutual panic. Little striped lizards flash up and down the sunny walls. But this was our first *orvet*. Coco released it carefully in a corner of the terrace just beyond our fig tree. It was strange to see him so protective, first of us and then of the harmless lizard. He cracked open his shotgun and pulled out a red shell from the barrel tube as he rocked around, steadying himself against the ever-shifting pull of gravity.

"I keep this gun to shoot vipers because one killed my baby sister. She was bitten over there," he said, pointing to his own house. "She opened the shutters, and *voilà, c'était mortel.*"

We were clearly much more at risk from a drunken neighbor in the yard with a loaded shotgun than from a viper. However, gathering up a pile of clippings is a likely way to get bitten. Since the legless lizard episode, I've collected many red shotgun shells in our *charmille,* and we confronted Coco with them, after which he readily admitted, though greatly embarrassed, to hunting doves, not vipers. Even if we allowed hunting, our property is in the village, and pellets would hail down on our neighbors. Still, hunting in the village is not uncommon. Bougé had warned us.

"*Attention!* It happens. I've been shot before. I was just behind the house, and the hunters fired from the *charmille.* I never saw them." He flapped his hand. "*Ça brûle!*"

Though spent, the pellets can still burn. Fortunately, he had been hit in the back. Bougé never accused Coco of shooting him, but there was a certain truth to his charge that Coco was a poacher.

Because of our encounter with the legless lizard and our culpability in endangering its life, we bought an illustrated guide called *La Puisaye: Oiseaux, Mammifères, Amphibiens, Reptiles, Orchidées.* It's remarkable that orchids should be the last in a list of animals, as if they, too, belonged among the region's indigenous mobile beings. The book contains specific research information that can be fully appreciated only by a resident. It notes that the last death in the region from a viper bite occurred in Rogny in 1944. The tragedy of war seemed compounded: a three-year-old girl, opening shutters on a village in occupied France, a viper there in the shock of light.

We learned the most about vipers from Bill Montgomery, Mary's nephew, who visited us years later. Besides being an accomplished painter and printmaker, Bill was a passionate herpetologist. From the backseat of our Peugeot, he'd ask suddenly, "Oh, could you stop!" Then he'd jump out to look at a snake that had been flattened into something that looked like a letter from the Arabic alphabet. Bill wasn't sightseeing in France; he was looking for vipers, preferably live ones. Unfortunately, he had to settle for those that turned up on the road. While vipers are not uncommon, they are not easy to find. They are very shy. Even the ones killed on the road are rare, because the crows, which are ubiquitous in our region, carry them away before anyone has a chance to see them. When Bill found one with fatal injuries that were hardly visible, he picked it up and laced it in his fingers. He held it gently to inspect the checked pattern down the spine and the black scales along the underside.

"It's spring, so the snake died trying to warm its awakened body on the asphalt," Bill explained. "They'll come out in the evening or morning."

Mary and I thought that we had two types of vipers, red and gray, but Bill said, "They're just variations of one species. This is an asp. You have asps and adders in Europe, but adders live in the north, as far as Sweden. Around here there are only asps, the more venomous ones."

Bill carried his prized roadkill out to the terrace steps, where he took Nikon close-ups. On sleepless nights in Elgin, Texas, he would etch the snake's likeness on a copper plate under a magnifying glass. Then the plate with its fine lines and shading would be stamped into dampened paper and colored for a field guide—the viper, the moment before it slips onto the road from the shaded cover of aquatint. It took Mary and me months to look at the fields and copses the same way again. We became focused on the road, intent on finding vipers.

The spring of our first legless lizard, I was mowing the lower garden, and the blade caught the slightly raised head of an *orvet*, the gentle creature. I had to toss it into the hedges. As Larkin writes of a hedgehog in "The Mower," "I had mauled its unobtrusive world / unmendably. Burial was no help." It was a moment of futility. There was no meaning in it; it wasn't a sign.

In the Night Glow of the Virgin

*T*he bells in the Église de Saint-Loup ring for Angelus at 7:00 A.M., twelve noon, and 7:00 P.M. The sequence is always the same. Marie Anne, cast and hung in 1860, the smaller high-pitched bell, rings three times three rings; then Isabelle, cast in 1639, sounds a much deeper tone and seems to ring randomly for a minute. Only before Sunday mass or for funerals or weddings do the bells ring together steadily for minutes at a time.

The first morning that we woke in the presbytery, Marie Anne and Isabelle literally rang us out of bed, since the presbytery lies directly under the steeple. Our French friends thought it a joke. Poor fools go to the country only to be deafened. "How go the bells?" Still, you not only grow accustomed to the bells but also begin to feel them set the rhythm of a country day. In the Bas-Bourg, the school bell chimes on the hour and half hour, like a mantel clock, a clear, distant sound. It has its own peculiar pleasure because the school, in our times, is the heart of the village. When a school closes, its village perishes.

One day about a week before the wedding, Coco came impetuously into the yard and grabbed me by the wrist, saying, *"Venez! Venez!"* leading me to the church, flashlight in his hand. I followed him to the porch of the church, which encloses a unique Romanesque portal made of limestone. It is framed by two pilasters, which support arcades carved with fretwork and zigzags. Above the simple half-circle arches, Moorish looking, a triangular facade rises to the level of the nave and is also decorated with fretwork. Next to the portal, there's a passage I hadn't noticed before, with a precarious wooden ladder that leads high up into the batfilled dark under the roof. Coco had his usual day of drinking and it suddenly came to him, regardless of what I was doing, to show me the *clocher,* the bell tower of the church.

The church has a huge atticlike space. The roof is a magnified version of ours, chinks of light coming through the tiles, showing the great shadowy oak structure where the bats sleep. Their droppings crunched under our feet as we crossed the length of the church. It is an odd sensation to walk across the nave to the transept, knowing that there are vast spaces below your feet. It's like going behind a stage, seeing the props. At the transept, there's another set of ladders. We passed from the realm of bats to the crisscrossing framework of oak beams suspending the green bronze rims of Marie Anne and Isabelle, above which the tawny owls had built their nests. All across the wood floors, mice and voles had been transformed into dried-out capsules of fur and bone. I can't imagine how the owls can nest beside the bells and still hear their weird calls and hissing, but they have chosen the highest prospect from which to launch themselves into the night air.

Coco led me to each double-arched window, with central columns, the southern window giving a panorama of the Bas-

Bourg, the seven locks like a giant's staircase leading out of the valley to the waterfall where the river passes under the Bridge of Donkeys. Beyond the island and up the slope toward Brénellerie, you can see the Arabian horses exercising in the fields. Below the slope, to the east, is the Briare Canal with its long line of noble sycamores rising far above the roof of the Vieille Colombe. To the west are the cemetery and fields. Then, pretending to be a sniper, Coco pointed out the north window at the presbytery and its grounds. He said, *"Je suis venu ici avec mes frères et mes soeurs et on a espionné le curé et sa gouvernante."* Besides spying on the curé and his housekeeper with his brothers and sisters, he'd watch from his hiding place the comings and goings of unsuspecting neighbors, seeing them miniaturized by distance in the summer light. He remembered how a Nazi soldier kept guard—a hostile owl—at the highest vantage.

For me, looking down on the grounds of the presbytery had the strangeness of an out-of-body experience, like a flying dream or the removed perspective of a departed spirit; an owl's view, the view of bats and swallows. I could see my family and friends in miniature—Mary working in the garden; Tom, her father, and Phyllis, Tom's third wife, parked in garden chairs, drinks in hand; Mary's nieces digging borders and planting peonies, tree roses, carnations, lobelia, poppies, and impatiens. My mother was there, and old family friends from New Haven, Charles from New York. Soon my father appeared as if out of thin air, a woman accompanying him as he inspected the fruit trees.

In our country house in Connecticut, my father had planted an orchard of dwarf fruit trees in careful rows. I remember so clearly filling the holes in the earth with water, gnats swarming around my ears, my father sweating, lowering the burlap bundles of earth and roots. Those trees were young and straight, hardly mature enough to produce more than a few pieces of fruit, as various as ours, humming with bees, but none so old and experienced. Some brood; others remain in the clutches of brambles; still others tower—all of them full of birds, even in the heartwood.

Our family and friends from America came early for our wedding, and from the bell tower with our elfish neighbor, I felt as if I had dreamed them there below, transported from so many other contexts of my life to come together on foreign ground. The spell was suddenly broken when Coco started shouting, "Ho-kay! Ho-kay," as always showing off his one English word. He continued playacting the sniper, knocking off our entourage, everyone looking up at us. Coco slapped my shoulder and gave his mischievous laugh.

My mother and Lee had been the first to arrive and were installed in the half-finished rooms of the presbytery. Lee is my mother's oldest and closest friend, a large woman with dark, attractive eyes in striking contrast to her aura of white hair. She grew up in the old Italian-American, now Hispanic, community of Fair Haven, attended Catholic schools, and has worked for decades as a nurse in the intensive care unit at the Yale–New Haven Hospital. Her high-pressure job requires some philosophical views of life. Lee will ask, "What are you coming back as? Whether you like it or not, we're all reincarnated, you know. So make up your mind." She is well equipped to care for people on the brink of alternative states of being. She is robust and full of *joie de vivre*, ready for drink and gab.

Lee gave us a miniature glow-in-the-dark statue of the Virgin Mary. "Jeffrey, I brought you the Virgin Mary because she'll bring good weather for your wedding." She insisted that we place it in the western window of the library. "Make sure she's facing out the window."

Europe is governed by anticyclones and depressions, high- and low-pressure systems respectively. When a depression drags its anchor over England, as so often happens in May, the bad weather comes in bands of heavy rain from the Atlantic Ocean and can go on for a month, even a whole season. That May had been very wet, the grounds and fields were deep green, and the wildflowers were so abundant that they made random gardens out of paths and country roads. The weather for the end of May was unpredictable, to say the least, since each day there were downpours and heavy gusts, then rainbows and billowy white mid-spring clouds. At night, the Virgin Mary cast her steady blue-green pall at her assigned window.

While Mary and I spent our weekends in the house and had added sparse furnishings, the presbytery, in our minds, was still a construction site. The walls, some of which had been recently taped and plastered, were still unpainted, rotted beams were exposed, and the ceilings still showed cracks and flaking paint. Dirt came up from broken tiles covered with cement and plaster. We had X-ray vision, the image lingering in our minds, of a building that had suffered long, progressive erosion from Polluche's to Père Jo's time.

Ultimately, through winter and early spring, Mary and I restored gaping, empty rooms, but it was Lee and my mother who seemed to jump-start the heart of the dead building. They opened the entire house to the air, washed all the windows, scrubbed decades of dirt off the woodwork, set up boxes covered with cloth as makeshift tables, and filled with wildflowers any jar or paint can they could find. They wandered off on treasure hunts at the edges of fields and in junk shops and malls. For them the house had been like a blank canvas ready to be filled with air, light, shape, texture, color.

These friends of thirty years, veterans of child rearing, mortgages, infidelities, family deaths, and failed diets, now so settled in themselves, plunged into their undertaking with all the joy of children playing out a compelling fantasy, yet with an inevitable sense of practicality and tastefulness. Their experience comes from years of sorting things out, judging one object against another, knowing what kind of person an object could interest, what kind of universe it should live in, what part of the soul it would touch—the whimsical, austere, romantic, cute, silly, or sad. They passed judgment on demitasse cups, pitchers, prints, candlestick holders, platters, lamps, and tables heaped in flea markets, auctions, antique shops, department stores, tag sales, and annual bulk trash collections.

As my mother and Lee reanimated the presbytery, swallows flew in through windows and open doors. They darted to the molding to chitter over Père Jo's office, then to the bathroom, where they perched on raw wiring that awaited a light fixture. Finally, they settled atop the hot-water heater in the kitchen. Monsieur Nottin had hung the large white tank near the ceiling in a corner, the gap making a perfect space for a nest. The birds chittered for hours, uninhibited by our comings and goings, as if we all were meant to occupy the space together. If we were to believe Lee, they could have been villagers in former incarnations and were looking for a *fête*.

Mary's family also arrived early to help us prepare the house and organize the second day of our wedding. We met them at Orly Airport, for us conveniently located south of Paris. Mary's sister, Margaret, and her nieces Margie and Frannie came from Austin,

Texas, and Tom and Phyllis from Highlands, North Carolina. They had met for a connection in Atlanta, flying together to Paris.

It was an important moment for me, meeting Mary's family, particularly Tom, her father. I had always found the experience of meeting a lover's father intimidating, and Tom was a formidable man in any case: tall, good-looking, a Southern gentleman, formerly a professor of chemistry at Tulane. He carried a large walking stick that his stepdaughter had bought for him when he visited her in China in the early eighties. The cane had a large dragon's head carved into it by the ninety-one-year-old man who sold it illegally before the open markets started to appear. The dragon faced forward from the handle so that when you spoke to Tom you had two dragons staring at you.

Driving back to Rogny, I had Margie in front and Tom and Phyllis seated in back. The others followed in a rented car. I had known Tom and Phyllis for an hour and learned everything about their harrowing winter, when several blizzards buried Highlands. They lived in the last house on Satulah Mountain, on the edge of the Smoky Mountain range. Tom tended to shout, since he had hearing in only one ear, poor hearing at that. His stepson shot him in his good ear the night he also shot down Nancy, Tom's second wife in their New Orleans garden. Such horrors frequented Tom, as if he were a character in a Southern detective novel.

"Three days we were stranded. No heat, electricity, or telephone! The army finally came to get us. They came up Satulah in troop carriers! Then we stayed in a Red Cross shelter, and it kept snowing!" We already knew that Phyllis's daughter had called the police; Tom was too stubborn to call for help himself.

Along the winding country road, Phyllis fell asleep while sucking on a piece of hard candy and woke heaving as if she were having a heart attack. Tom, only half awake himself, when shouting about the blizzard, noticed nothing. I pulled into the parking lot just in front of the old Roman amphitheater; Phyllis choked wildly beneath the grass-filled seats that overlooked a spooky scene. Mary, Margaret, and Frannie pulled up to see Margie beating poor Phyllis on the back. Finally, a bright yellow piece of lemon candy shot out, to everyone's relief, on the silent, ancient ground. When Phyllis got back into the car, shaken but grateful to breathe, Tom sat in the same position, as if nothing had happened. "We had biscuits and tea mainly! Even the Red Cross was unprepared!" A scenic Burgundy drive, Phyllis's near-death experience at the amphitheater: poor tired man, he could hardly tell the difference.

When we arrived at the presbytery, a two-humped camel, a zebra, and a llama marched around the Liberty Tree on the place de l'Église. A donkey with a cart followed, playing recorded calliope music through two loudspeakers. They were led by a clown and an acrobat in a red sequined leotard, all of them a little weary from the routine. The camel was draped with advertising for the one-ringed circus that had set up its tent on the Quai Sully. From time to time, a lion's roar rose up to the Haut-Bourg from the canal. The little parade seemed an impromptu arrival ceremony for Mary's family. It marched off down the rue Gabriel-Landy, where Coco stood with trusty Dan in the doorway of his modest house, doffing his cowboy hat and taking deep bows to the clown and acrobat and then more bows to Mary's family, who discreetly hid their horror at the sight of our drooling neighbor.

After all the introductions and a tour of the presbytery, Mary's family settled in at their *gîte*, just below the Haut-Bourg, next to an old *boulangerie* and the Quai Sully. There they'd take a nap with the camel groans and deep grumblings of the lions passing through their dreams. We planned to go to the circus late in the afternoon. None of us had ever seen the roving European kind: large red trucks and trailers, with performers, handlers, and animals all living and traveling together, a nomadic life of bare survival on the social periphery.

The animals marched through the town, and then they were staked to a grassy area along the canal, with barges passing slowly by and kids roaring at the lions caged in one of the trucks. By the time everyone had awoken from that heavy sleep that provokes the strange sensation of forgetting where you are, facts slowly reassembling in a foreign light, there was a downpour. We passed by the tent, and not one child had shown up for the show. The acrobat was standing at the entrance of the tent with one of the animal handlers. She had black hair tied back and wore a bright red cape all the way down to her bare ankles. In all of her makeup and sequins, she gazed at the rain, a performer without an audience.

Nothing is less French than opening one's house to the world. While every other house on the *place* was locked up in the evening, the shutters on the presbytery were wide open. Only a few of the windows had curtains. Anyone passing could hear us talking, see us in the long evening light that comes in from the west, or watch us in the light of dinner candles. Our neighbors turned their heads away as they passed our windows, particularly Monsieur Bougé, who went through the greatest gyrations to be discreet, to show his deep respect for the inner sanctity of the home. We made it difficult for him as he passed at least twice a day to tend to his childhood house next door.

It's not in our nature to shut out the world, particularly in the country, full of changing light, joyful sounds, and fresh scents.

Even at three in the morning, as I wander down the hall to use the bathroom, what could be more stunning than the view from the Virgin Mary's window, the whole valley lit by the moon? I'd watch the insects that flew in through the open windows, the transparent wings of one soon trembling in the filaments of a web. A crane fly tapped all legs in a corner as if searching for an opening to the fourth dimension. Later I found Mary standing in the refrigerator light, wearing nothing but bottoms, guzzling water. I'd follow her from hall to hall back to bed, the way discernible only by starlight. The grounds outside bound in stillness. Finally, we'd climb into bed, into the horrible sheet tangle. The bottom sheet didn't fit the bed, and the feathers in the comforter had shifted all to one side, causing Mary to battle with it, one leg in, one out, over the shoulder, off the shoulder, tossing it off altogether.

"Damn these sheets. They're never right. Can we get up and straighten them?" Twenty minutes later the battle recommenced. "Goddamm sheets! They're after me!" The sheets took on a life of their own.

If Mary betrayed any signs of losable cool, it was over the sheets. She worried about how we'd get fifteen sets and keep track of them over a two-week period. We'd reserved all the *gîtes* we could in the area, including three from Fougère. In France, sheets and towels are not supplied at rentals. With all the guests arriving, we had to come up with them ourselves. We had no choice but to ask Jean-Louis and Ariane and our friends in Paris. In the end, we stockpiled sheets, in all their various colors and sizes, from four different households besides ours. Mary decided that each sheet had to have an identification, a color-coded mark indicating from whom it was borrowed and to whom it was to be issued. The sheets were to be the primary responsibility of all guests. Each set came with Mary's explicit instructions for care and return; they were to be guarded like flags of honor.

After the first washing, the sheets lost their markings. They were being matched up arbitrarily. Then they began to vanish altogether. Picnic cloths? Rags? Sails? Who knows? It was impossible to get our guests to appreciate the full magnitude of the problem. "What's with Mary and the sheets?" For Mary, when the sheets got out of control, there was no order in the universe.

Everyone was satisfied with the explanation that Mary was just displacing anxiety to the sheet problem. But then there was the problem of towels. Of course, Americans use towels once and put them in the wash, so the towels wandered off from the guests to whom they were issued. The towel crisis followed the same hysterical pattern as the sheets. "What's with Mary and the towels?"

Other schemes were more successful. We learned that the village had a number of chairs and long fold-up tables and that we could use these at absolutely no cost. In fact, two of the town workers seemed happy to deliver them. They were an odd couple, one a burly, bearded redhead, unusual in France, and the other much smaller and wiry. When they arrived at the presbytery, they couldn't believe what they saw. *"Personne ne se marie dans un chantier."* No one gets married at a construction site. They paused to look in wonder at the rotted beams dug out of the walls, and they shook their heads with genuine worry. We stored the tables in the living room because if it rained we would set them up there and in the library. The workers passed them through the front window hardly saying a word.

One of our main resources was the *épicerie*, or grocery store, situated in the center of the village. An enterprising man named Monsieur Guillon, who had an uncanny resemblance to Richard

Gere, ran the shop with his wife, a short pleasant woman with hair spun to twice the size of her head. The *salon de coiffure* in Rogny seems to offer only two colors, as the village women are either radioactive redheads or toxic blondes, Guillon's wife being among the latter.

In France, it is virtually impossible to buy a bag of ice. It comes in blocks or shavings, and we needed to cool a bathtub full of white Burgundy, Sancerre, and *crémant*. Mary asked Guillon if he could get ice for us.

"Madame, I can put several bottles of Volvic in the freezer for you." Freezing plastic bottles full of mineral water was a perfect solution. As the water melted, we could offer the Volvic at the tables. It must have been a trick he learned serving so many barges. Guillon also had access to Rungis, the famous hub of France's food distribution, located next to Orly. He could get us all the fresh fruits and vegetables we'd need.

We ordered pâtés from our *boucher* in Paris, Monsieur Bajon, a little man with black hair and a red scarf who sang out, *"Bien sûr, monsieur! C'est parfait, monsieur! Exactement comme vous voulez!"* as he skated on the sawdust of his tile floor. While Monsieur Bajon provided the epitome of *commerçant* theater, his work was pure artistry. He would skate out of the freezer with a rough cut of lamb or veal and carve with his array of knives a sculpted crown roast or tie a perfectly corseted *rôti de veau*.

Quatrehommes, our *fromagerie* on the rue de Sèvres, was a veritable museum of cheeses, where we stocked up on Beaufort, Époisse, Sainte-Maure, and Aveyron Roquefort. A mountain of *baguettes* would come from the *boulangerie* next to the lock across from the *épicerie*. We would pick up *jambon persillé*, a Burgundian specialty with ham, garlic, and parsley in gelatin, when we went to see Monsieur Pillot, our wine producer, for Santenay and Chassagne-Montrachet in the Côte d'Or. We accumulated sacks full of plastic utensils, plates, and glasses along with paper napkins and tablecloths.

While Mary and I stockpiled the necessary ingredients for May 29, I thought of Emma's country wedding in *Madame Bovary*.

The table had been laid under the wagon-shed. It was laden with four sirloins, six fricassées of chicken, a casserole of veal, three legs of mutton, and, as a center piece, a handsome roast suckling-pig flanked with meat-balls cooked in sorrel.

Certainly, no single person had prepared such a feast. For our country wedding, the cooking, decoration, and choreography were all in my mother's hands. The day would follow her scenario, and one of the strongest patterns in my mother's life is that her mind becomes lit up with scenarios that rarely take into account the risks of any given situation. Every venture she undertakes has about it an aura of apocalypse—whether it's having a child at sixteen or making a dinner party. She says defiantly, "I know I may crash and burn. I can't help it." She forces her scenario into being and fits everyone into it, unwittingly or not.

She has always been a rebel, leading insurrections often against her own best interests. After her father's death and the house fire, she had spent a year going to libraries and movies instead of to P.S. 131 in New York. She had financed her days stealing milk and the *Times* from neighbors' doorsteps and pocketing the money her mother had given her to buy them. She was sent to boarding school, where she refused to speak, using her self-inflicted isolation to read through every book in the library or fall into dreams while ironing and cooking for the school, the everyday chores required of the students. Even her voracious reading was seditious; Kains's *Five Acres and Independence* led her to raise a family in a quixotic natural world, removed from T. S. Eliot's "Hollow Men." The house of my childhood was filled with the books, records, and pictures of her adolescent heroes: Gandhi, Thoreau, Whitman, Graham Greene, C. P. Snow, Sartre, Camus, Coltrane, Ella Fitzgerald. The FBI came all the way out to our little country shack to ascertain the extent of my mother's complicity in the communist malignancy. Then, in confirmation of their suspicions, she was carted off to federal prison for trying to lie down on the deck of the U.S.S. *George Washington,* in Groton. She was protesting the installation of nuclear weapons on submarines.

In recent years, my mother has turned her rebel spirit against any obstacle to pleasure and comfort, a losing battle given the chronic maladies that arrive with age. However, she will go to any effort or expense to give a party for her friends. May 29 would be her creation. She would plan, cook, orchestrate, and where better than in a Burgundian village? Of course, the presbytery, so recently raised from the dead, with its half-sized refrigerator and rusted-out stove, threatened her plans with an array of hazards.

Coco found ways to join the preparations. Mary's nieces, Margie and Frannie, were busy working in the garden, and Coco insisted on digging holes for their peonies and roses. The women couldn't understand a word of what Coco was saying, thinking that the town drunk was angry with them for some unknown reason. They both stood stiffly with their arms crossed while Coco talked nonstop, trying to teach them the proper use of a shovel. It didn't occur to him that the two American women had ever used a shovel before. Coco didn't believe in flowers, but he believed in helping neighbors. He then decided to hack back the ungainly lilacs that had passed their bloom, and he poured gasoline on the cut branches and burned them in the orchard. This brought Bougé over in fury to accuse Coco of being an arsonist. *"Idiot! Vous êtes un criminel!"* Bougé thought that Coco was once again trying to burn down his childhood home.

The night-glowing Virgin began to assert her powers over European weather patterns; days grew clear, sunny, and hot. Only so much digging and planting in the garden or cleaning and preparing of the presbytery could be permitted our early-arriving guests. We planned several excursions, one of which was a private viewing of the Haras de Cottard.

Mary and I had first visited the *haras* in the winter when Rogny was still veiled from the material world by wood smoke, on days that hardly woke under a solid sheet of gray sky. The Haras de Cottard held an open house and exhibition of their Shamilah Arabians. These horses are purebred, in all age groups, champions in Europe, the States, and Canada. Their presence in Rogny seemed a child's wish answered by a genie. Arabians are the poster horses that children sleep under. In the damp winter in Rogny, region of moss, lichens, and ferns, the Arabians went on display in all their desert mystique.

Arabians have a visceral magnetism, as if they were, in their strength and beauty, the physical materialization of some part of the human spirit, their size complementing the human body. No other animal, in all our history, has transported us so faithfully into nightmares of our own making and into the realization of our highest aspirations. Arabians are the oldest breed, depicted in Egyptian statuettes dating back to 2000 B.C. and in rock carvings in ancient Nejd and Syria. They are the horses of Ishmael and Solomon. Muhammad proclaimed that the path to heaven was through the care of horses, and at the same time such care was an earthly pleasure, a gift. The desert Bedouins, over centuries, had bred Arabians for strength, speed, and endurance. The Arabian horse became the vehicle of Islamic expansion through Egypt, northern Africa, and Spain. The Muslims were so aware of the horse's superiority that they forbade the sale of Arabians to Christians, but still in conquered territories the Arabians' traits were passed on to other breeds. In fact, Arabians have been used in the upgrading and development of all other breeds.

A large crowd came to Rogny for the open house, more than the exhibition hall could handle. Before the show, we had a chance to pass by each stall. The horses seemed to sense Mary's passion for them, her sureness around them that comes from a lifetime of riding. Mary spoke to each one—Ménestrel al-Shamilah, Julia Bea, Musknitsa, Creativa, Padron's Mist, Neschara, Karaganda, Vojvondina.

We were among the earliest to arrive in the showroom, at Mary's insistence. The walls around the arena were covered top to bottom with show ribbons. When the lights went out and music was pumped into the arena and when the shafts of spotlights circled with mounting intensity, I knew that here was the horse breeder's version of the NBA. With music blaring, Nadir, the premier stallion, flashed into the pool of light, his tail flying like a black silken flag of the Bedouins, his muzzle greased to show the shining flare of his nostrils. Running by his side was a trainer in his white billowy shirt, breeches, black boots, crop in hand, dancing with the horse, all to heavy-metal rock music and the incitement of the other trainers banging their crops at the edge of the ring.

Nadir introduced the long procession of champions, fired and greased, each an embodiment of alertness and energy, going through the intricate choreography with its trainer. The centerpiece of the choreography was the moment when the trainer held the butt end of his crop up toward the muzzle of Ménestrel or Musknitsa or Padron's Mist. The horse fully extended its long neck into an arched curve called *mitbah*, showing the distinctive angle at which the head and the neck meet. The more extravagant the curve, the greater the horse's agility in moving its head dramatically in any direction.

Toward the end of the show, after the yearlings were shown, recent buyers were presented with their frisky young horses that jerked them around the exhibition hall. Then Nadir made his last appearance, half horse, half god, flooded in light, drums and bass beating the audience into a communal tachycardia.

After that open house, the Haras de Cottard became Mary's horse dreamworld, requiring several visits each weekend to watch the trainers exercising their perfect animals. By May, the new colts were springing into the air or cavorting around on giraffelike legs, each colt worth more than a very fine house. In fact, one horse might be sold to several owners who breed them at different ranches. Others were bought for status. It seemed no small irony that members of the Arabian royal family came to our obscure village in France to buy the horse their own culture had created.

Mary arranged with the *haras* to have a private showing of the Shamilah Arabians, sure that family and friends who had come for the wedding would be as awed by them as she was. The proprietor of the *haras* was more than pleased to make an appointment. Mary told everyone, "She thinks we're rich Parisians looking to buy a horse."

We went from stall to stall, some holding mares and colts, others stallions, all the horses we knew, Ménestrel, Julia Bea, Musknitsa, Creativa . . . Mary cooing to each one, the heat slowing the world down into flies and warm odors. My mother and Lee quickly had enough of the heat and left early for the cool rooms of the presbytery. But Mary's family stayed on, her nieces just as mesmerized by the Arabians. They shared Mary's passion for horses, and one had to conclude that it was somehow engendered in the women of the family. Mary had had Tabu, who died in her arms. Frannie had had a geriatric mustang called Smoky, while her daughter has Summer and Star. The trainer brought out Musknitsa and coaxed her into a *mitbah*.

Mary's father stood in the heat, wearing a checked wool hat, skeptically watching the chestnut stretch its neck into an absurd muscular arch. He and Phyllis habitually overdressed. It was as if they were ready at any moment to be received at a château. Out in the direct sun by the pasture, he was miserable. Besides, his interest in horses did not extend beyond how well they fared at the Fair Grounds Race Course during his New Orleans days. Finally, he ran out of patience. "Aren't they going to ride that horse? Ask the monsieur if they ride the horses."

"But, Daddy, they can't ride the horses—the bits and saddles leave marks and calluses. The hide has to be flawless."

"What's the point of horses you don't ride?"

"They're perfect. They're the most beautiful Arabians in the world!"

"For thousands of dollars you buy a horse to look at?" Tom shook his stubborn, eighty-six-year-old, half-deaf head. They stood side by side, chemist and molecular biologist, father and daughter, caught in the old American stalemate, arguing the merits of beauty versus utility.

Les Noces: Le Premier Jour

On the twenty-eighth of May, midafternoon, Mary and I took a bath together in a huge tub at the Château de Prunoy, while Christabel, resembling a fluffy white bird in a white nest, sat happily in the bidet next to us. It was the first quiet moment that we had had in days, and after several weeks of rustic living conditions in the presbytery, we luxuriated in our noble room. It was situated in the northeastern corner of the château, the floor-to-ceiling windows giving a view over the vast lawns, the sun leaning panels of light against the wallpaper, adding warmth to the pale pink pattern. Tobé had chosen our room for us, knowing that Mary's favorite color was pale pink, and a fresh arrangement of pink roses awaited our arrival. In the distance, dark clouds passed with gray skirts of rain, while the air was charged with the chatter of late-spring birds. We could hear voice and piano, fragments of Schubert, drifting up the staircase, Tobé practicing in the salon. The evening was preparing itself.

Because of the small size of the château, we could invite only family and our closest friends for the first day of the wedding party. The second day would be a much larger group. Guests arrived, parking their cars on the crunchy gravel, and checked into their rooms. They hung up suits and dresses and then excitedly gave each other tours of their extraordinary rooms, each totally different in color coordination, style of furnishing, prospect, and lighting. Our group occupied the entire Château de Prunoy, an establishment of appealing eccentricity, with good-natured cats and dogs allowed to roam the halls freely and some of the Oriental rugs emanating the faint odor of cat piss.

Large gold-framed mirrors hung in the halls along with portraits and attractive engravings. The unpolished *parquet de Versailles* floors creaked with the dislocations of age; statues and busts silently stood in corners or sat on mantels or marble fireplaces. Despite all the care in decoration and the elegance of the furnishings, the château's charm was unpretentious. The building's scale wasn't altogether imposing, nor was its asymmetrical L-shape with a single tower covered in ivy. The shutters, in desperate need of reconditioning, reminded me of ours. The service was cheerful and relaxed, appropriate to the country atmosphere of the place. We had forgotten Christabel's food, and when I asked the receptionist if we might have a little dog food, she replied, *"Excusez-nous, monsieur, on n'en a plus.* We only have some cat food. *Mais les chiens adorent la nourriture pour chats."* They were feeding their own dogs cat food, having themselves run out of dog food, and it was true: Christabel preferred cat food. Certainly for a bowlful she'd abandon her nest in the bidet.

It's a privilege to spend a night in the ancient, historied building. Few have the means to live in the old châteaux of Europe, so their survival depends on creative efforts to generate resources for their restoration and maintenance. Like the Château de Prunoy, many châteaux have been transformed into hotels with restaurants, and the proprietors have formed various associations. Others, like the Château de Saint-Fargeau, have become museums, educational centers, or the sites for concert series and regional events. Still others, like the Château de Boutissaint in our region, use the associated forest as wildlife parks where wild boar and their striped babies, called *marcassins,* follow you at the edge of their large enclosure or where as you walk into the domain, you will see herds of huge deer running, as if they were only half material among the trees.

At the Château de Prunoy, Mary and I soon encountered our first major crisis. The Reverend Brown, a longtime family friend, had generously agreed to write and perform a ceremony for us in the garden. Unfortunately, just before the wedding he was afflicted with Ménière's syndrome, an inner-ear ailment that causes vertigo. He did, however, fax a text to the château, and the receptionist delivered it to our room. The Reverend Brown meant to work out the ceremony with us when he came. He had had the chance only to jot down some notes, which by themselves seemed odd for the occasion. The writing was dense, philosophical, and filled with literary, religious, and mythological allusions. Most of our English-speaking guests would have difficulty understanding it, much less our guests from France, Germany, and Italy. I felt a wave of desperation. Without the text, we had no ceremony, just the picnic.

Mary didn't want a religious service. She's a scientist and an atheist. While she thinks an ordinary ghost is "implausible," the Holy Ghost is clearly "unfathomable." Even as a little girl in the Episcopal church, she thought that God, the Father, was fine, and saw him as a Michelangelo fresco. God, the Son, was fine, too, up on the cross. But God, the Holy Ghost, she didn't see a need for.

She imagined someone at Mardi Gras wearing a white sheet. The dove is the symbol of the Holy Ghost, and when I mentioned this to Mary once, she replied, "Do you mean when we have *rôti de pigeonneau* we are eating the Holy Ghost?" Much to the chagrin of Mary's family, which has an honorable line of southern Episcopalian ministers, Mary managed to get herself expelled from Sunday school, where the class had been studying maps of Egypt and Palestine and the route of the Exodus. She couldn't accept that God would kill so many Egyptians, first the children with a plague and then the pharaoh's soldiers in the Red Sea. Mary had the temerity to ask, without raising her hand, "How do you know the stories in the Bible are true?"

"Indeed, Miss Crumpler?" the teacher replied, believing Mary's provocation was merely a way to amuse the class.

"Well, I don't believe it." Although ordinarily shy, Mary even now feels emboldened when challenging authority, particularly righteousness without a semblance of reasoning.

When the idea came up of having the Reverend Brown, an Episcopalian, preside over our wedding, Mary was worried. I argued that he was different.

"He isn't like a real minister. He doesn't proselytize in the least."

I recalled the wonderful evenings I'd spent at his cottage in Rhode Island, talking about poets and philosophers whose works the Reverend Brown could speak of so eloquently and refer to with such facility, quoting Saint Augustine and Thomas Aquinas. The Reverend Brown was our own Angelic Doctor. I should have anticipated a difficult text. I told Mary that I had fished with him for blues or bonito at the breachway where he invariably lost the fish in the strong current at the last instant, leaving only the consolation of admirable cursing and swigs from a bottle of Labatt's. Mary remained suspicious until I made my final point. "Besides, he plays the cello."

"Well, he can't be bad, then," Mary finally conceded. She had played the cello for many years and still dreamed of going back to it. That the reverend played the cello made all the difference, and suddenly he could do no wrong.

I read the text to Mary while she was relaxing in bed, wearing nothing but a towel in her hair. She might panic over disappearing sheets, but situations like this didn't fluster her in the least. She agreed that the text was difficult but that it had authority and a true sense of occasion. She reasoned that it was the delivery that counted.

"We have more performers coming to our wedding than anyone could ask for. We'll just put them to work. They'll love it. We'll just assign parts for them to read."

Mary was absolutely right. We had, to mention a few, Tobé who adored performing, and her husband, Steve, a Yale medical professor, who is an outstanding speaker. We had Yehudi Wyner, a music professor at Brandeis and a composer and international performer, and his wife, Susan Davenny Wyner, who had a major singing career. Finally, we had Charles Siebert, an essayist for the *New York Times* and the author of several books, who loved to tell stories and do impressions. This was our assemblage of performers for the ceremony.

With great relief on my part, we dressed. Mary wore a sheer pink dress with a flower print and gold studs with three rubies. When she put on her pearls, she declared, "This is max!" and we descended to a reception room, which was paneled from floor to ceiling in warm walnut and had banks of windows on both sides with views of the courtyard and the great expanse of lawn. Our guests, with glasses of champagne, had already begun the first wedding party without us.

Mary and I made the rounds separately introducing people who had already introduced themselves to one another. I was half engaged in the talk and half abstracted by the novelty of the moment; how freely friends and family mingled, even though they were imported from the disparate parts of our scattered lives.

Just as Mary had dressed to the max, so did our guests, looking their best for the château banquet. Anna, an Italian scientist who worked with Mary, was the most conspicuous with a back line that plunged so daringly that one could only conclude she was wearing nothing but the dress. By contrast, Ghisseline Plissis, another scientist and friend, dressed in a manner the French call BCBG, *bon chic bon genre,* a term from the eighties that has recently mutated into PAN, Passy-Auteuil-Neuilly, wealthy Paris neighborhoods. Not only did every piece of Ghisseline's clothing fit a theme of color and style, but also her makeup and hair were flawless. Her body seemed immune to all the natural forces of disorder that affect the rest of us. Arriving late was our Paris neighbor Thérèse, a television producer, who wore a red micro-miniskirt, and her hair, which had just grown back after chemo, seemed colored to match it. Each costume was an adventure.

For weeks before the wedding, Phyllis, Mary's stepmother, would call up either Margie or Frannie, deeply worried that they'd show up at the château in jeans. She had rescued her old prom dresses from the depths of her closets. "Dear, I've brought out my prom dresses for you and Frannie. You will need them at the château in France." She'd forget that she called and call again, terrified that poor Margie and Frannie would be considered peasants if they didn't wear her prom dresses. Mary had told me how during her high school and college years in New Orleans, dressing up was a way of life. All the girls had special dresses and shoes for "formals," which were mainly held at social clubs, the evening filled with dancing and drinking rum-laden Cuba libres on the sly. The whole notion of "formals" was a foreign world to me. I grew up in the caste system of Levi's, Wranglers, and Lee's, and our socials were held at political cafés that stank of patchouli and were plastered with cartoon posters demanding someone or other be freed or declaring someone or other was a pig. In any case, Margie and Frannie managed to convince Phyllis that they had no intention of coming to the château banquet dressed as peasants. They, in fact, had dressed elegantly and were busy talking to my friend Charles. Phyllis wore red silk with an elaborate print, a scarf tight around her neck, like a gypsy princess.

I finally introduced my father to my father-in-law-to-be. The two men, one a New York Jew and the other a Southern patrician, could hardly strike a greater contrast. Tom was twice my father's size, both in height and girth, and with his neat white mustache and dark blue suit, his dragon cane ever vigilant, he seemed all the more imposing. The distinguished professor was versed in the decorum of social occasions, having devoted the later part of his life to cocktail parties and the horse races. My father, on the other hand, at every social situation I could remember his attending, and they were few, acted as if he'd been given the wrong address. Despite his allergy to alcohol, he sipped down a glass of champagne like a can of Sprite. His face turned blotchy, so that he resembled a perplexed raccoon.

Tom boasted, "The Crumplers have a long line of notable ministers, you see, including a bishop from up in Charlottesville.

He was Mary's great-grandfather on my mother's side." Tom could have been holding court at the Fair Grounds Race Course.

My father, who fled his psychotic mother out of sheer self-defense, understood instinctively that "good family" was no family. Bishops didn't exist on any plane of his reality. He was more interested in Charlottesville as the place where in 1943 he got clobbered as backup quarterback for North Carolina State. My father had been accelerated in grade school by two years and was, if not the youngest, then the slightest quarterback in N.C.S. history. He could get killed on the football field but was too young to enlist. Still, less than two years later, just before the end of the war, he'd come to France as an officer on a liberty ship. He took a train in a snowstorm from the flattened vestiges of Le Havre to freshly liberated Paris. Our wedding was the first time he'd been back.

Before the concert, a storm had moved in. The lights continued to flicker, and the old windows of the château rattled while Yehudi played the piano. The guests enjoyed another round of champagne while wondering if the lights would go out altogether and the wedding would turn into a pajama party lit by candles or a night of intrigues in a mysterious old château.

The wedding, after all, was already unconventional enough, particularly for the French. We were beginning with a banquet and ending with a picnic. French weddings begin at the *mairie,* since French law requires a civil ceremony before the church wedding, where one sometimes sees a procession of cars arrive, one with an effigy of the groom hanging by the neck from a makeshift gallows in the *coffre,* the trunk. Sometimes the bride is hanging, too. These dangling effigies simply reiterate the French expression regarding marriage—*se mettre la corde au cou,* to hang oneself. I prefer the tradition called *enterrer sa vie de garçon.* A group of friends build a small *cercueil*, coffin, and at a prenuptial party for the groom they fill it with bottles of wine and then bury (*enterrer*) the coffin full of wine in a secret place. When the first child is born, the wine is exhumed for another celebration party.

The storm passed in fifteen minutes. Even with some distant rumblings of thunder, the black *merles* whistled their pure songs in the large chestnut trees as if giving us the all-clear signal.

"*S'il vous plaît, Madame Malawista vous invite au salon pour commencer le concert,*" announced the hotel receptionist, and the guests settled in their seats around the baby grand piano. Tobé appeared smiling and our little crowd applauded, relieved that the evening had been restored to its former good cheer.

The concert began with Tobé and Yehudi performing short selections from Schubert, Liszt, and Tchaikovsky. They were love poems set to music. Then Steve made his concert debut by singing admirably with Tobé "Là ci darem la mano," a duet from Mozart's *Don Giovanni*, Mary's favorite opera. Yehudi had known Mary for years. He wrote a piece called "La Blanche et le Vert: Petite Histoire Nuptiale," specifically for us, and it was the centerpiece of the concert. The title was a play on our last names: Weiss and Greene. The piece was too much fun not to perform twice before the finale, "Fugue for Tinhorns" from *Guys and Dolls*, along with which Mary's father bellowed, " 'We've got the horse right here. His name is Paul Revere.' " His hearing aid was whistling like an angry lifeguard. All through the concert, the tall château windows brightened even though we moved toward night. We had drifted into one of those endless twilights that seem to define late spring in the French countryside.

Seven circular tables had been set in the banquet room. Mary and I were seated with Jacques and Lena, Mary's oldest friends in

France, and Frédéric and Odile, who had lent us their house in the Saussois, not even a year before, precipitating our obsessed search for the presbytery. We were served Chablis with our entrée, *gelée de foie gras aux artichauts*. Each table became an island of talk and laughter, until Tobé halted the crowd to announce that her table was a reunion of everyone who had been at the house party in Tuscany where Mary and I met.

"We all thought their behavior was scandalous!" Tobé shouted out. " 'Where's Jeffrey? Where's Mary?' we'd ask. Oh, they're walking the dog again. They nearly walked that poor dog to death! Imagine all that dog would tell if she could talk."

We could see where the evening was headed. The *blanquette de veau* had been served along with Santenay and a few more damaging anecdotes. Tom finally hit his stride after drinking all day and stood up to tell stories in his slow Virginia accent. "One time Mary left marbles on the staircase. She was no more than three years old. I didn't punish her. Instead, I asked, 'Don't you know how dangerous it is to leave marbles on the staircase? Wonder if I fell on the stairs? Wonder if my back was broken? Wonder if I couldn't work and feed the family?' Little Mary said right back, 'It would teach you to look where you were going.' "

With a good laugh at his own story, he launched into a catalog of family dignitaries. "Now, Mary's great-grandfather on my mother's side was the bishop from Charlottesville."

Mary turned to me and whispered, "Fuck the bishop!"

After the bishop, the ministers, farmers, historians, and businessmen had all been listed, Tom raised his glass and said, "Welcome to the family."

When the *clafoutis*, a heavy custardlike dish with fruit, cherries in this case, finally appeared, it was badly burned. We didn't know whether to blame the cook or the Crumpler family tree. The beneficiaries turned out to be the château canines, who managed to slip through the surveillance of the busy staff. They found their way around the banquet room to supplement their cat food diet with burnt offerings of cherry *clafoutis*. With Christabel under my arm, I gave a toast in English to the generosity of our friends. Mary gave a toast in French. Then, leaving the château to the whims of our friends, we were the first to retreat, past mirrors and statues, upstairs to our room.

Les Noces: Le Deuxième Jour

During the busy week before the twenty-ninth of May, my mother conducted experiments on wildflowers. She had to find out which ones could be readily found in large quantities and were sturdy enough to last a whole day, to decorate the rooms of the presbytery and the tables out on the terrace. She and Lee would stroll down to the *charmille* or wander out in front of the church, choosing and clipping. They searched along the canal or trespassed in the fenced-off *domaines* of the cement-colored cows and the dumbstruck sheep. They stopped along the little communal roads to Aillant and Dammarie or drove as far as Châtillon-Coligny or Bléneau, all for wildflower reconnaissance. They came back with a mass of flower types in two armfuls and set up the presbytery as a laboratory, each room having at least one arrangement of wildflowers, each arrangement differing in size and composition.

In late May, you can find wild carrot, dwarf elder, cornflowers, forget-me-nots, wild roses, bluebells, violets, white campion, red clover, field daisies, yellow and purple vetch, ragged robin, milk thistle, early poppies, buttercups, wild pansies, dock, mouse ears, and renegade rape. Orchids also proliferate in the damper parts of the region in late spring. That year, more than any since, was spectacular for wildflowers. During my mother's experiments, we had our favorites—the most intense in color or the most exotic. Then we'd cheer on the poor things while they wilted. Field poppies and the purple, spidery ragged robin wilted almost instantly. Apparently you have to burn the stems or seal them with wax to stop the bleed-out of moisture. The yellow milk thistle withered; the mouse ears drooped.

While the wildflower experiments continued, my mother salvaged empty plaster tubs, paint cans, and buckets that she found piled up in the stables, waiting for a bulk trash removal. Some were too rough looking and had to be covered with cloth or paper; others kept their labels—Xylodecor, Enduit Band, Valentine . . . Somehow the less-than-elegant containers enhanced the airy beauty of the wildflowers, and the combination seemed a natural symbol for a wedding in a house under reconstruction.

On the morning of the second day of the wedding, my mother, Lee, Margie, and Frannie all left the Château de Prunoy very early. My mother plunged into the preparation of a feast for over fifty people. Lee and Margaret set off for fields and hedges that had been targeted earlier and searched for the specific types of wildflowers approved for the wedding. They also brought back stems of yellow grasses and gray-green bearded wheat. By mid-morning, our large bathtub was brimming with wildflowers.

My mother assembled the arrangements, a plaster tub for each table set up on the terrace, buckets for the doorways steps, and paint cans for the buffet table in the library. Any flowers might have served, but those that had passed the makeshift laboratory tests were often lacy, airy, and delicate. Most of the arrangements were composed of wild carrot, dwarf elder, buttercups, red clover, vetch, bluebells, and campion. The table where Mary and I would sit featured a paint can full of cornflowers and wild carrot.

By the time my mother emptied the bathtub of wildflowers, it refused to drain. Leaves, petals, and stems dammed up the trap, and when Mary and I arrived from the château, we found Coco and what seemed like half the men in town in our bathroom, trying to figure out how to take the bathtub plumbing apart. *"Ne mettez pas les mauvaises herbes dans la baignoire,"* Coco scolded, wiping his mouth. He wouldn't relent. *"Je n'ai jamais vu de pareil!"* I have never seen anything like it. Who puts weeds in a bathtub? This was the first of the endless *"Je n'ai jamais vu's"* that would define a contentious relationship between my mother and Coco that has lasted for years. Both are stubbornly convinced of the efficacy of their ways.

While Coco continued to complain about the *mauvaises herbes* in the bathtub, three of the strangers were on their hands and knees unscrewing the trap. My mother went on preparing a white lasagna with morels, letting the fuss and criticism evaporate on their own. She made the pasta by hand and sautéed the duxelles, which she minced and then squeeze-dried in a cloth. Then she chopped up fresh parsley to mix into the ricotta, mozzarella, and Parmesan filling. Meanwhile, Mary was hysterical over the ruined bathtub and the invasion of the house by drunken strangers who seemed to enjoy taking the trap apart like a puzzle. They were eager to help the Americans who did not know any better than to put weeds in a bathtub and have a wedding in a *chantier*. Americans are like children. Mary wasn't prepared for a bathroom full of men giving her advice.

To continue the inauspicious beginnings, my mother had to cook the mushroom lasagna in an oven too small to hold four baking dishes. She carried two of the dishes across the place de l'Église to try them in Ariane's oven, but that one was much smaller even than ours. My mother's solution was to place bricks on the rusted-out bottom of our oven to support a second row of dishes, which shortly bubbled over, filling the presbytery with a cloud from molten sauce and cheeses.

While the oven smoked away, my mother began the adventure of preparing the layers of wedding cake, an alternation of chocolate orange and white orange. She checked the lasagna to determine which parts of the oven gave the most reliable heat. The oven was operating on its own impulses, veering between semitropical mildness and the volcanism of an iron forge at full blast. Ultimately, the cake layers would come out unevenly, but under the circumstances they proved more than acceptable. The buttercream frosting turned out to be much more problematic. As if the whimsy of the oven weren't enough to deal with, the refrigerator, as it happened, didn't cool sufficiently to stiffen the mixture. It was like thin plaster that never hardened.

We began to anthropomorphize each appliance—mutinous bathtub, capricious oven, stingy refrigerator—my mother soldiering through steam clouds and frustration, determined to rule each peevish spirit. She baked the lasagna and the cake, snapped and steamed kilos of asparagus, composed the salads and dressings, and cut up and decorated the *pâtés*.

When the air cleared and the men from town went over to Coco's for a triumphal drink after cleaning out the trap, the buffet tables were set up with elaborate arrays of *pâté, jambon persillé,* and salads. The Xylodecor cans stood at the center with their fresh sprays of wildflowers, concentrations of local beauty. The bathtub was refilled with water so that frozen bottles of Volvic could chill the *crémant,* Sancerre, and Chassagne-Montrachet. Of course, the labels would float gently off the bottles and dam up the trap again, but I could clear it myself.

My mother assembled a cake that was architecturally uncomplicated but profusely decorated with the garden's edible flowers—pansies and violets. Though the buttercream frosting was a little loose, my mother improvised, getting enough of the buttercream to act like stucco. In spite of her chaotic methods, in the end *elle se débrouille,* as the French say. She manages. Now it was up to everyone else to create the moment—to sour it or to add to the wonder.

How we found an hour to dress I don't know. Mary put on a silk skirt that I had bought for her birthday, the palest peach. I had also given her an elegant, though simple white silk blouse to go with it. Mary's favorite climbing rose in the garden was the very color of the skirt, and my mother picked one rose and fixed it into Mary's long hair, all so carefully put up. She was stunning: the beginnings of silver in her hair, the peach rose, her smart blue eyes. We were both finally at ease, not only about the preparations but also with each other. We were not a young couple starting out. We were not beginning a family. Ours was a marriage of the middle-aged—nothing was expected of us. We were getting married, in our own backyard, because we were thoroughly enjoying ourselves and our life together.

The guests arrived with geraniums, rose plants, lamps, roasting pots, prints, trays, blankets, bowls, utensils, and even a slice of a meteorite, all carefully wrapped or tied with bows and ribbons, waiting to reveal themselves. The *crémant* was opened, and the emissaries from the different quarters of our lives were once again introduced to each other: Boris's daughters, writers, friends from graduate school, colleagues from Mary's laboratories, our new friends from Rogny, including Deluche and Ariane and Jean-Louis, friends from New Haven, and, of course, our families. Since this was a wedding/housewarming, Mary and I led little tour groups around the grounds. Our wedding guests were stylish but overdressed and wrongly shod for an orchard or a *charmille* or even for walking on the rough floors of the polyplaqued rooms or climbing the winding stairs to the vast, dusty space of the *grenier*. They inspected stables and drifted among the fruit trees or visited the statue of Christ down the prayer alley, *crémant* sparkling in their plastic wineglasses, rabbits scattering into the sheep pastures.

I wonder how different our wedding was from parties held on the grounds of the presbytery in years past. Our celebration was only the most recent. We see occasional weddings at the church, the place de l'Église packed with cars, the families gathering at the front of the church, camcorders recording the scene. In Père Jo's time, the wedding party could drift into the lower garden of the presbytery. Père Jo would be a natural catalyst of celebration, his presence animating the grounds.

May 29 was by far the hottest day that we had had that year. Everyone was looking for hats and for more cold wine or Volvic from half-frozen bottles. I gave out the hats that I had—baseball style with NFL logos of Cowboys, Bears, Giants. I wore them for tennis or jogging. Our guests were scattered throughout the presbytery or laughing and chatting in the shade of the Judas tree. They wore suits and baseball caps. Finally, Tom, in his black suit, dragon-headed cane glaring before him, shouted out, "What is this, a Quaker wedding?" He meant, "Get on with it."

Steve Malawista took over the role of minister, rabbi, priest, emcee, whatever you want to call it, with a mix of propriety and panache one would expect of an esteemed professor of medicine. The shade of the pear tree made a perfect stage. Mary and I stood at the center, with Tobé, Yehudi, Susan, and Charles by our sides, each scanning over his or her section of the photocopied fax sent by the infirm Reverend Brown. All the other guests formed a semicircle in the glaring midafternoon sun, unsure of what would transpire, since this was the first wedding that they had attended under a pear tree. Steve established his authority. "I am standing in place of the Reverend Brown, who could not perform this ceremony due to illness. Now we, friends and family, are gathered here today to honor Mary and Jeffrey's marriage . . ." His delivery was so natural that everyone fell into its spirit.

Tobé stepped forward, in a sheer flower-print dress with a bow tied in front, and launched part one of the reverend's text, which started with references to two C. S. Lewis books, *Till We Have Faces*, remythologizing the Cupid and Psyche myth, and *The Four Loves*, delineating the versions of love according to the Greeks— friendship, affection, Eros, and agape.

Then Susan took over. She wore a white blouse and dark summer dress, her long hair partly braided, flowing down the front of her shoulders. She held a straw hat in one hand and read the reverend's summary of a story that Nikos Kazantzakis attributes to Francis of Assisi. It was about a knight who, having returned from the Crusades, begs for the love of a beautiful woman and attempts to solve the riddle she poses, one that in the end educates him about the true nature of love.

Yehudi began the third and most difficult part, the Reverend Brown's analysis of a poem of mine called "On Augusta," which refers to a level of intimacy in which one lover, even when separated from the other, can experience the world through the other's eyes. The poem was based on Byron's letters to his half sister, Augusta, with whom he had an incestuous relationship leading, in part, to his exile. But the Reverend Brown turned the focus of his analysis to François Bonivard, who was imprisoned at the Château Chillon. At one point I stood forward and read the poem beside Yehudi, who was wearing a wacky blue-and-white engineer's hat that was the envy of the other guests.

Then my friend Charles took on the text's most liturgical part, which gave a definition of agape-love through references to the self-offerings of Isaiah, Hosea, and Jesus: "We make, O Lord, our glorious exchanges. What Thou has given, we now return to Thee, that in turn, we may receive Thyself."

The rotation of readers ended with Steve's delivery of the final section, which referred to one of my poems where I describe worshipers praying to the east.

When Adam and Eve were cast out of the Garden, the Lord God placed an armed seraph to the East of Eden. Now, why did God do that? Is it not in order that, in attempting to return to the Garden, Adam and Eve could not reenter without looking, even if peripherally, into the eastern light? No matter how disjuncted or oblique one's reference to the east may be, the referent is yet that same light—which plays lovingly and searchingly upon our clumsy efforts at love, until we have faces.

There we were, under the pear tree, the reverend's text finished at last. The garden might not have been Eden, but it was ours. Steve turned to Mary, who had stood silently through the reading, and began, "Do you take—" Mary interrupted with a loud "You bet!" to immediate applause. Mary's suggestion of having our friends read the reverend's text was a stroke of genius. Soon the shade of the pear tree lit up with camera flashes and kisses. Everyone enjoyed the drama. Amid the commotion, Margaret whispered to Mary, "We can read, too, you know."

Plates were filled at the buffet, and everyone chose a place at the tables on the terrace. Mary and I sat at the one table that ran perpendicular to the others, the deep green lawn, the orchard, and the Loing Valley at our backs. The seating at our table had been assigned to my father and Angela, my mother, Tom and Phyllis, and Steve and Tobé. After Phyllis asked Steve one too many times if they had met before, Steve sidled up to my mother and said, "You know how you always worry that you have Alzheimer's. Well, you don't. But she does," nodding toward Phyllis.

It would be a year before we knew how tragically correct Steve's diagnosis had been that day. I think often of poor Phyllis as she was then. She was unsure of herself, apologetic and self-effacing by nature, yet she seemed a cheerful and warmhearted woman and in perfect health. We thought she was only confused, jet-lagged, disoriented by travel, so it was easy to make allowances when she repeated herself or introduced herself more than once. In retrospect, her most telling symptom was anxiety. Once, when Margie, Frannie, and Margaret drove off on a tour, saying they'd be back by six in the evening, Phyllis telephoned us at the presbytery, looking for them. Then she called Fougère, Ariane, and Jean-Louis, and finally the *gendarmerie,* thinking that they had all been abducted. At the time, we were appalled when Tom would shout at Phyllis for becoming excessively agitated. "Honey, just forget about it!" Now we remember how well his shouting worked.

The afternoon grew hotter. The wildflowers stood up nobly, though the leaves of the dwarf elder began to droop, then the clover dipped its sugary tops. Even the rose in Mary's hair grew a little tired. My mother's mushroom lasagna was a hit. It was nothing new to see her bask in compliments, stumbling through the list of ingredients, asked a dozen times for the recipe. She had always been a wonderful cook, but over the years cooking had become a passion. She often attributes her talent to her years working in a lab. She makes an analogy between biochemistry and the kitchen. In truth, her success is part chemistry and mostly imagination and bravado. At the end of the meal, the wedding party toasted her and stood and clapped.

The gifts emerged from their wrappings—lamps, framed pictures, and meteorites all on display on the terrace in the late-afternoon light. Finally, the pansy-and-violet cake appeared. The very moment Mary and I cut into the cake, Marie and Isabelle rang seven o'clock Angelus. We have become accustomed to such coincidences.

When the heat broke and the sun angled over the *charmille*, casting shadows of our guests against the presbytery, swallows began to race above the lamps, frames, and dishes, crossing our terrace, and darting straight for Polluche's stone wall, dodging at the last moment up and over, to make a hard turn behind the dovecote across the orchard. When they reached the stables, they turned back and came across the terrace again. Then, as in the moment when the first stars appear or when you pass from your last thought into sleep, the swallows metamorphosed into bats. Their black flicking circle filled the last spaces of constricted light. Finally, the tawny owls launched themselves into the spotlights that shine on the church steeple. Some of our guests took turns wearing the curé's black felt hat that I had found in the stables. They took pictures of each other with Polluche's wall and the church in the background. The hat, Père Jo's, was a synecdoche for the spirit of the whole man. Other guests filtered away to catch a train to Paris or go back to their hotels and *gîtes*. Some lingered, singing communist worker songs, popular during the late sixties.

I have always been the first up, even as a child, and the following morning, while everyone else was still sleeping, I stepped out onto the terrace and a scene of disappearances. No moment of the presbytery has lingered so clearly in my memory, and for all the photographs taken the day before, there were no photographs taken the day after, when no scene could have looked more pleasantly spooky or better told a whole story with only bits and pieces of remaining evidence. But it wasn't just the story of the day before; it was the story of the night. It was as if one wedding had finished and a second had begun, one in which the wedding guests celebrated with rainwater.

It had rained in the night. I'd slept through it. The little statue of the Virgin, having served her office of bringing us a cloudless wedding day, had then allowed a rain to fall so that it filled the plastic wineglasses. Some had been abandoned half-filled with wine, so they had turned pink or palest yellow. Others were limpid. The alley between the church and the presbytery sent its corridor of light across the tables and benches into the dense foliage of the nut trees that cast the cool shade that the wild strawberries love so much.

I walked from table to table, the paper tablecloths soaked, the colored napkins scattered along with the gift wrapping, stuck to seats, half folded in the grass, or balled up and soggy. The paper plates and white utensils were all skewed, as the guests had left them after taking last bites. I thought of our guests, in the presbytery, the *gîtes*, and nearby hotels, some at the Château de Prunoy, their made-up hair unmade in sleep, traces of makeup on their eyelids, suits and dresses hung in armoires. Their shutters, I'm sure, were closed on the noisy light that comes on a clear morning after night rain, the birds' ecstatic racket.

I find it strange that I never seem to know, until I'm alone and disassociated, how happy I am. It's as if I need a delay. I need that moment like the morning after, standing amid the remnant trash of celebration, to feel contented. I seem to need both the happy event and the shadow of the event. There were the buckets of flowers on each table, and one on each side of the doorway. The experiments had worked; few had completely wilted, though the rain had weighed them down. All had been cut from along the roadside in the morning, less than twenty-four hours earlier, by Lee and Margaret and then arranged by my mother, now all sleeping in the aftermath. The flowers had lasted into the second wedding, the one that is made up in thought, finished happily, transformed into rainwater.

Feu de la Saint-Jean

*T*en months after our reckless purchase and only one month after the wedding, Mary and I triumphantly finished our first room, the library. It was not an arbitrary choice; it required the least effort and expense. Its elaborate paneling, half the wall space, was already in excellent condition. The rest we plastered, taped, then painted a dead white, which American friends called "resale white" and French called *"froid,"* cold. Mary and I loved the clean white space of our one finished room; to honor the room properly, we decided to fill it with rustic French furniture.

Almost all the small villages in the Puisaye have a cycle of tourist events in summer: tag sales, antique shows, expositions of animals and regional products, historical spectacles, bicycle races, art shows, dances. The two official events are the Foire de la Saint-Jean, June 24, to celebrate the shortest night, and Bastille Day, to honor the mobbing of the fortified Paris prison on July 14, 1789.

At any of the summer events, someone might be selling furniture. Often it is set out on the village sidewalks next to battered vans, vendors seated as if in a disordered living room from which the house itself vanished. Three kinds of furniture are available. First there are genuine antiques, brought from city to village so that customers take museum prices to be rural bargains and think that they are being rewarded for being shrewd enough to venture into the country to buy. Then there is poor quality or rotted furniture, stripped, stained, and restored to look like rustic pieces of great value, as verified by their immoderate prices. And finally there is furniture stolen from country homes.

For our one proudly finished room, we began to haunt tourist events looking for, as one might say, steals. And certainly, we found such countryside touring much more pleasurable than plastering, painting, or slinging cement. One early summer day, we saw the typical Day-Glo sign announcing a *vide-grenier* and furniture exposition in Briare and soon found ourselves on a sidewalk under a plane tree in front of a handsome buffet, priced above what we'd want to pay, but not absurdly so.

"*Louis-Philippe, noyer massif,*" the vendor announced, with a quick smile, not typical of French salesmanship. We suddenly felt ill prepared—solid walnut was not a problem, but we ran the dates of various Napoleons and French kings through our heads. This vendor seemed to specialize in Louis-Philippe, since all the pieces resembled one another in style.

"*C'est très beau mais beaucoup trop cher pour nous,*" Mary said, explaining that the buffet was beyond our means.

"*Qu'est-ce que vous cherchez?*"

It was this question—what are you looking for?—that triggered a yearlong relationship with Monsieur Lelièvre, a man who scavenged a life on the margins of French society. He wasn't alone.

He had a sidekick, an attractive young woman, very small, always smiling, with dark hair and dark eyes. We would soon learn that her name was Sophie. In contrast to Sophie, Lelièvre was huge, not so much in height as in muscular mass and the broadness of his shoulders. One could easily see him as a marine or a rugby player. His red hair, what was left of it, was cropped very short. He never spoke to his little partner in our presence, but they had established a system of eye cues for when to pass a cigarette or give a light. Since they smoked constantly, these exchanges were frequent and well practiced, like those of a skilled dental assistant passing tools. When Lelièvre launched into a speech, he tilted his head and leaned slightly forward so that it was impossible not to see the perfect hemisphere of a single lipoma, cyst, tumor, whatever it was, on the side of his neck.

Lelièvre was a purposeful man, open in a way that the postsixties generation in France seemed to demand, with no tolerance for social strictures and survival-of-the-fittest commercialism. He was, at heart, a young French socialist, one who had loved his former job maintaining machines in a local box factory. With the factory's closing, he was forced into restoring and selling furniture to survive. He worked all the local expositions. The day he asked us what we were looking for, Mary told him that we had just bought a ruined presbytery and needed furniture like the Louis-Philippe buffet but had assumed great expenses and couldn't justify acquiring such a fine piece.

Lelièvre answered that he had another Louis-Philippe buffet that hadn't been restored but was, in fact, even finer. He would sell it to us for half the price that he could make off it if he repaired and refinished it. Because he needed cash—*liquide,* as the French say—he was willing to part with it, in its rough state, for a much smaller profit. Lelièvre gave little Sophie another eye cue, this one meaning "Look after things." He then joined us in our Peugeot, Christabel charging with excitement into his arms, anxious to size up the stranger as friend or foe, the huge earnest Monsieur Lelièvre holding the mitten-size white dog as if she were a bomb.

He pointed the way to Châtillon-sur-Loire, a town that historically had great power and influence in the region but now, with the slump in local industry, had become impoverished and dreary. He directed us up a steep slope and into a mazelike *lotissement,* a low-cost, treeless housing development, and somehow distinguished one garage from dozens of identical ones that might have coffered the Louis-Philippe buffet. A friend had temporarily lent the garage space to Lelièvre, who used it for storage and as a makeshift workshop. We learned that he, in fact, was living in the broken-down, blue spray-painted van that sat in the drive in front of the garage. A clutch job had clearly been interrupted, leaving us to wonder how Lelièvre moved his furniture.

He opened the garage, and I helped him muscle the buffet out into the sunlight. It reared back about fifteen degrees because worms and rot had completely devoured its back feet. The worms and rot had also made gaping oval holes in the back panel and several shelves; otherwise, according to Lelièvre, the buffet was a treasure. He proved this by rubbing its front surface with light steel wool dipped in Star Wax. Warm nutwood emerged out of the gloomy finish of moldy neglect and dark nineteenth-century stain. One need only glue new legs on the back, replace a few panels, and strip and refinish the exterior. We were instantly won over and happily bought the rotting piece for our ruined presbytery.

At the time, we should have given more thought to Louis Philippe as a symbol. After the Revolution, what need had France of this last Bourbon king? What need did we have of his ruined furniture? The Liberty Tree was planted in front of the presbytery to celebrate the abnegation of Louis Philippe! On the other hand, it was the Liberty Tree that tried to root up the Haut-Bourg in general and the presbytery in particular. We debated such associations, none of which made much sense.

The next morning, Lelièvre and Sophie showed up while Mary and I were making love. A bang came at the door, Christabel erupted into hysterics, and Mary and I scrambled for our clothes— Mary usually answering first while I failed to erase the evidence of what we had so obviously been doing. Our visible disorientation from *coitus interruptus* didn't faze Lelièvre in the least. He came in and took a cigarette from his little assistant, without even looking at her, lit his, then held his lighter to the side for her while preparing to launch into an introductory course on how to restore the Louis-Philippe buffet that he was delivering. Mary ran off to get a pencil and paper to take notes.

"En forme?" he asked dryly, using the sports expression the French employ to inquire whether you are at the peak of your performance level. Sophie smirked, but in a sweet way that made it impossible not to have a crush on her. I figured his casual attitude was typical of the sixties generation, "tutoyering," kissing four times, twice on each cheek, instead of the conventional once. I couldn't help imagining Lelièvre, who always seemed *en forme*, smoking dope and making love to his attractive companion on the imitation sheepskin rugs at that moment loosely wrapped around our newly acquired buffet. There in the middle of the *lotissement*, Lelièvre would fuck and fix the clutch and project his next quick sale, all at once.

The buffet came more or less as a kit. Lelièvre brought fragments of some even more hopeless furniture that could be cut, pieced, and glued to replace its missing or rotted parts. He carefully explained the restoration process, and Mary scrupulously wrote down each step, noting specifically the types and brands of anti-worm and antimold sprays and the most effective stains and waxes. We were so pleased with our ruined buffet and its price that we asked Lelièvre to contact us if by chance he came across a nice armoire. Confident of finding us one, he took our numbers: work, Paris, Rogny. While he couldn't receive a call in his home, he could at least drive his home to a nearby phone as long as the clutch held up.

We took the opportunity to show the presbytery to Lelièvre and Sophie. He looked over each room thoughtfully; then in each he started a new lesson on how to restore fireplaces, doors, stonework, and floor tiles. Apparently, just after he lost his job, he had lived in Brittany, where he learned to refinish furniture and paid for his lodging by doing restoration work on the old house that he lived in. His dream was to buy such an old house and open a furniture shop. In his present state, that dream seemed far off. But he informed us that he acquired most of his furniture from friends and associates in Brittany.

When he reached our one finished room, he said that he bet that the paneling in the library, which we had just freshly painted, was made of a beautiful hardwood. He pulled out his penknife, asking if we would mind if he scraped some paint away from a small patch to take a look. Sure enough, light rosewood appeared, and he offered to stain the wood for free if we uncovered the paneling. Mary gave me a sinking look. Suddenly we saw ourselves refinishing furniture and swabbing paint remover while the rest of the house collapsed around us. What slowly began to occur to us was that Lelièvre would be happy to live in our house in exchange for helping us restore it. We gave the idea consideration, since Mary and I gravitate naturally toward disaster. The proposition seemed fair if we were open-minded enough for a small-scale, socialist utopia, sharing meals with Lelièvre, listening to his lectures, and swapping smirks and clouds of smoke with beautiful little Sophie. But finally we were afraid they would move in forever and we'd lose our private world.

A week later we received a call from Lelièvre; he had our armoire. Of course, we weren't obligated to buy it, but there was no question in his mind that once we saw it we would want it—Louis-Philippe, after all. We arranged to rendezvous in Châtillon-sur-Loire; there wasn't a chance in hell that I could remember which garage in the *lotissement* our armoire occupied. However, after we'd joined Lelièvre and Sophie and wound through the maze, we would have had a difficult time missing it: the armoire stood like a monolith on the drive in the late-morning sun. The price was ridiculously low, and the purchase was made before the second exchange of a cigarette for a light.

The next weekend, after another feverish grasping for clothes, the armoire arrived safely—in the blue spray-painted van—though its doors had to be reattached, along with molding along the top. The delivery of something so large is an event on the place de l'Église. The Marteaus, Jean-Louis, Ariane, and Coco migrated to the blue van in front of the presbytery. Coco insisted on helping Lelièvre and me carry the huge armoire; Sophie carried the hardware and tools. We must have looked like a funeral procession hauling a coffin large enough to contain a whole family, the residents of the Haut-Bourg filing behind us. Once stood up in one of the bedrooms, the armoire was majestic. Lelièvre, assisted by his attentive Sophie, reattached and adjusted the huge doors; then he shimmed the feet so that the armoire wouldn't rock around the sloping tile floors.

We were so pleased with our purchases that we asked Lelièvre to find us next a set of drawers, a bookshelf, a bathroom dresser, and even a set of front doors. We decided to refurbish the Paris apartment as well. For such a large order, he assured us of greater bargains, taking measurements of the front door as he left. It is very un-French to discuss one's expenditures; however, Mary and I, unable to contain our delight, announced the ridiculously low price to the audience who stood admiringly in front of the armoire. Each nodded, with arched eyebrows, and muttered a thoughtful *"Pas mal, pas mal du tout."*

Only Coco gave a great, cheery, albeit saliva-befuddled grin of approval, offering a hearty single handshake. No one appreciates a good deal so much as Coco. He took this happy occasion to invite us to the Feu de la Saint-Jean, for which he had been charged with the construction of the bonfire that weekend. Coco considered this responsibility a great distinction, and our presence at the town celebration would be an honor. We assured him that the honor was ours, despite not really knowing what the Feu de la Saint-Jean was.

I plunged into serious research, starting with *feu,* and in *Le Petit Robert* I found nearly two whole pages listing expressions using "fire." There were the predictable expressions *feu de l'inspiration* and *âme* (spirit) *de feu* and the stranger *adorateurs du feu,* the celestial *feux du firmament, Feu Saint-Elme,* and *les feux de l'aurore* (dawn); the violent *à feu et à sang* (with fire and blood) and *baptême du feu;* the comical, rarely used *pantalon feu de plancher* (too short—pants with the floor on fire); the sexual *avoir le feu au cul* (to have a burning need for ass); and finally the religious *feu de l'Enfer, feu de Dieu,* and *le feu sacré.* Of course, the columns included flaming, firing, and burning, but there was no Feu de la Saint-Jean. The Larousse continued in the same vein—*le feu est à tel endroit* (embarrassment), *le feu de l'été* (summer heat), and *n'y voir que du feu* (to understand nothing).

I began to read messages into the definitions. I looked up "bonfire" in French, *feu de joie,* which means literally fire of joy. In English, bonfire means the more morbid "bonefire," triggering visions of a dark ritualistic world of early Europe transported over centuries to our little canal village for the Fête de la Saint-Jean. But every French kid knows that the Fête de la Saint-Jean means a *feu de joie* and *feu d'artifices* (fireworks), dancing and general mischief.

The night of the twenty-fourth, Mary and I heard the Bléneau band crank out a march, in competition with firecrackers and bottle rockets. Christabel scurried into the bedroom in a fit of shaking, as she always does at the first rumble of thunder, crack of a hunter's gun, or popping of fireworks. She couldn't come with us even on tranquilizers.

Off we went down the slope, past the *mairie,* the school, and the post office, to the Quai Sully at the edge of the canal, where in the past the circus had hoisted its tent, the mattress dealer set up his beds, and the *brocanteurs* (secondhand dealers) laid out their *vide-grenier*—grimy glasses and bottles, rusted tools, and worn-out tires. But that night on the *quai,* a massive tepee of rough-cut planks had been assembled, towering two stories high. It stood about the size of a small barn, which was what, as a child, I had misunderstood a bonfire to be—a barn fire. This was no coincidence: the only such fire I had seen was a great barn fire started by lightning. It lit the horizon like a misplaced dawn, *faux* (false) *feux de l'aurore.* A fire engine from Bléneau was parked next to the majestic tepee, right at the edge of the canal, presumably to pump water directly from the canal should the whole village accidentally catch fire. Meanwhile, the Bléneau band blared away, brass drowning out fifes and clarinets while snare drums and triangle seemed to have moved on to a different march.

Mary and I were shocked by the size of the crowd that had formed, filling the *quai,* streets, and bridges of the village. Pleasure barges had tied up on the far side of the *quai,* two deep in places. The town boys studiously kept the crowd in *feux croisés* (a cross fire) of bottle rockets and firecrackers. And there was Coco, in the middle of it all, the master of fire-making, the charcoal burner's son, lit up himself with the *feu de l'alcool.* It was his party.

The Bléneau band disassembled temporarily, and after brief ceremonial speeches were amplified through the loudspeakers set up next to the post office, music was piped out to the crowd, and Coco, bowing and doffing his cowboy hat, turned and marched up to the wooden tepee, lighter in hand. Clearly some fire starter had been added because in a matter of moments the fire worked evenly around the circumference of the great pile of planks, which soon sent a blaze towering into the night sky, illuminating the whole village. The schoolchildren, led by their *institutrice,* took one another's hands and formed their version of a snake dance. They coiled and uncoiled, undulating through the crowd to the recorded music, all cast in firelight. Coco began to work the crowd, holding out his hat to take contributions for his artistry.

The light of the fire was intense. It cast magnified shadows of the dancing crowd far up into the trees and over the sides of buildings, and if you looked away from the fire itself, you had the same vision of the fires of Saint-Jean that villagers had had over the centuries. Now each time I stand before the bonfire, the vision of shadows in firelight comes to me, but during our first, the character of the flaming tepee began suddenly to change. The color of the flame deepened, and a great column of black smoke rose. The crowd sensed before we did that something had gone wrong; they stopped dancing and turned to watch the bright tepee transform into a malevolent volcano. The crowd moved back. Even the Bléneau *pompiers*—firemen—seemed jarred from their complacent daze. Coco began to curse— *"Quelle connerie! Quelle connerie!"* In helpless disgust, he wiped the saliva from his lopsided mouth. Mary and I half expected a wicked *sorcière* to appear and make some hideous demand on our defenseless village. Then the whole tepee-turned-volcano collapsed toward the canal, revealing, at the heart of the disaster, burning tires. The Bléneau *pompiers* strapped on their black gear and shiny silver helmets and confronted the evil blaze, looking more like gladiators than firefighters.

Coco is a disfigured clown, but he is also a proud man. Someone had sneaked tires into the center of his bonfire during his afternoon nap, a prank directed at him personally, and he took it hard. He did not emerge the next day from his little house, nor did he serve *pastis* or *gros rouge* to his usual flow of comrades. We didn't even see him shut up the church. Let the damned thing shut itself up. Everyone in the Haut-Bourg felt Coco's wound. He seemed increasingly complex—the prideful woodsman, the poacher, the elfin spirit, the deformed jester, the spiteful brooder, the remorseless drunk, the resourceful innovator, the singular man-child of the place de l'Église. Still it was only a matter of days before we were watching him feign heart attacks on our terrace or pretend to hang himself from the belfry. He was making dinner for Madame Briançon and zooming off for a *verre* at the Saint-Mathurin, to the familiar whine of his moped, Dan in full bark chasing the fumes.

Mary and I soon learned that there isn't a worse place for catching up on sleep or making love than a country house. Christabel tries to kill the postal lady who comes on her bike and puts the mail in the window behind the *jardinière,* the flower box, or Nottin or Deluche stops by with a new heater or an estimate, or Lelièvre calls with exactly the piece of furniture we are looking for. Several weeks after the calamitous Feu de la Saint-Jean, Lelièvre called to announce that he and his petite Sophie had established a legitimate place of residence, no small feat. The French are generally very reluctant to rent because of strong laws favoring tenants and a deep conviction in the privacy of private property. Certainly, Lelièvre's itinerant lifestyle couldn't have been a sterling recommendation, so we concluded that he had probably lied about his circumstances. But we were happy for him, and for ourselves as well, since we had an actual phone number where we could contact him should we have a sudden yen for a chair, bureau, or side tables.

Lelièvre also called because he had found our set of drawers for Paris. He gave us directions to come see it at his new domicile, situated east of Châtillon-sur-Loire toward Sancerre, off the main road. In fact, the house couldn't have been more isolated, far up a winding dirt road, finally appearing between woods and a field of sunflowers. We recognized the blue van, with its transmission once again disassembled; the set of drawers was set out in a muddy drive surrounded by a muddle of uninterested hens. The house itself was so run-down and remote that we half figured Lelièvre had simply decided to move in. Who would know? Perhaps an old farmer was locked up in a closet. The house came with a large shed, where Lelièvre could restore and refinish furniture when he wasn't working on his chronically dilapidated van. We wrote a check for the set of drawers and for a mahogany bookcase that Lelièvre had saved as a surprise for us, and he invited us into the house for a glass of wine and a lecture on local economics.

Sophie turned off the TV and greeted us brightly, offering seats in the main room, which served as a kitchen, salon, and guest room and preserved a distinctive blend of odors from cigarettes, marijuana, and mold. A friend of theirs, a young black man, was abruptly gathering up his things, making plans to meet later, and looking under the table and the woodburning stove for his shoes, which, it turned out, he had left outdoors. After his disheveled exit, we were treated to glasses brimming with the worst aperitif wine that we'd had in years. To our hosts' delight, we nodded approval of its notable sweetness while complimenting their good fortune in finally finding a place to live. We expressed our wonder at how well Lelièvre managed in difficult circumstances. This compliment led to an eye cue for a cigarette and a dissertation on the joys of working in the box factory at Ouzouer-sur-Trézée just south of Rogny.

At first I envisioned large cutting and folding machines, but the kinds of boxes that Lelièvre's former employers made were for jewelry, leather goods, and expensive watches, like those by Cartier and Hermès. Fancy boxes or not, I was skeptical of any glory claimed for working in a factory. My first job had been in a dress factory, to earn enough money to travel to Europe. My factory was divided into three distinct levels of hell—cutting room, sewing floor, and packing room, where I was relegated as unskilled labor. I had an abusive foreman who shoved my head into a rack of dresses during inventory because I kept losing count, and at lunch, I'd sit with a sandwich and listen to men who had worked there for fifteen years. They knew the mysteries of how to pass a day, half working, half smoking and drinking among the bolts of material. Meanwhile, I had a partner who would slip unexpectedly into the twilight of diabetic shock. I still think of him when our diabetic neighbor, Madame Briançon, binges on the cakes she makes for herself and the ambulance races up to the Haut-Bourg to revive her amid the crumbs.

Lelièvre said that what he'd liked most about working at the box factory was being part of an *équipe,* a team, and I pictured a huddle of big guys like him, a rugby team making jewelry boxes. Lelièvre had maintained the machines, and this involved some education and mechanical skill, so at least his job wasn't the deadening repetition that characterizes most factory work. At the end of the day, he would fish in the Loire with his factory *copains,* buddies. This point led inevitably to a lament on the great tragedy of the Loire, that once noble river now shackled to the cooling towers of numerous nuclear power plants.

The closing of the box factory was not a unique event; the economy of the region had slumped so deeply that young people like Lelièvre had to leave or scramble to survive (devising an income in the shadows of the general system). According to Lelièvre, the older generation had benefited most from the system, retiring with healthy pensions, investments, and savings, and was now, paradoxically, keeping the region alive after industry had collapsed as a result of the high cost of labor. The retirees buy inexpensive country houses in the region and renovate them, and then depend on small local businesses, including, of course, furniture dealers.

With his trademark smile, Lelièvre gave us two bottles of his precious stock of wine, which was a touching gift, if less welcome than we led him to believe. We crossed the chicken-filled yard, with a bottle each, and parted on Lelièvre's promise to deliver the furniture to Paris within two weeks. There were handshakes all round, and a last glimpse of the chest of drawers and the bookshelves standing in the mud against a backdrop of sunflowers.

It took no fewer than six months and a dozen broken appointments before the blue van arrived happily in the heart of Paris. Half the broken appointments were blamed on mechanical problems—clutch, fuel pump, brakes—surely all plausible. The other half involved unforeseen demands and mysterious personal problems. We had begun to worry. But there Lelièvre and little Sophie were, as if transported from another world. Sophie, to my disappointment, had cut and frosted her hair, making her look cheap and unnatural. Along with the furniture, Lelièvre delivered the extraordinary news that they had acquired an old *crêperie* in Brittany, which he planned to transform into a combination workshop and showroom. However, the transaction would take a year to complete.

That winter, Lelièvre found our front doors. We couldn't wait to drive to his muddy, chicken-filled yard to see them, even if it meant enduring the hazards of Lelièvre's wine, two bottles of which rolled around on the floor of the car for months before, with modest ceremony, we gave them to Coco. The doors could not have been better; they were eighteenth century, the same epoch as the presbytery itself, elaborately carved scrolls on both sides, and solid oak. They were masterpieces, and Lelièvre promised to refinish and hang them for us within the next two weeks.

Four months later he and the van and the doors arrived. Mary complained about his broken promises, and he answered with a smile, "Well, have you finished the buffet yet?" He had noticed it still standing in our living room just as he had delivered it, tilted like a troubled boat. Without another word of complaint, we implicitly agreed that all projects have lives of their own and thus are always completed on schedule, whatever that schedule ends up being. And, as with all projects in the presbytery, hanging the doors was much more complicated than we'd anticipated. The plaster and loose mortar that framed the doorway had to be chipped out and resurfaced with cement. The project took several weeks, since the cement had to be completely dry before the doors were hung in place, stained, and weatherproofed.

We were away when Lelièvre finished the job, but we stood proudly before the doors, basking in all the compliments of our neighbors on the place de l'Église, though the compliments were accompanied by endless suggestions and discussion about attaching a rainskirt and the problems of expansion and contraction in summer and winter. The last few times we saw Lelièvre, he was without Sophie. We didn't mention it. The last time Mary spoke to him, he confessed that major changes had occurred in his life. What could they be? Had he lost little Sophie? Did the Brittany deal fall through? Had he had trouble with the law?

It has all remained a deep mystery. An acquaintance of mine in Paris told me that he never buys furniture in the country because 75 percent of it is stolen and this bothers his conscience. Often I wonder if the presbytery isn't, in part, a warehouse of stolen goods or if sometime someone will knock, saying, "These are my doors!" But mostly, though it has been years, I hope we'll see Lelièvre and little Sophie seated again amid furniture on a village sidewalk, in a room without walls.

Summer Sonatas at the Église de Saint-Loup

*E*ven out in the provinces, it is not uncommon for churches in France to moonlight as concert halls. Some have a summer series with chamber music and recitals. If the town is large enough and the church is heated, it is possible to find winter concerts as well. But in a village like Rogny, where there are seven hundred and fifty inhabitants and on the east side of the church the walls are buckling, it would never occur to us that a concert would be held next door at the Église de Saint-Loup. Nevertheless, on one of the hottest days in late July, a full-size concert piano was hefted out of a delivery truck from Auxerre and flyers went up at the Club de l'Amitié, the *boulangerie,* and the Guillons' *épicerie,* advertising that the Barlis, father and son, would perform violin and piano duets at the *église* that coming Saturday.

While we worked in the yard, gardening and scraping and painting the back shutters, we began to hear Beethoven's "Le Printemps" coming from the church. The Barlis were practicing in the late afternoon. The notes could be heard across the Haut-

Bourg; they'd float out of the church to Coco's little house and over to the Marteaus', Bougés', and Roussats'.

After a half-year of construction work on the presbytery, in our new life among farmers, woodsmen, artisans, widows, thieves, and drunks, "Le Printemps" seemed to waft in from another world. Mary adored Beethoven and classical music in general, still nostalgic for the days when she played the cello in a chamber group. When she heard the music, she was at first shocked and then spellbound. Still wearing her gloves and boots, her knees caked with garden soil, she slipped out the terrace door and stood quietly by the church to hear the music better.

We learned from Ariane that the Barlis had a country house in Rogny and had, as a onetime offer, volunteered to give a concert, provided that the village rent the piano. The mayor leapt at the chance to associate himself with the Barlis and show his commitment to enhancing Rogny's cultural life, which consisted solely of an Expo d'Art: recent watercolors from the local *maison de retraite*, or retirement home. Ironically, the concert took place only weeks before the mayor disappeared. For the Barlis, this concert was not just a generous performance for the pleasure of the villagers; it would be the debut concert of Olivier Barli's twelve-year-old son Guillaume.

The Barlis were among the most notable families in the area. Olivier Barli's father had been a tenor at the Paris Opera, and his mother was an accomplished concert pianist who taught Olivier to master the instrument. Olivier himself became the director of the Issy-les-Moulineaux conservatory and recorded solo albums of Chopin, Schubert, and Bach under the combined names of his Polish-immigrant mother and father, Barli-Majewski. Olivier's son may not have been a true prodigy, but he wasn't far from it. By the age of twelve, he had already won numerous competitions and was studying music at such an accelerated pace that he was a child among accomplished young men at his music school. Olivier's parents had recently died, and it seemed fitting that his son should give his debut concert in the village that his musical grandparents had chosen as their home.

Two days running, the Barlis came up to the place de l'Église for their afternoon practice session. Since Olivier parked his Honda next to the presbytery, I was able to catch a glimpse of both father and son. Olivier bore an uncanny resemblance to Benny Goodman, and I swore he knew it, in heavy black-rimmed glasses, checked sport coat, and bow tie. His son was a smaller version, a miniature Goodman, except that he wore the distinctive government-issue, socialized-medicine oval glasses. The two Goodman look-alikes disappeared into the church, but then their music emerged: sonatas of Beethoven, Bach, and Handel. Mary would exit by the garden door, lured into a scene of swallows swooping along the alley, full afternoon sunlight projected over ancient stone walls, and music suffusing the air around the small country church.

Apart from Ariane and Mary and I, the inhabitants of the Haut-Bourg had no use for the Barlis' music. Coco was particularly annoyed about the concert because he felt personally responsible for the massive black piano that lurked in the church for nearly a week, and in the past there had been worrisome thefts and vandalism. Just the winter before, someone had stolen the church's central heating system, which consisted of a propane tank with a screw-on burner that resembled a loudspeaker. The curé, out of desperation, posted a large note entreating the thief to return the heater. It said, *"Frère Voleur, après le dégel, prière de rendre l'appareil de chauffage pour le bonheur du plus grand nombre.*" Brother Thief, after the thaw, please return the heater for the happiness of a larger number of people.

No one has seen the heater since. Along with the added responsibility of the piano, Coco was also annoyed because he would be obliged to stay up much later on Saturday night than was his habit in order to lock up the church after the lingering audience finally filtered out.

On the night of the concert, Mary and I had only to dress up, step out through the garden door, and pass into the makeshift concert hall. The town exerted the maximum effort to make the Église de Saint-Loup look presentable, despite its mold and its detaching plaster. A large Persian rug had been rolled out over the *dalles funéraires,* the inscribed stone slabs that conceal the medieval bones of Jehan Douart and Madame Mahaut under the floor. A red carpet had been placed down the alley under the church nave, and two large bouquets of peach-colored gladioli in floor vases stood sentinel on either side of the piano. The town had even brought in special spots and halogen lighting, along with video and sound recording equipment. But of all the transformations, the audience itself was the most striking. While Mary and I recognized the mayor, his assistant, the doctor and his wife, and a few other familiar faces, we were seeing a different side of Rogny and the region—these were the Parisians, and Mary and I were in the unanticipated position of being observed with some curiosity, first because we were Americans and second because we had bought the ghost house next to the *église*. I felt self-conscious; Mary was oblivious. She just wanted to rush to the best seats with the best view of the musicians at work.

One of the most unnerving experiences in the arts is the incongruity of a child performing with such mature emotion. How can a twelve-year-old feel what a middle-aged adult feels? A good performance is so much more than a technical exercise; it is expression and interpretation, things that can be coached but not taught. When I was a kid, I wanted to play the saxophone because I loved my father's Coltrane and Charlie Parker records and was dazzled the times he would take us to live jazz broadcasts at the RCA studios in New York. However, we were too poor to buy or rent a saxophone, and my father, who played clarinet from time to time, insisted that a clarinet was the same thing as a saxophone, which, of course, it wasn't. Even so, as one of my childhood torments, I played my father's clarinet and took lessons when the money was available. At ten, I auditioned for the school orchestra, which was dominated by precocious girls playing violin and flute and a few boys who played trumpet, saxophone, and trombone.

On my first day, the music teacher made me play in front of the whole assemblage of children, who fidgeted restlessly, barely able to restrain themselves from making their own noise. The teacher chose a piece I couldn't play and berated me into tears that lasted the whole hour after I had been exiled to third clarinet, something I hadn't even known existed. Everyone knew that I was the worst musician on the team, and whether I actually played or not made little difference, so long as I stopped when I felt the reed stiffen into a treasonous squeak. I decided that music was unforgiving and cruel, yet each time our little children's orchestra performed, I experienced the exhilaration, terrible as we were, that one only gets from music—adding one's notes to a much larger collaboration, thus becoming part of a much larger self. Nevertheless, I still felt the sting of my music teacher's cruelty, and I remember the sense of liberation that came with quitting the miserable instrument.

But that night in the Église de Saint-Loup, I watched what few musicians experience—the Barlis, father and son, performing at a level so high that they seemed to transcend their instruments.

The concert began with a speech by the mayor, who heaped prodigious praise on the Barli family and copious congratulations on himself for raising the funds to rent the piano. Of course we were all asked to contribute at the end of the concert, to offset any budgetary deficit. When Olivier and Guillaume, in formal black-and-white concert regalia, finally entered from the back of the church, they basked in the goodwill and happiness of their family, friends, and neighbors. The applause finally muted, and Olivier took a moment to explain the significance of the evening, thanking the audience for its role in inaugurating the career of the twelve-year-old. The boy then stepped forward, and together the Barlis launched into "Le Printemps."

Olivier embodied the grace and poise that come from a lifetime in the world of performance; his gray-eyed son stood before the audience with all the intensity of the possessed, his small body invaded by a demon of virtuosity. We watched in wonderment as he played Bach's "Adagio de la Sonate." In the middle of the concert, each Barli performed solo. Olivier played a mazurka, nocturne, and polonaise by Chopin; the gray-eyed spirit attacked Veracini's "Le Largo." As an encore, they played a sonata by Handel. The final applause appeared to exorcise the demon, and we found ourselves standing up with the rest of the audience to applaud a reserved, though smiling, boy as he took stiff bows.

We joined the line to introduce ourselves to the Barlis and lavish praise on them. Mary confessed to having come from the presbytery each afternoon to eavesdrop on the rehearsals. This brought on a flash of recognition to Olivier's face. At the same time, there was the roll of thunder from a summer storm, which had suddenly disrupted the evening. *"Vous êtes les étrangers qui ont acheté le presbytère!"* We admitted that we were those foreigners, Americans to be precise, and Olivier thought immediately of other Americans. To our surprise, he knew one who had come to the concert. Amid more frequent and increasingly violent rumblings of thunder, he introduced us to Anna Chapelle, the first resident American we had encountered in the region.

Anna Chapelle was a tall, handsome woman in her fifties, with an authoritative bearing. She had married a French businessman and raised children and worked as an administrator. Anna and her husband had renovated a very large carriage house about thirty kilometers away. It had belonged to a château that no longer existed. Since Anna's husband had a passion for nature, they acquired vast tracks of wooded land, the château's forest, that provided enough fox, deer, wild pigs, rabbits, badgers, and game birds for Monsieur Chapelle and his family to observe to their hearts' content.

The night of the concert produced the kind of violent storm that Madame Savin would surely have ascribed to God's vengeful campaign against her Renault. But this was summer, and summer storms are common; they are especially intense where we live. Above the valley, at the very edge of the steep slope, we are fully exposed to the wind, and lightning explodes above the church steeple, rattling the owls that must have gone deaf anyway from Isabelle and Marie Anne's clanging for Angelus. We invited Anna and several of her friends over for drinks and a short tour of the presbytery; the Barlis concluded their triumphant evening with their audience gasping at impressive thunderbolts that punctuated exclamations of musical pleasure and admiration. Finally, a superbolt lit the entire region and extinguished the electricity. Mary and

I were obliged to light candles, which cast a dim, shadowy aspect through the rooms, hinting of their former life.

With drinks and candlesticks, we escorted our new acquaintances through the house with its one finished room. As we passed rotted beams and half-cemented walls, our guests' faces had clearly, even in the candlelight, that expression of dismissiveness that comes with experience and says silently, "Good luck." Still, Anna was amiable, and she reciprocated for the candlelit tour by inviting us to her carriage house for a party that would feature a private concert by the Barlis.

To the audience leaving the concert amid the sudden downpour and wind, the presbytery must have looked as it had two hundred and fifty years ago, when Polluche lit the rooms with oil lamps and candles. But the point for them was to get home as soon as possible; our acquaintances left shortly, like the others, the cars starting up all at once as if for a demolition derby. The storm only compounded Coco's annoyance with the concert, since he had to lock up the church in drenching rain in what was the middle of his night.

Summer storms at the old presbytery are not unlike those at my childhood home in Wilton. The Wilton house was also on top of a hill and exposed to whatever fury storms had to offer, whether ice storms, blizzards, hurricanes, or electrical storms. My mother was particularly fearful of thunderstorms, and not without cause. As soon as such storms began, she would pick out a book and go to bed, pulling pillows all around her head, preparing for a hard landing. Out front was a telephone pole with a sizable condenser to which lightning was particularly attracted. When lightning hit, there wasn't an instant between flash and deafening pop; it never sounded like ordinary thunder. For a long time we assumed that we had a margin of safety because the condenser acted as a lightning rod. But one time it didn't, and lightning charged into the house through the TV aerial and burned out every electrical appliance, including the electric water pump in the well room. Before going to bed with her book, my mother learned to disconnect the aerial, leaving the wires dangling on the front porch. God forbid that a stranger came to visit at the wrong moment.

By the end of the summer, Mary and I had been thinking a good deal about my mother. During the spring days that my mother spent preparing our wedding, the presbytery had bewitched her. She wouldn't listen to her own trepidation or to the good advice of her friends but began to talk about retiring to France, even to our remote village. At the beginning of August, we received a letter.

> *I have been doing some serious thinking and considering of options, and since one of the possibilities involves the two of you, you must do some serious, honest thinking and talking also.*
>
> *In a year or two, I will be retiring. It has become apparent that I will not be able to stay where I am, as expenses and taxes are outstripping the income of the house. Therefore, I'm going to have to move—where to?*
>
> *One of the thoughts that I have had is that if I could have a room in the country house and space for a garden I could retire there.*

She went on to explain that her best friend, Lee, was planning to move to England and that her other friends were considering various retirement plans which didn't include living their whole lives in one of the poorest cities in America. My mother supposed that she would have a better chance to make friends in France, a proposition that seemed absurd, particularly in our village.

My major concern is that you would be unhappy under these circumstances. You know what my personality is like. It won't improve with age, only more of the same. You would have to be happy with that. I want you to divest yourself of all sentimentality and think with hard and tough heads. We should all think of this possibility joyfully or not at all.

My mother lived near downtown New Haven in a white Victorian house built by a Yale professor for his new wife, a Belgian princess. It was the kind of house walkers paused in front of to look at the roses on the white fence or the weeping cherry or the star magnolia. Paradoxically, while I have been moved to restore the shack and solitude of my childhood, my mother aspired to recapture something of her aristocratic ghost world, coming up with schemes that have allowed her to live beyond her income. Her major problem has been the city of New Haven, which has throughout its history vacillated mostly between depression and recession, while Yale conveniently saw itself as a part of a quaint New England town. When New Haven was established in the seventeenth century, it respected the autonomy of neighboring townships, with the consequence that its tax base was circumscribed to a small area. With years of white flight, vanishing industry, and then Reaganomics, the tax burden fell on homeowners, at least the ones who hadn't defaulted or abandoned their buildings altogether.

The house my mother lived in had been converted into three apartments so that she could live on the first floor while renting out the two upstairs ones to pay for the mortgage and other expenses. Over the years the value of the house increased, and my mother took out additional mortgages, which increased her payments. Then taxes skyrocketed and property values dropped. My mother was stuck. She could hardly make a go of it when she had her full income from Yale; there was no way she could live in her own house if she retired.

When we received the letter, Mary and I were mostly concerned about my mother's friends leaving New Haven. We were far from convinced that she would be bold enough to make the move, and Mary and I never thought with "hard and tough heads" about anything, least of all my mother's living with us. We wrote back immediately, telling her how concerned we were about the desertion of her friends and that we were committed to helping her achieve happiness during her retirement. We had enough extra space that one room didn't seem much of a sacrifice. Anyway, we felt that having some options would console my mother.

The concert party with total strangers was the sort of social occasion that Mary and I ordinarily avoid, but Mary suggested that the Barlis might turn out to be friends, the sort that my mother referred to in her letter. But recruiting friends was not the only reason we went to the party. The Barlis were engaged for a repeat performance, there was a restored building to investigate for new ideas for our own, and finally, Anna had been very kind to invite us.

The day was exceptionally hot, and after an arduous search for the carriage house concealed in the depths of a forest, we found ourselves sweating in an audience of perspiring French businessmen preparing to listen to the Barlis perform "Le Printemps" under the glassy gaze of deer heads, stitched-up foxes, snarling badgers, dehydrated squirrels, and dusty partridges.

The carriage house turned out to be a nineteenth-century farm building that had harbored ox-drawn wagons with tall hayracks. The arching cut-stone doorways had been transformed into luminous banks of windows, and above the large open space, where businessmen sat instead of wagons, the Chapelles had built a mezzanine in dark-stained wood with a surrounding balcony and an angular staircase. To one side of the room was a gaping false fireplace constructed for vases filled with dried flowers; on the walls the taxidermal bonanza was broken up only by swords, rifles, painted leg traps, and engravings of bucolic prospects and landscapes.

Greeted with cordial applause, the Barlis descended from the mezzanine and positioned themselves under a fierce-looking wild pig. While the audience lacked the ebullience of that in the Église de Saint-Loup two weeks earlier, we witnessed the same unnerving transformation. Again, the twelve-year-old played like a demon. Inevitably, the Barlis drew the audience into their unique sphere of charm, father and son beautifully paired.

When the concert ended, with satisfaction all around, the audience rose quickly to seek out wine and conversation before the feast was served. For Mary and me, that moment was like a shipwreck, and we moved away from the debris to the well-kept grounds in the waning heat of oncoming night. We discovered that we were not the only ones marooned in alien waters, when Olivier and his wife, Laurence, drew us into conversation. The virtuoso violinist had turned to a boy once again, now joyfully humiliating one of the Chapelles' retrievers by throwing it invisible sticks. His sister, Pauline, boisterously protested her brother's mischief. Both Laurence and Pauline played cello, but apparently neither had pursued her instrument with the same ardor as the father and son. But all in all, without their instruments, the Barlis seemed a cheerful, unassuming family, and Mary and I felt charmed to be accepted into their company.

While we chatted with the Barlis, other guests passed and offered compliments and small conversation. One guest, who seemed drawn to us as if by bad karma, was a middle-aged, pipe-smoking *polytechnicien*. *Polytechniciens* are a distinct breed of Frenchmen who go through a very selective *concours*, or competition, to attend one of the Grandes Écoles, where for four years they are told by other *polytechniciens* that they are the most intelligent people, not just in France but in the entire world. He gave a reserved nod of recognition to Olivier and introduced himself midsentence of something I was saying about American literature.

With raised eyebrows, he asked, *"Expliquez-moi, en quoi les Américains ont-ils contribué à la culture?"* Explain to me, what have Americans contributed to culture? Then, with great satisfaction in needing no response, he turned his broad back and strolled away; Americans had contributed nothing.

Olivier rendered a spontaneous impersonation. *"Expliquez-moi, en quoi les polonais-juifs immigrés ont-ils contribué à la culture?"* Explain to me, what have Polish-Jewish immigrants contributed to culture? He mocked the *polytechnicien* while referring to his own ethnic background to show solidarity with us. While we didn't know whether or not Olivier and the Barlis would make good friends for my mother, they were decidedly becoming ours.

To avoid further damage, I kept my mouth shut while I watched the final preparations of *méchoui*, which had been smoking all evening in a pit near three tall poplars. *Méchoui*, a popular Arab dish, is prepared by skewering a whole lamb on a spit and roasting it in a hole that is dug a yard wide and a foot and a half deep in the ground. Red-hot embers are kept at a constant temperature while the lamb is turned slowly and constantly basted. Apparently, the kidneys are an especially prized delicacy. The whole operation requires careful attention so as to avoid over- or undercooking. The goal is to serve golden-brown, well-roasted, crackling meat. According to Arab tradition, when the meat is done, it should be served immediately and eaten only with bare hands, which are washed later with special rose water. I couldn't help anticipating all of us—businesspeople, hunters, musicians, and one *polytechnicien*—ripping apart pieces of the poor lamb right off the spit, but in reality the animal was cut up and served on several platters, with couscous and North African salads.

By the time full dark arrived, all the guests had left, and Anna suggested that the Barlis and we take a swim in the new pool out back. The pool itself was a most peculiar sight, with its blue aura startling between the edges of the forest and a harvested field. Bright light shot up from below the surface, suggesting a landing strip for UFOs. Anna lent Mary and me her kids' bathing suits, which, surprisingly, fit us, and we went to the landing strip looking more like shadows than whole beings.

Another summer storm was coming. Lightning became frequent enough to keep the forest lit in the distance, and a line of clouds pulled a dark blanket over the constellations. The Barli kids were oblivious, diving toward the pool's sunken lights, wrestling, hugging. Laurence spoke calmly about her and her husband's fears for Guillaume. There are hazards for child musicians, and for several years the Barlis have been consulting an orthopedist. The boy was growing around the shape of his instrument.

As we swam with the family of musicians, I remembered how on hot summer nights my parents would pack up dinner and drive us to Great Pond, just in the next town, and we swam well after dark. My brother and I would race halfway out to the lit-up cottages on the far shore. My mother and father, swimming, too, blurred into the dark, with the stars overhead. There was one thing that we were sure my mother would love, and that would be swimming in Anna's pool.

In This Together

*E*very year I fish in the Loing River between Saint-Fargeau and Saint-Privé. Trout season begins in early spring when the days are blustery, so casting is often difficult. I try to place my lure just downstream from where the clear rushing water meets a deeper pool, dark under scattered shadows. I like to cast as far away as possible from the desired spot. If the trout sees me, I'll have no chance; accuracy is everything.

When I was growing up, hardly a day passed when I didn't walk the length of the Hop Meadow River, where it coursed through our property in Wilton. There was a natural dam at one end where a stretch of rocks, rounded by glaciers and river flow, made a small waterfall. The river passed rapidly over a bed of moss-covered rocks until it relaxed suddenly where the banks widened and the river grew deep enough to make a swimming hole. The river then hurried on into the deep woods of water company property, and it came quickly to a tall waterfall at the edge of the Pound Ridge Reservoir. There was no shortage of other creatures—crayfish, bluegills, pickerel, suckers, and young bass, the frogs trilling as they jumped from the banks. Painted and spotted turtles gathered on rocks, their black backs absorbing the warm sunlight. The river in summer was framed by water iris, tiger lily, and Indian paintbrush and patrolled by dragonflies and damselflies. Even in winter I'd walk across the snow-covered meadow to look into the water, at nothing but the black riverbed.

But on the Loing River in a sudden gust of wind, my lure sails into the branches of an oak tree. At the same time, as if in a Japanese movie or a dream, a flurry of petals falls around me and then scatters across the water, since I am standing near an abandoned pear orchard. In another age, at the Loing River, one would have seen Jeanne d'Arc, just a month before the siege of Orléans. She passed through with her renovated army in 1429, gathering troops and provisions. The towns along the Loing have marked on plaques and monuments the points of her passage. Considering these events, I realize that aside from a peppery odor and the clarity of their waters, the Loing and Hop Meadow have little in common. The notion I had of re-creating a country life similar to the one I grew up with was absurd. Even if Mary and I had bought a mill and lived above constantly rushing water, little would have been the same. The choices that I've made in my life have transported me to a completely different land.

Our river in the New England woods remained mostly wild, only dammed here and there to make a pond. The woods themselves were crisscrossed by stone walls where once there were eighteenth- and nineteenth-century farms. Stone foundations remained as depressions in the leaf cover. When the reservoir was drained, foundations of farmhouses and mills appeared along with black stumps of rotted trees.

In contrast, the Loing was used for centuries to float logs, which means that it was linked to a complex of lakes and ponds tightly controlled to assure sufficient depth and power to keep the logs moving. Those lakes and ponds also control water levels in the locks of the canal. The confluence of the Loing and the Seine is less than eighty kilometers from Paris, and along the way the Loing passes the strategic cities of Montargis and Nemours.

Certainly, in Wilton there was nothing like the engineering feat of the Briare Canal. Our village camped twelve thousand workers in the early 1600s, and the local nobility was ordered, first by Henry IV, later by Louis XIII, to supply them with food and provisions. The construction of the most ambitious canal in the world was a part of an even larger plan to cultivate forests, restore and develop farmland, and expand the network of transportation by building and modernizing roads and waterways. In Paris, at the same time, the Louvre Palace was enlarged and the Pont-Neuf constructed.

The canal is an engineering wonder, the seven locks rising thirty-two meters (over one hundred feet) up the steep edge of the Loing Valley. Once the canal was finished, an efficient transportation route opened up from the south of France to Paris, and the port of Rogny, which had known primarily piled logs, began to see a great variety of commerce. As one might expect, tariffs were posted in 1639 on every imaginable product—grains, fruit, nuts, beans, wine, liquor, fish, meat, cheese, skins, oil, wax, textiles, metal, glass, ceramics, and fuel. Such exotic foods as almonds, figs, olives, pomegranates, and limes passed through the small village of mainly woodsmen and peasants.

In our time, the canal bypasses the seven locks, just off to the right, leaving them marooned in the side of the hill, for tourists to photograph and ponder. The first two locks still have water in them and are populated by frogs and small fish that live among large green clouds of algae. If you lean over, you can watch swallows and bats fly in circles beneath you. The edge, however, is unnerving. There are no railings. One afternoon Mary and I were eating a quick lunch of *charcuterie* at the Auberge du Canal, where the patron is Madame Charnier, a tall, haggard woman in her fifties. She owns a *dogue allemand,* a huge gray dog the size of a donkey that often sleeps stretched out in the street or in the bar, where it takes up half the floor space. Mary remarked that there were no railings around the locks. "*C'est dangereux.*"

"*Mais oui,*" Madame Charnier responded. "*Évidemment! L'année dernière, une femme a reculé d'un pas pour prendre une photo. Et voilà, c'était fini.*" A woman had stepped back for a photograph, fell, and ruptured her liver. It seems that such accidents in France are just a matter of bad luck—*pas de chance.* In the States, the basins of the locks would be ringed with railings and warnings, not to mention graffiti.

The seven locks are still used for tourist events. In late July, Rogny organizes a spectacular fireworks display, renowned throughout the region. Up to twenty thousand people come for the music, lasers, balloons, and skyrockets, and each year a theme is featured—sorcery, ecology, or history—in a narrated speech, the high points punctuated by an array of rockets. The town sets up bleachers and Monsieur Guillon sells *saucisses, merguez,* and *frites,* as does the butcher, while the *boulangerie* sells ice cream, pastries, and sandwiches. When the crowd fills the town, I get a vague impression of the twelve thousand workers camped around fires in 1604.

The only other use for the seven locks is as landmarks for pilots training at low altitude. During the week, two or three Mirages fly in tight formation so low over the presbytery that you can see the colorful light display on the control panels, and because they come in just over the house, you don't hear them until the engines seem to explode above you. The pilots, training from the base in Châlon-sur-Saône, line up the steeple of the eleventh-century church with seventeenth-century *écluses* (canal locks) and set their guidance systems for practice bombing of Rogny's little bridges. Warplanes flying over Rogny are nothing new, and I'm sure many of the residents remember vividly the bombing campaigns of the Nazis and the Allies along the Loire. There is even a small church nearby that has been claimed by the woods, the bomb damage exceeding the local will to repair it. No one has a monopoly on war. Around Wilton, we had our battlegrounds for the battles of Drum Hill and Ridgefield, where a clapboard house proudly announces a cannon-ball lodged in a wall or the graveyard allows an inscription for the British dead: "Our enemies in life, our guests in death."

The differences between Rogny and Wilton are vast, but two years after Mary and I bought the presbytery, I was faced with the astonishing irony of sharing a country house with my mother again. My mother had tried, as an impetuous teenager, to create an alternative life in the woods, living off the land with her artist husband, her two children, a small herd of wily goats, and a Noah's ark of various small creatures, domestic and wild; now, in the later part of her life, she had decided to move to France and live in the presbytery. She had been sitting on the back porch of her house looking out at her small fenced-in garden, the city of New Haven rising in the background with stubby towers and a yellow Citibank sign hung in the sky, and she thought to herself that she could be sitting right then on the presbytery terrace. Mary and I had had clear warning in her letter that asked us to consider her coming "with hard and tough heads," but we failed to believe that my mother would make such a radical choice.

In part, what made my mother's moving to France seem so improbable was that she had developed fairly severe agoraphobia. It took years of learning muscle relaxation techniques and breathing exercises before she ventured out of the New Haven area. Whenever she traveled, she went well armed with books on tape, crossword puzzles, a tangle of knitting, a pillow from her bed, a medicine cabinet's worth of emergency supplies, and, most important, a trusted friend by her side. With all these comforts and distractions, my mother would courageously set off for the precipice. Her terror comes most fiercely in traffic jams or starting out on drives of even moderate distance. She turns on a book on tape and does crossword puzzles simultaneously, loudly asking the name of some sports figure in seven letters across. My mother's decision to move to Rogny seemed paradoxical: she defied her anxiety-filled imaginings yet was led on by uncensored dreaming. Her friends were dumbfounded.

For two years before retiring, my mother read pop psychology books on aging, and she joined support groups of people who were committed to reinforcing in one another a comfortable self-image. My mother had spent a lifetime living beyond her means and worrying about it. She had struggled on her own since running away from boarding school, and now that she was in her sixties, with an array of ailments, she was determined to live beyond her means and not worry. As she had written us bitterly the previous summer, taxes in New Haven made it impossible for her to retire in her own home.

My mother is fond of saying to me, "We grew up together." In a sense, she is right. In Wilton, she was a teenage mother, and in New Haven in the sixties she ran the house like a commune, with a series of boarders and our various girlfriends moving in and out. I can't say that my brother and I made my mother's life any easier, not because we fought with her or rebelled, but because she struggled so hard to make life work, and we were acutely self-involved. After my father left, the theme of the household was "We're all in this together!" It is a mentality that we never completely grew out of, and several decades later my mother was resolved to renew the complicity, which would take some getting used to by Mary.

The winter before my mother's planned arrival, only the bathroom and the library could be considered finished. The walls and ceilings in each unfinished room had to be plastered, taped, and painted; the beams in the living room needed cleaning and preservative. The cement and plaster around the cut-stone blocks framing several windows were still crumbling, and the windows themselves needed reconditioning with scraping and glazing. Two holes remained in the ceiling from water damage; each had rotted supporting beams. Counters and cabinets had to be built and installed in the kitchen. Finally, electric heating elements had to be mounted under each window.

It was clear that I couldn't do that much work alone, and as a solution my mother wrote, "If you both agree, I can arrange to have John Lasky come for a month to six weeks to live in the presbytery while working on it. I can find a cheap ticket on Moroccan Airlines or some such, and I'm sure neither the ticket nor John will cost you much."

My mother has always been obliged to find misfits, drunks, artists, loners, and nuts, not to mention her own sons, to do work for her because she can't afford real workers. The relationships were always personal. It wasn't a matter of hiring a Jamaican woman to clean; my mother would end up giving her free driving lessons on Saturday mornings or taking her to the flea market or the women's clinic. My mother would make dinner for her roofer who developed a sudden terror of ladders, or she would entertain her carpenter's notion that with just the awesome powers of concentration he planned to grow back his missing index finger. She called her electrician Sparkles because he flirted with everyone—men, women, children, and dogs—with his sparkling blue eyes, and then there was Mr. Highsmith, her handyman, who would never work on Saturdays, even if water was pouring in through the ceilings from thawing ice jams; he was a Seventh-Day Adventist.

Among these workers, my mother developed a close friendship with John Lasky, who was a housepainter and a periodic devotee of AA. Lasky was about fifty years old but seemed to have the perpetual youthfulness that certain obsessive-compulsive people have—limitless energy and black hair without a strand of gray. Although his nose was large and he often gave a pumpkinlike grin, revealing a large gold front tooth, Lasky was definitely good-looking. He grew up in the trashed-out city of Waterbury, Connecticut, where he spent his childhood taking regular beatings from his alcoholic father. Still he managed to grow old enough to drink and deal out beatings himself, until finally he landed in jail. His girlfriend at that time vanished with their child into the Hasidic community in Brooklyn. Lasky joined AA, knowing that alcohol made him crazy and he would surely kill himself or someone else in the end if he didn't give it up. As with drinking, Lasky did nothing halfway; he became a good artist, an accomplished musician, and a committed activist, while painting houses to earn an ascetic living. Other than his passions, he needed nothing but a simple room, a subscription to *Mother Jones,* and membership in the Sister City (New Haven and Leone, Nicaragua) Project. He ended up living in my mother's basement in exchange for painting the house, which took two years between other jobs. He managed to save money for annual trips to Central America, where he'd go to see firsthand the people who were victimized by the CIA, whose sole purpose he felt was and would always be to cause damage and misery throughout the world to pave the way for American corporate profiteering.

As peculiar as Lasky was, he became a good friend of the family, and it seemed only natural to invite him to come to Rogny for a month or so and pay him to help us get the house in order for my mother's arrival. Our goal was to make the northern part of the house completely livable; any work completed on the south side would be welcome, albeit unexpected.

It was a rainy, miserable late January when Lasky moved into the house, and Mary and I were embarrassed by the conditions we subjected him to. Our vision had always been to shut off half the house in winter, thus saving on heating costs. Through the EDF, France's electric power company, we also subscribed to a plan called *éffacement jour de pointe,* EJP, which was very advantageous for second-home owners. Through its nuclear energy program, the EDF became so efficient that it could sell electric energy to the European power grid. In the winter, on cold days when the demand is at a peak, EDF could tap extra power through its EJP program. The power company reserves the right to charge EJP subscribers ten times the normal electricity rates over twenty-two weekdays from November to the middle of March. On those EJP days, however, the normal rates would go into effect from midnight to 6:00 A.M. For subscribing, we saved 30 percent on our yearly electrical costs, and we assumed we'd use the house only on weekends in winter when the rates are normal. We installed a system that automatically shuts off our heating system on EJP days to keep electricity consumption to a bare minimum.

Lasky would be the first person since Père Jo to live in the house full-time during the worst days of winter, and because that winter was so cold, almost every weekday during Lasky's stay was EJP. Lasky was forced to haul in logs for the Godin woodburning stove in the library, where he would sleep, and for the large kitchen fireplace.

I was sure that Lasky would lose his mind, living like a hermit in the presbytery. But he set up a music stand beside the illuminated window of the Godin stove and unpacked his violin and flute. He set out his reading material—this time Edward W. Said on the Palestinian situation—and unfolded his bed from the convertible couch, where he spent the night strangling sheets and blankets, or so it seemed. Lasky was installed and ready to attack the ceilings and walls of the presbytery.

The inhabitants of the Haut-Bourg didn't know what to make of Lasky. After all, no one imports laborers from America, and laborers don't ordinarily play the flute and violin after midnight. In the winter, the *mairie* always displays a lurid black-and-red poster warning against *travail au noir*, jobs done without paying the required value added tax, 20.6 percent on all labor. Labor contract negotiations often include what is paid for by cash and what by check—cash suggesting *travail au noir* and a check showing a tacit respect for TVA and possible fines and jail terms. Small jobs in the region are commonly paid for in cash. But having an American working in the presbytery was a situation outside the scope of normal transactions—was this *travail au noir*, an illegal alien working in France, or just a friend helping out?

Meanwhile, Lasky was confused and upset about his neighbors. He called me to ask, "Who's trying to blow up the Renault out front?"

"That's Madame Savin," I replied. "Her husband told her she always had to warm up the car before driving it. Her husband is dead, and she thinks she's being extra prudent. She races the engine, and no one can talk her out of it."

"Prudent? Maybe if this were a drag strip."

I assured Lasky that Madame Savin was also prudent about the gearshift and tended to crawl to and from the cemetery. "It's unlikely she'll crash through the wall."

"And who's the crazy drunk creeping around here?"

The illegality of Lasky's presence was not the immediate question; establishing the reason for his presence and his relation to us was. The only way to set things straight was to include Lasky in the general activities of the Haut-Bourg, which centered on *gros rouge* and *pastis*. Coco was determined to show solidarity with a fellow worker by banging on the windows, shouting *"Venez! Venez!"* When Lasky opened the windows, Coco would playfully grab his shirt and point to his little house, where he wanted Lasky to join him for a *pastis*.

Lasky was repulsed by the miserable, deformed drunk and couldn't understand a thing Coco was saying, which only made Coco more insistent. *"Venez!"* Finally, after being dragged into Coco's modest living quarters, Dan lying calmly on the bed, Lasky understood that he was expected to participate in Coco's customs of hospitality and *boire un verre*.

Lasky knew little French: *"Non, non, je n'aime pas ça!"* Coco wasn't about to accept such reluctance and poured two inches of urine-colored *pastis*, followed by some water, into a dirty glass; instantly two clear liquids became one yellowish, opaque one. The problem was that Coco was offering Lasky a glassful of instant hell. In angry frustration, Lasky continued his refusal in English. "I don't drink! I don't want it! Let me go!" And he walked out.

How do you explain AA in a small French village where almost everyone drinks, at least with lunch and dinner? The inhabitants who drink all day seem to lead lives as productive as those of the ones who don't. No one falls down drunk on the streets in Rogny, and no one is homeless or without medical care. Père Jo would be called, for all intents and purposes, a scandalous drunk in the States; to the hardworking people in Rogny, his drinking seemed to be a source of humor and a reason for affection. Ultimately, the misunderstanding between Coco and Lasky led to an escalation of tension. Both were stubborn; Lasky's refusal of Coco's *pastis* was taken as disdain. Mary tried to explain to Lasky that Coco was the tutelary spirit of the presbytery and should be respected, to which Lasky responded that Coco was nothing more than a stinking drunk, and who would know better, Lasky added, than someone who'd been through it? It wasn't the dogma of AA evangelism that drove Lasky's contempt. It was just contempt for the predictable behavior of drunks, behavior he recognized in himself.

Coco took it upon himself to make sure that Lasky was doing a proper job, which led Lasky to close all the shutters on the street side of the house to keep Coco and everyone else out. Work progressed in the house at an astonishing pace. Every two or three days, we ordered more supplies from Zerflou, the professional building supply house. They would deliver tape, taping compound, plaster, acrylic and oil paints, and various tubes of caulking material. Lasky attacked two or three rooms at a time. As the plaster and compound dried in one, he painted in another. On the weekends, I'd come and work on the heavier construction with his help. This included hanging cabinets, final cementing, and removing plaster from a central beam.

Lasky and I worked well together, which is not always the case with middle-aged men who have set ideas about how things should be done. However eccentric, Lasky, I could see, was a skilled professional. He could work even with materials that were not exactly the same as in the States, although not without a great litany of complaints about their inferiority. In turn, I think, Lasky respected my courage in trying to tackle the disaster of a neglected house in a country other than the States. Perhaps what helped most was that I nodded in meek agreement with his charge that the U.S. government was sucking the lifeblood out of Castro's Cuba and that every American citizen was directly or indirectly culpable for the assassinations and genocide in Nicaragua, Guatemala, Honduras, and El Salvador. Lasky announced that he had never enjoyed playing his flute and violin as much as in the presbytery, in front of the hot Godin stove. He painted or taped for a few hours and then played some Handel on the flute and bluegrass on the fiddle.

"Every night I've been dreaming of my father. Even while painting I think of the stupid bastard."

"Are you still angry?" I asked him.

"Hell, it's just funny that I should even be thinking of him now. I can even hear him in my head."

"What does he say?"

"Well, it's not the same abusive crap. It's different. I don't know, but I think I understand him better. I was wild when I was a kid. I mean really wild. And my father would fight in bars and later with me. He wasn't stupid, though."

"What was he, then?"

"Complex. He was definitely complex."

I told him the house might be haunted, but all the spirits are good-natured. So I urged him to take his father with him when he left, even if he had been elevated from "abusive" to "complex."

In spite of Coco's occasionally banging on the shutters and Madame Savin's engine roar, and in spite of the grim, dulling cold, Lasky seemed content to work, play music, and carry on internal dialogues with his father. He hardly went out except to buy bread and vegetables and occasionally cheese. His vegetarian meals focused on the potatoes that he insisted on baking in the fireplace, although the stove worked fine. Occasionally, someone would leave him some partridges or a pheasant, thinking Lasky might enjoy them. He'd call, "Someone left birds on your windowsill. What am I supposed to do with them?"

Mary and I experienced the odd sensation of growing accustomed to finished rooms. They were obviously cleaner and brighter, the cracks and peeling paint were gone, and the holes patched, but on the whole they didn't look so different from when we first saw the place after the painters had come through spraying white over everything above the floor tiles, including some stiff spiderwebs in the corners. It seemed as if after two years we had arrived where we had started, in our prelapsarian bliss. Lasky worked so obsessively that rooms throughout the entire house were taped, painted, and plastered regardless of where we were with various other restoration projects. At last, Lasky's part was finished, the shutters were reopened to the place de l'Église, and the midnight flute and violin music vanished, leaving only the whirring owls. We learned that Lasky had volunteered to monitor elections in El Salvador, and then he planned to travel in Central America and Mexico on the money he had made helping us.

The narcissi, crocuses, forsythia, and quinces had come and gone, along with the tulips and the fruit-tree blossoms. Madame Savin had gone back to Châtillon-Coligny, where we'd see her in the market clutching a framed portrait to her heart. At first we were certain the picture was of her husband, Claude, but it turned out to be an image of the thorn-crowned Christ. March and April were gone, and we entered the month of lilacs, roses, and wildflowers, and the month when the French celebrate workers (Fête du Travail), victory (Victoire 1945), holy spirits (Pentecôte), and mothers (Fête des Mères). There couldn't be a nicer month than May for my mother's arrival, almost exactly a year after our wedding picnic on the terrace.

My mother had packed up a lifetime of furniture, rugs, books, lamps, kitchenware, and lawn chairs, with a gritty determination not to let her wild imagination get the best of her, her mantra being, as it had been for several years now, "If I crash and burn, I crash and burn." Doubts would flood in; she couldn't stop them. As persistent and dark as they were, she just let them have their say along with all the other voices swirling in her head. Her friends wept on the phone and conspired in private emergency gatherings, wondering how to prevent her woeful error. In the end, they consoled themselves that my mother would certainly return in a year, defeated by homesickness and insolvency.

The day of my mother's arrival had been carefully choreographed. She was coming with her friend Lee, and they would both be toting massive suitcases, several of which were to be taxed for "excess." My mother was also bringing her heavily tranquilized golden retriever, Zouzou, and her freaked-out, wobbly Maine coon cat, which meant two animal carriers, one of them the size of some small French automobiles. My mother's sack of antianxiety tools had tripled in capacity, filled with extra pillows so that if things became too tough, she could put the pillows over her head and pretend she was dreaming.

Mary was upset because we couldn't meet my mother in our little Peugeot 205 alone, and we thought it an extravagance to rent a van just for a trip to the airport. But she enlisted Ariane and Jean-Louis to follow us up to Orly in their red station wagon, which was no small kindness given that we had to leave at 6:00 A.M. because my mother's arrival time coincided with peak morning rush-hour traffic around Paris. My mother and Lee emerged weary but victorious among the horde of glazed-eyed travelers. Ariane shouted, *"Bienvenue! Bienvenue! Comment s'est passé votre voyage?"* She gave my mother and Lee enthusiastic welcoming kisses.

By the time we all arrived at the baggage area, the two animal carriers were already circling on the carousel next to luggage, taped-up boxes, and what looked like tires for a Cadillac. Zouzou, with head lowered, was staring blankly through the bars at passengers and customs officers before curving off once more behind the black rubber belts and then reemerging. Ava was simply a doped-up ball of fluff at the back of her carrier. We rescued the animals and recovered suitcases, packing two cars to capacity and setting off to make our way back to Rogny.

Mary and I moved out of our bedroom next to the kitchen, and my mother moved in, immediately securing her newly won territory by placing several photographs on the fireplace mantel. Most were shots of her closest friends and my brother and me as children in Wilton. The rest were of crashing green ocean waves and New

England sunsets. Zouzou collapsed in a stupor, the cat disappeared into the *grenier,* and my mother immediately busied herself with unpacking familiar things. It was her way of taming the strangeness of such a big move.

Mary and I sat in the library with Lee, who whispered, "You are not going to believe what's coming." Her eyes widened. "The whole house." She laughed incredulously and continued, "I helped your mother pack. The whole house is coming."

A freighter at Jersey City was being loaded with a container of my mother's possessions—the furniture, paintings, and books that I grew up with, the things that inhabited the house in Wilton.

Nesting

To our dismay, my mother's furniture landed in the shipper's warehouse in England. Two weeks later, after some confusion about where Rogny was exactly, an enormous truck arrived, entirely out of scale with the place de l'Église. It seemed to have come from a world of giants, and all the inhabitants of the Haut-Bourg assembled on the *place*, midmorning, to marvel at it. The truck had a two-part trailer, so it was forced to circle its wagons around the little Liberty Tree.

At the time, the rooms of the presbytery had only the sparse furnishings that Mary and I had acquired during our profitable relationship with Lelièvre. The Louis-Philippe buffet was still docked, with its habitual tilt, against a wall in the living room, but the celebrated armoire had migrated out of the bedroom into the hall. We had acquired a few tables, a small chest for the bathroom, and chairs, but that was about all.

With the arrival of the truck and the bustle of the movers, my mother's desks, tables, beds, couches, chairs, rugs, lamps, and paintings quickly sought out their preferred spots in the various rooms. Garden furniture was stacked in the stables, and trunks, boxes of books, and excess chairs marched up to the *grenier*. The work progressed well into the afternoon before the occupation of the presbytery was complete. Then the driver revved up the loud diesel engine and tried to maneuver the truck out of the precarious confines of the *place*. When he looked in his mirror, he saw Coco, the French version of a damaged leprechaun, circling his dusty black cowboy hat in the air and shouting *"Ho! Ho!"* as the truck reversed, narrowly missing the newly painted shutters along the front of the house. Once liberated, the truck vanished quickly with a roar interrupted only by the shifting of gears.

For days, my mother emptied boxes and trunks and arranged furniture. On top of every desk, table, and bureau, and on all the mantels, objects of porcelain, brass, and silver appeared. Clothes, bedding, linen, glassware, and china filled the closets and drawers. She hung several large paintings by my great-grandmother, who in a distant part of the century had been awarded the Prix de Paris for her work. I had known the paintings all my life, and one still had blisters from the fire that destroyed my mother's childhood home. Another was a formidable portrait of my great-grandfather Charlie, who was an industrialist and an English lord. In each window on the place de l'Église, my mother placed *jardinières*, terra-cotta window boxes, planted with cascading geraniums and blue petunias; then, on either side of our carved eighteenth-century front doors, Lelièvre's recent installation, she put large Chinese ceramic vases also filled with geraniums. More boxes were opened, and more objects appeared, while the *grenier* and the stables overflowed with cardboard and wads of packing material.

Mary was stunned. Her simple country home had become my

mother's manor. We were left with one room, a bedroom on the garden side at the far end of the house, which we stubbornly kept in a half-finished state. It had a piece of *polyplaque* leaning against the bricks of an old chimney that I had uncovered. For a bedside table, Mary kept a rush chair with a broken back, and for decoration we hung a poster of birds—*Les Oiseaux des Montagnes et de la Forêt*. Meanwhile, my mother triumphantly announced, "The presbytery is now a home."

The furniture actually arrived in a variation of the Trojan horse scheme that fooled even my mother, who had come up with it. She had originally planned to rent an apartment in Paris, furnish it with her own things, then sublet it short-term during the summer at a high price while she lived rent-free in the presbytery from May to October. The income from the sublet would offset her annual rent in Paris. She had spoken to several short-term rental agencies who assured her that her scheme would work. Thus, while Mary was shocked by my mother's occupation of the presbytery, she understood that the situation was temporary, until my mother was able to find the perfect apartment and could put her well-studied plans into action.

Meanwhile, the villagers, who had observed the fits and starts of a dead house being revitalized, now saw it for the first time in fifteen years lit up every night with the living. If they passed slowly in a car or walked along the place de l'Église, they could see warm light inside a stone house. Beyond the white shutters, the geraniums, and the clean windows, they could see the portrait of my great-grandfather above a wing chair and brass lamps. They could see my grandmother's desk below a still life of irises. They could see, beyond the wood-burning stove, the table at which I ate as a child in Wilton. They could see ferns on pedestals, panels of Japanese prints, kitchen cabinets in pale oak, and handmade tile counters, all brightly lit.

In the fully furnished presbytery, I'd wake to the peacefulness of 3:00 A.M., and I'd get up to read for an hour or so until tired enough to sleep again. Christabel would shuffle out to lie next to me while I listened to the whir of owls announcing their comings and goings from the church and the stars lit up the orchard, confusing a bird into premature song. Wonderful books seemed all the more wonderful, such as Yourcenar's *Memoirs of Hadrian*, where Hadrian, in his lengthy epistle, reflects on sleep:

> But what interests me here is the specific mystery of sleep partaken of for itself alone, the inevitable plunge risked each night by the naked man, solitary and unarmed, into an ocean where everything changes, the colors, the densities, and even the rhythm of breathing, and where we meet the dead.

At that moment I'd be sitting in the *salle de séjour* in a chair across from the portrait of my great-grandfather Charlie that his wife, Tillie, had painted shortly before taking her own life. She'd co-opted Rembrandt's style of painting the figure illuminated by a single outside source of light, so that the unlit parts of the body blended with the dark background. The strokes, however, were bold, postimpressionistic. When I look at the painting in its large, unadorned gold frame, I try to see something of the family features in my great-grandfather's face, but there is nothing I recognize of myself in Charlie's nose, eyes, or hair. It could be a painting of an utter stranger, except that it had followed me from childhood to a room that I had restored in a historic French building. If I live long enough, perhaps I'll see more of myself there, nights when the others are sleeping and I look up from a book and think about Charlie, that good-natured man, who, unlike Tillie, lived happily without millions, choking on cigars into his late nineties.

My mother had two priorities on arrival at the presbytery. The first was to buy a used car with an automatic transmission and air-conditioning, and when we asked Monsieur Servais, the *garagiste* in the Bas-Bourg, where we might find one that had such exotic features, he contracted his dark eyebrows in thought, as though the problem were more metaphysical than practical. He muttered *"Ce n'est pas évident"* several times to himself.

The *garagiste* in Châtillon-Coligny was equally perplexed and sent us off to Montargis, where the largest Peugeot dealership in the region was located. We quickly learned that automatic transmissions are unpopular because the French like their cars nervous, as they say. Also, having a car with automatic transmission means you don't know how to drive. Air-conditioning gives you bronchitis, which soon after leads to pneumonia. Getting one feature or the other seemed possible. But getting them together was like looking for a flying saucer.

In Montargis, the dealer shook his head after scanning up and down his printout describing the cars in his lot, and we asked if he minded our looking at his cars anyway. My mother, Mary, and I split up, wandering about the vast lot, when Mary spotted a gray Peugeot 405 with *climatisation* on the dashboard and a shift set in "park." With a sense of triumph, Mary confronted the dealer with the car. "So how do you explain this?"

My mother's second priority on coming was to link up to the

rest of the world with television and radio. She had a satellite dish installed atop the far side of the stables where it would be obscured from view. However, the oblivious workmen broke holes through the slate roof, sending Monsieur Bougé over to complain about their sloppy work and defend his nut tree in case we misplaced the blame for the damage. We took note of the sloppy work and had Deluche patch up the holes, but to our horror Monsieur Bougé cut down the nut tree anyway, fearing that the old tree would collapse on our roof.

Mary protested to Monsieur Bougé, "But the insurance would pay for a new roof."

Monsieur Bougé was taking no chances.

We felt a considerable twinge of guilt—a nut tree had been executed for threatening our satellite dish. The dish was pointed toward the southeastern sky along the orbital track of Astra satellites, and to my mother's disappointment she received almost exclusively German channels, which would neither entertain her nor help her to improve her French. With the help of some English friends, she managed to obtain an illegal decoder so that she could receive French channels in France, along with a few more British and American channels and, strangely enough, National Public Radio.

My mother would cook, read, paint, write letters, and garden, and there was always that familiar American cadence in the background of, perhaps, an ex-addict interviewed about his new book or some tired discussion of thwarted idealism. It was as if my mother had created a comfortable ghetto of American voices. Suddenly I saw our little family in the light of friends and neighbors in New Haven, whose parents or grandparents could speak only Swedish, Italian, or Spanish.

Along with full residency came interference. Coco complained, *"Quelqu'un va voler les vases chinois!"* In this case, he reflected everyone's concern, including the mayor's, that surely the Chinese vases that my mother used to decorate the front steps of the house would be stolen. My mother's French was poor, and needless to say, she had to struggle to understand anything Coco said, which induced Coco to shout at her, something my mother never took kindly to, even when it was well intentioned. Coco, the frustrated, self-appointed protector of the presbytery, enlisted Mary to explain to my mother that she was asking to be robbed. My mother said, "Nonsense!" Coco shook his head, the geraniums grew very happily in front of the house, and the Chinese vases were never stolen.

Coco enjoyed doing odd jobs for my mother, some for pay (my mother always paying twice what he asked) and some as a *bon voisin,* a helpful neighbor. Like the other women in the Haut-Bourg, my mother began to cook soups for Coco and buy him gifts, which he invariably stashed away in a drawer with scores of others that he didn't know what to do with. She would listen to his complaints about his various physical ailments—colds, pulled muscles, and chest pains—and then daydreamed as he scolded her about leaving her car unlocked or the front windows open. To him, my mother, by tempting fate so openly, virtually intended to turn innocent villagers into criminals.

The first job for which my mother hired Coco was a public disaster. Hardly anything grew under the Liberty Tree except for a couple of daffodils, some tufts of wild grass, and a patch of Coco's parsley. Coco planted parsley everywhere—in front of the church, in our yard, and in one of Madame Briançon's flower boxes. My mother decided that the Liberty Tree had to have a bed of impatiens beneath it. With Mary translating, she discussed the project with Jean-Louis and Ariane, the Marteaus, the Bougés, and Coco, all of whom said it wouldn't work. Still my mother bought the impatiens and offered to pay Coco to dig up the ground under the chestnut tree and plant them. Coco agreed so long as his patch of parsley would remain untouched— *"Ne jamais transplanter du persil car ça porte malheur."* Never transplant parsley because that brings misfortune. My mother was convinced that she was doing a great service for the village, which was, after all, on the tourist circuit and should be full of flowers in the late spring. She only hoped that the other inhabitants of the Haut-Bourg would, in appreciation, help water the impatiens.

The French believe that *marronniers,* or chestnut trees, suck all the water out of the ground and that it is impossible to grow anything under them. This is just one of many odd French beliefs about certain trees. For example, they believe that cold air drops out of walnut trees. If you take a nap under one, you risk dying of pneumonia. And at New Year's you must place a chip of oak on the mantel as a kind of good-luck house-insurance policy. My mother was told, *"Vous ne devez pas planter les impatientes sous un marronnier."* You must never plant impatiens under a chestnut tree. They'll never get enough water. This turned out to be a self-fulfilling prophecy because no one bothered to water impatiens that were doomed to begin with, and in spite of politely approving of community projects, the French tend to mind their own onions, as their expression goes, something my mother wasn't doing. She made a feeble effort from time to time to revive the impatiens between severe droughts, but in the end all but a few stubborn sprigs died off, giving way to weeds again and to the seemingly indestructible parsley.

My mother's failure hadn't gone completely unregarded. The town responded with its own effort at beautification. One day a truck sent by the *mairie* parked next to the Liberty Tree, and the ground, in a matter of minutes, was turned over by the same two workmen who had just the year before delivered tables and chairs for the wedding. They scattered an even dusting of grass seed that grew into a mop of green grass that no one bothered to mow. It was clear to all that the *marronnier* chose to suck water away from impatiens but not from grass, weeds, or parsley.

While my mother was busy setting up our house, the swallows, redstarts, *merles*, finches, tits, and wrens were busy setting up theirs—May and June are high nesting season. The birds made good use of shreds of tape and packing materials they found in the stables. They'd weave them in with the moss they gathered from the grass and the trees. Above all, for nest building, they treasured hair. On the terrace on sunny mornings, my mother brushed her long silver-gray hair, and then she would brush Zouzou and Ava, the Maine coon, who had finally ventured out after days of hiding in the *grenier*. My mother left their hair for the birds, who seemed delighted with the building supply bonanza. We watched them gather my mother's hair and Zouzou's and Ava's and fly off for the stables, the *pigeonnier*, or hedges of *charmes*.

Birds nest all around us, and in late spring anyone who goes into the stables is berated mercilessly by parenting birds. They try to monopolize attention while the babies know instinctively to duck down into their nest as if to avoid an incoming artillery barrage, a maneuver which becomes increasingly futile as they grow rounder and more fully feathered.

When I'm working on a major project and digging down to fortifications—say, under the bathroom floor—I think back to the unimaginable world almost two millennia ago and realize that those inhabitants, the Gauls and Romans, would have seen, in their own time, the same bird populations as I do, the same migratory cycles of Siberian birds of prey in the winter, the songbirds returning in March. They would suddenly notice the day starting and finishing with songs that they hadn't heard for months, songs that I recognize from another life, growing up in Wilton. The swallows arrive late, when they are good and ready, when spring has prepared for them a world of natural comforts—warm weather, a feast of insects, nearly endless evenings.

One of the most peculiar sights is the migration of the *grues cendrées*, the gray cranes. Parts of the sky fill with them, and often their flight is circular, soaring far above any other bird. Monsieur Marteau stood in our yard and explained, "They fly straight until they pass over the Loire and the cooling towers at the *centrales nucléaires*. Then they become muddled and fly in circles."

My mother could understand French better than she could speak it. She knew that Monsieur Marteau was completely wrong and felt compelled to correct him. She'd just seen a nature program, probably in German, showing the unique way that *grues cendrées* conserve energy.

"That's not it at all!" she protested in English. "They circle on the updrafts to gain altitude and then soar long distances without flapping their wings."

Monsieur Marteau had no idea what she was saying. He was still considering the horrible effect radiation had on the cranes' guidance system. They were just flying in hopeless circles. Perhaps something equally dreadful was happening to us without our realizing it.

———

On warm mornings in late spring, Mary loves to take a cup of coffee and make an inspection tour of her hardy flowers. On one such day, she found a baby *merle* at her feet. I had cut the grass the evening before, so the abandoned bird was hard to miss, hunkered down, too afraid or weak to move. When Mary presented her find to my mother and me, the three of us peered at the cartoonlike creature with its oversized head that wobbled drunkenly about on a scrawny neck. My mother dug out some cotton and gauze pads from her cabinet crammed with emergency medical supplies and made a nest in a French coffee bowl, where the *merle* was subsequently placed with mouth wide open, ready for its morning feeding. I offered to go out and dig up some worms, but Mary said that the worms had to be partly digested by the parents before the baby bird could digest them itself. This, of course, left the perplexing question of where to find partly digested worms.

"I can go to the butcher and ask him to make ground beef or chop up a *saucisse* for our bird," I offered.

This was met with uncertainty. Mary said, "Well, they're not crows or owls. I don't know if *merles* would eat meat."

"Besides worms, they eat cherries," my mother added.

"They do?" I imagined a cherry larger than the bird's head.

In fact, *merles* are just like American robins that have been spray-painted black, except for the bright yellow beak. We didn't know the first thing about nurturing a wild bird. As kids, my brother and I stole some pigeons from a nest in a neighbor's barn, but they seemed neither wild nor fragile. It felt normal to hold a pigeon, pet it, and teach it to fly. But wild birds seemed forbidding, an invisible barrier separating them from us; they live on some other natural plane apart from ours. We invited wild birds to live in proximity to us by putting out seeds or nailing up supports for their nests. We let them fly in and out of the house. But confronted with the *merle*, I couldn't help feeling what I felt, growing up in the country: wild means *Do not touch!*

Mary rushed out the garden door to rouse Coco from his afternoon nap and get him to help us, as he always did in our moments of distress. Coco seemed to know everything about the forest and had probably raised birds from the wild himself. We all watched expectantly as he came in and examined the *merle* in the coffee bowl, offering a callused finger to the quivering box of the bird's open mouth. *"On doit lui donner du pain trempé dans du lait."* Why hadn't we thought of that? My mother soaked a little bread in milk and used a small silver salt spoon that had come all the way from New Haven to fill the tiny, expectant throat.

Coco boasted that he had raised many birds over the years and said that he would be willing to look after ours. We were all relieved, since our schedules made the task difficult for Mary and me, and my mother wasn't too keen on assuming the burden of feeding a *merle* every few hours. What better foster parent than the man from the forest? Coco marched home with the bird in the coffee bowl, which he placed in his cupboard. The *merle* was dead by morning.

The next weekend, as she inspected her border garden, Mary found another bird. This one, however, was newly hatched and icy cold. My mother and I stared in disbelief as Mary came into the house, warming in her hands the near-dead thing with transparent skin, eyes set in black rings, and a mouth big enough for the bird to swallow itself. With the stubbornness of a youngster undaunted by large, heartless forces—adult realism, natural selection, whatever—Mary demanded the ugly little bird's rescue from certain death.

The new bird seemed doomed, but my mother outfitted him with a teacup nest inside a coffee bowl. He was clearly too small to be a *merle*, so we decided he was a *chardonneret*, since we had seen many in the garden that spring, the males so flashy with yellow feathers and bright tricolored heads. *Chardonnerets*, or goldfinches, are small songbirds that the French named after *chardons*, the thistles that they love to eat. Mary said, "Let's call him Charles. Charles is far easier to say than *chardonneret*."

We were all relieved that this time we had a vegetarian in our care; there would be no need to explain to the butcher that we wanted something that resembled half-digested worms for a baby bird. An English visitor had conveniently left us a box of Weetabix, which my mother mixed with milk and fed to the bird with the silver salt spoon. To our astonishment, within an hour of being warmed up and filled with Weetabix, Charles revived with all the vigor of a miniature Tyrannosaurus rex.

Soon our French neighbors began visiting to pay tribute to Charles, who was most of the time merely a gaping mouth quivering in space. They tried to prepare us for the inevitable— *"Les animaux sauvages ne peuvent prospérer que dans la nature."* Wild animals can only survive in nature. Jean-Louis came in and mused over Charles in his teacup under the newly installed counter lighting. Jean-Louis had recently undergone a carotid artery procedure. You could see the scar that starts at the corner of his left jaw and curves gently toward his chest and under his shirt. When he ponders a question, he pauses, gazing at middle space, as if putting together the parts of a disassembled world. In this case, with his index finger across his lips, shushing an unseen presence, he offered his conviction: "Only the parents can provide Charles his necessary nourishment. It comes through their own digestive systems."

Despite his pessimism, Jean-Louis, a man more sensitive than most to the tenuousness of life, looked at our little survivor with admiration and every few days came over to see if he was still thriving.

Charles demanded feeding even when the dark hole of his mouth looked like a little cement mixer full of Weetabix; contenting him became an endless chore. I couldn't help but sympathize with bird parents slaving under the tyranny of nests crammed with the likes of Charles. Now when I see birds coupling recklessly in the air, crashing through branches, a mess of frenetic wings, I want to say, "Think of what you're getting yourselves into."

My mother knew better than anyone. While Mary was a nurturing presence, my mother had become mother bird day in, day out. Every hour or two, she dutifully filled with Weetabix the eager mouth inside the teacup. During the week, Mary required daily reports on how Charles was faring; my mother had been eclipsed as the important new resident of the presbytery. On weekends, Mary took over, spending hours caring for Charles and talking to him about what it means to be a bird. Whenever she gardened or ate lunch with us on the terrace, the coffee bowl with Charles in the teacup was set down beside her.

Charles had conquered Mary's heart, but it was my mother's schedule he adapted to as the weeks went by. My mother would go to bed at midnight or just after and get up at ten or sometimes later in the morning. Those were not exactly bird, let alone baby bird, hours. Charles got his last spoonful of Weetabix long after the rest of bird life had settled down in the sheltering darkness of bushes, hedges, and rafters of outbuildings. He would hear the morning cacophony of bird songs long before his own mother bird roused herself bleary-eyed to load up the automatic coffeemaker and mix his milk and cereal. When Mary and I came down, we were surprised by the change in Charles—he slept until ten or eleven in the morning before demanding his Weetabix. We thought he was plummeting into dissipation; my mother certainly was. For the first time she could sleep as long as her heart desired, and she was taking full advantage of an undisciplined life.

Charles quickly graduated from the teacup to the coffee bowl, and his translucent reptilian skin produced fuzz and pinions. Even when he was a horrible, most unbirdlike thing, he would climb to the lip of the teacup, turn, and poop. It was a remarkable instinct we had no idea baby birds possessed—Charles refused to live in his own excrement. We speculated that his nicety—and a sudden gust of wind—might have been the cause of his original fall.

Soon Charles was able to stand on our fingers, nibble and peck, and chirp bird declarations. Whenever I think of birdsongs, I'm reminded of the analogy that's been made between birdsongs and human songs, that there are only five thematic categories: "Good morning!" "I'm here!" "I'm hungry!" "Let's make love!" and "Good night!" By the time Charles had expanded his repertoire from "I'm hungry!" to "I'm here!" we realized that we had made a significant error in identification: white bars appeared on his wings, bars not found on a *chardonneret,* and his feathers were muted browns and grays. These discrepancies sent us to several guides and a revised identification—Charles was a *pinson des bois,* a chaffinch, a bird renowned in France for its gaiety—*gai comme un pinson*—based on its *ramage*—its singing, chirping, and warbling. We could expect Charles to become a virtuoso.

Once he had reached fledgling age, Charles had entirely adapted to my mother's decadent hours and spent the days listening to NPR or TV or hopping onto her shoulder or head as she read in her big wicker chair under the Judas tree. With great ceremony,

Mary bought Charles a cage at a local *animalerie* so that he could spend the warm June days outdoors and strengthen his wings and legs, flicking and chirping between perches. Everyone, including Jean-Louis, who had become a Charles devotee, was present for the first attempts at flight, which consisted of dropping Charles to the ground while Mary gasped with horror and Zouzou sniffed the damage. This technique was enhanced by a slight toss, which only increased Mary's alarm and Charles's velocity and, so, the impact of his crash. He was not a precocious flier.

By the time my mother was living in the presbytery, we began to mark the passage of summer by its *fêtes,* and already the Fête Nationale had arrived. For the Retraite aux Flambeaux, on the eve of Bastille Day, children and their parents marched up the hill and sang for us while they stood in the half-light of their *lampions,* candle lanterns tied to long sticks. We stopped in the middle of our dinner to stand on the front step, listen, wave, and applaud. Then the parade of lanterns would march off and descend toward the canal by a series of streets named after birds—chemin du Colombier, allée des Fauvettes, rue des Hirondelles. The presbytery next to the eleventh-century church was once again a living part of the village. Children came to borrow a bicycle pump or play with Zouzou or marvel at Charles, who was almost full grown.

On the Friday following Bastille Day, when we arrived on the place de l'Église, we met Jean-Louis, who had visited Charles that day and informed us that he was sick. He could neither walk nor fly. *"C'est mauvais! Charles ne peut plus ni marcher ni voler."* We rushed in to see for ourselves, and it was true—Charles was crippled. When he moved at all, he flopped on his side, his right wing hung loose, and his right foot curled lifelessly under him. It seemed, particularly to Mary, a cruel irony that Charles had lasted long enough to show us the complete folly of our intervention—that instead of having a new hatchling succumb quietly on the cool morning grass, we'd end up helpless witnesses to a mature bird's thrashing about, rolling on its back, fighting to right itself. The next morning we went to see the veterinarian in Bléneau.

I have to confess that I am suspicious of Parisian vets, who cater to overbred dogs and cats and charge their clients psychiatrists' prices. One had diagnosed Christabel's cough as epilepsy and prescribed phenobarbital, which might have turned her into a barbiturate addict, not that she couldn't have used some kind of sedative.

Country vets, by contrast, seem heroic, going off to dilapidated farms on calls to save, mend, maintain, or euthanize horses, cows, sheep, donkeys, and goats, and holding, too, a Saturday clinic for dogs, cats, canaries, and rabbits, which they also save, mend, maintain, or euthanize.

The clinic in Bléneau is run by an unusually attractive young couple, Docteurs-Vétérinaires Vassallo. Madame le Docteur is a beauty—wholesome skin, short brown hair, soft eyes with long lashes, and a lively smile; Monsieur le Docteur has whatever is the French equivalent of a clean Ivy League look. On occasion, a young dark-haired colleague fills in, and every time we have consulted him he has insisted on using his poor English and demonstrating his da Vinci–imitation mirror writing.

With a Maine coon cat, a golden retriever, and a Maltese, we were regulars at the Saturday clinic and in fact received a discount for our plurality of pets. On this particular visit, it was Monsieur le Vétérinaire Vassallo who greeted us brightly, shook our hands, and led all of us into his *cabinet*. Nodding at the large *marmite*, a cooking pot, he asked, *"Et qu'est-ce qu'on a ici?"* What we had was not the kitten, rabbit, or tortoise he was expecting, nor was it the canary or parakeet he envisioned when we announced that it was *notre oiseau* Charles. Docteur Vassallo's handsome jaw dropped perceptibly when we lifted the antispatter screen and he saw the *pinson des bois* staring up at him from the coffee bowl, chirping angrily for Weetabix. Mary explained that we had raised Charles from a hatchling and then sadly pointed out the curled foot and lowered wing.

To his credit, Docteur Vassallo confessed that he had little experience with patients of Charles's sort, but nevertheless began carefully to examine Charles, who wiggled and chirped energetically, opening wide for the inspection. Docteur Vassallo listened to the bird's heart, checked both shiny black eyes, and finally unraveled the atrophied foot to get a good look at it. He then asked Mary about the bird's diet. Mary's answer— *"lait et Weetabix"*—led to a solemn hum-filled pause before the verdict: Charles had a vitamin D deficiency. This was hardly encouraging news. Docteur Vassallo explained that birds cannot assimilate vitamin D in the form found in people food; during Charles's rapid growth the vitamin deficiency had resulted in the laying down of defective bone. The damage was irreversible, leading Mary, her eyes already wet, to ask if Charles had a prayer.

"Un tout petit espoir vu son état de vitalité générale." Charles had a slight hope based on his general vitality, and we were instructed to go to a local pharmacy and ask for vitamins for birds. Docteur Vassallo had some in his *cabinet* but only in twelve-month supplies for whole flocks of ducks or chickens. I picked up Charles's *marmite,* and we all thanked Docteur Vassallo for taking the consultation seriously. Mary took out her checkbook, Docteur Vassallo

protesting, *"Mes tarifs sont en fonction du poids du client."* I charge by the patient's weight.

The pharmacy, it turned out, had exactly the same bird vitamins as Docteur Vassallo, which meant that from one liter we had to take ten microliters twice a day. Mary brought micro-pipets from her lab to measure out the prescribed amounts for dilution, and she and my mother scrupulously fed the vitamins to Charles, but we were all prepared for the worst.

During her first summer in the presbytery, my mother tacked up a sign at the Guillon's *épicerie* offering free English lessons, and a few students showed up irregularly when they weren't out somewhere hunting for work. She began to frequent the Bar de l'Écluse, where she drank tea or bright red Campari and struck up somewhat inept, albeit good-humored, conversations with the regulars. She never ventured far into the countryside, but she visited all the nearby villages or took Zouzou for a run beside the large pond called l'étang de la Grande-Rue. Friends visited her, and her sister even came all the way from California for a stay. My mother was the familiar smiling American with the large yellow dog at the Tuesday and Thursday market in Châtillon-Coligny. She soon had a circle of people she saw regularly.

As always, young people gravitated to my mother. She even got to know the two orphans Véronique and Jo, both of whom still lived with Madame Bourgeois in a house only moderately more spacious than Coco's. Their parents had died in an accident on one of the notoriously lethal French roads. Madame Bourgeois had managed to bring up the two by herself, and now Véronique, the elder, works at a nearby home for the aged, while Jo, trained to work with handicapped children, is forced to take odd jobs, like most of the young people in the village. On weekends, she sings in a rock band called Jukebox, which performs once or twice a month at the Club de l'Amitié or the Bar de l'Écluse. Véronique and Jo have shoulder-length black hair and dark gentle eyes, and both seemed shy. Because they both ride motorcycles, I'd wave, not knowing whether it was Véronique or Jo who passed, pretending not to see me. The ritual of my waving and their not seeing me was the extent of our relationship for two years.

On a Friday in August, Mary and I came down to the presbytery to find the washing machine disassembled in the kitchen and Véronique and Jo, to whom we'd never spoken a word, hovering over the parts with wrenches in hand, removing a wayward sock jammed in the track of the tumbler. I've worked on cars, repaired plumbing, and installed electrical fixtures, but I had always considered broken-down appliances the domain of an expert who had the special tools and enough training to know what to expect once inside the machine.

"This happens to us all the time," Jo announced in a disarmingly soft voice. For years they'd taken apart Madame Bourgeois's washing machine and managed to double its life span. Jo handed me the sock, which looked as if someone had shotgunned it off the line, and Véronique began to reassemble the washing machine. We had the impression that, shyness notwithstanding, the two young women could do anything.

Amid all the comings and goings that day, while Véronique and Jo worked on the washing machine, Charles flew out the kitchen door. Against all odds, he had survived. The claws on his curled-up foot had atrophied and fallen off. Charles steadied himself on one good foot and one stub. He began to fly about each day in the kitchen, sometimes spending hours on the hot-water heater or on the mantel next to decorative dishes and Dutch tiles. But his personality had changed completely. Even after fledging, Charles had greeted everyone with cheerful chirping. After his recovery, he scolded and pecked viciously. He glared angrily. He agitated himself in every way to make clear how much he hated us. He flew to the washing machine to berate the two young women and then harassed my mother when she went out to her kitchen garden. Charles had beaten insurmountable odds, and it was time for him to join the natural world, where he had had a near-fatal start. My mother, on the other hand, had moved in to stay.

Les Jardins de Curé

*I*t is 1958, and l'Abbé Jean Camus, robed in his black *soutane,* is standing on a stage set up just in front of the ten-foot-high terrace wall. In provincial costume, twenty-five girls, having just performed *danses folkloriques,* are lined up next to him. Behind them all is the presbytery, above which you can see the 1848 Liberty Tree rising like a thundercloud of leaves, its branches stretching almost the whole length of the building. Along the staircase is a pear espalier with August fruit swelling on branches trained to fork skyward. The light falls across the faces of the curé and the children at an angle that means that the day has passed well into afternoon. Long tables are stacked with linens, food, games, paper goods, and pottery to be sold for charity. Other stands are for the lottery, wine tasting, and—more food—*saucisses frites*. Perhaps the children are about to begin their games—throwing darts at balloons, running races, or playing the equivalent of Père Jo's *Jeu de Massacre*—while their fathers compete against one another at carbine shooting and trapshooting in the neighbor's field. All this is followed by more dancing, a film with a religious theme projected in the *grenier* of the presbytery, and the *dîner champêtre*, a rustic dinner with costumes and decorations based that year on the theme "La Provence," with Mediterranean colors—blue and radiant yellow.

I know all this because I read No. 38 of the *L'Écho des Grands Bois*, typed up in the curé's office, which now is the room we call the library. The occasion is the *kermesse*, August 17, 1958; at the time I was six and on the cusp of memory myself, but on another continent entirely. Many of the children lined up on the stage are exactly my age at the time and must, naturally, be implored to stand still for the annual photograph, which, in its decoratively cut border, is, in the end, half the size of a dollar bill.

The French, in the fifties, were enmeshed in all the errors, paralysis, and humiliation of relinquishing exploitative colonial rule in Vietnam, followed by inglorious fighting in Algeria, which was considered by many to be France itself. Every issue of *L'Écho* contained, during the late fifties, a section called "Nouvelles de Nos Soldats," where l'Abbé Camus summarized letters and postcards that came from soldiers in Bir-Hamoudi, Aïm Kerma, Sidi-Salem, Thrempt, Laghouat, Ben Aïchoune, El Affroun, or Ouëd-Djec. There is not, in any of the summaries, a word expressive of a doubt, a shadow, or a fear. L'Abbé Camus, imposing his sense of decorum, relays only reports on the night stars in the desert, expeditions into the mountains, half-tracks zooming through the desert heat, playing *pétanque*, or soldier-swimmers in the calm North African sea. Only once does the curé note, in an open letter to the soldiers, that he has heard, and is touched by, confessions of fear and disorientation.

Meanwhile, in *L'Echo des Grands Bois*, l'Abbé Camus recounted his more innocent personal stories. In one, he had forgotten to procure a trophy for the trapshooting competition that was held at the *kermesse*. When Monsieur Pelletier came to claim his prize, Camus gave him his *sucrier*, a silver sugar bowl, which, given its value, was much appreciated. Several weeks later Camus was invited to a dinner by the *famille* Pelletier at the Château Brénellerie, where he was served coffee with sugar from the same fancy trophy. Monsieur Pelletier insisted that Camus take back the *sucrier*. After all, he'd won the trapshooting contest, and that was plenty of glory without taking the curé's *sucrier*. Camus was relieved that he hadn't thrown away the top.

The next year Père Jo edited *L'Écho des Grands Bois* and completely transformed the *organe de liaison pour la paroisse*—the parish newspaper—into a tabloid, with articles syndicated by the Catholic Church and advertisements for Vedette washing machines, Crédit Agricole, and Motoconfort. "Nouvelles des Nos Soldats" was replaced by "Nouvelles Catholiques," Catholic news from around the world. You wouldn't know that a war was on, that kids from the village faced the horribly effective guerrilla tactics of the National Liberation Front. L'Abbé Camus was promoted and reassigned to Sens, and the soldiers didn't know Père Jo well enough to send him their news, much less their confessions.

Looking at the photographs of the *kermesse* of 1958, it is hard not to recall the extreme changes France experienced that year. For a decade, there were so many changes of government that the French would joke about who would be running France the following week. Then de Gaulle was made premier and given, for six months, all powers, using them to dissolve the government and form the Fifth Republic. Divisions in French society had deepened over maintaining French rule in Algeria, where de Gaulle had given the *pieds noirs,* the progeny of the original French settlers, assurances of French rule while negotiating on autonomy with the National Liberation Front, a contradiction that spawned the makings of a *coup d'état* by four generals in Algeria. Even the franc was on the verge of being redefined, one hundred old francs to one new franc, a move that would befuddle the French for decades. In spite of all the turmoil, you can see the children going about the traditional activities of the summer church fair, which combines celebration with the raising of money for both the church and the poor.

Over the years in Rogny, *kermesse* had been held in the gardens of the presbytery, and such gardens, called *jardins de curé,* have a particular mystique in France, their name connoting enclosure, charm, and meditative calm. In reality, communities were obliged to support their parish priests, and the *jardin de curé* meant a loaned garden. The gardens varied in type and were not always associated with the grounds of a presbytery.

While gardening might seem to suit the spiritual life of all curés, some had groundskeepers and other forms of help. Others lived on such scant incomes that they grew much of their own food. Their *paroissiens,* members of their flock, might donate flowers for funerals and mass and fruits and vegetables. Nevertheless, the curé was obliged to maintain a garden. Some curés became notable for developing hybrids of fruits—"god apple," "Jesus grapes," or "Saint Antoine strawberries." There are numerous rose and camellia hybrids named after bishops and abbés. Some curés became botanists. For example, l'Abbé Bertholon published an article called "De l'Électricité des Végétaux." Inspired by Benjamin Franklin, the abbé invented an electro-vegetometer with which he electrically stimulated plants to see if he could enhance their growth.

Our friends and neighbors tell us that in all probability the entire terrace had been occupied by plantings of fruit, vegetables, and herbs. In fact, just after we bought the presbytery, we found in it a large gray cabinet solidly constructed of simple boards and shelved with wood recuperated from wine cases. It was filled with spiderwebs, dust, and yellowed newspaper. We dubbed it the "bishop's cabinet." On the inside of its door, we found a calendar from the fifties that listed the ideal moments for planting beans, carrots, radishes, lettuces, eggplant, and squash. We took this as circumstantial evidence that the curé had used the cabinet to store seeds and gardening tools. Throughout the stables, we found old implements for clawing, hoeing, and picking at the earth, all of them rusted beyond usefulness or obsolete.

The children had lined up for the *kermesse* photograph in exactly the spot where Mary first pierced the sod to make her border garden on the terrace. We had bought a house in Burgundy because, in large measure, Mary wanted a flower garden of her own, even though she had never gardened seriously before. She had dozens of houseplants at home and in her office, along with several window boxes, but turning over earth, putting plants in the ground, and watering them were new adventures.

The presbytery grounds had only climbing roses, clematis, honeysuckle, and lilacs, with a few renegade daffodils and tulips; Mary could hardly wait to attack the sod with any groundbreaking instrument she could find—fork, pick, hatchet, trowel, or shovel. She kept herself in excellent shape, first by riding horses and then after the accident to her back by milder exercise. But after a day of forking out squares of sod and shaking out loose soil, her hair fell out of place and she looked like a disheveled floppy-eared rabbit. She announced that she couldn't walk. She abandoned her tools in the middle of the yard. Only a hot bath, some *paracétamol,* and several glasses of Pouilly-Fumé could ease the stiffness sufficiently that she could cheerfully brag about her day's exploits against the sod.

Over several weekends of work, pain, *paracétamol,* and Pouilly-Fumé, she had dug up the entire length of the terrace and, modestly, planted lobelia and carnations, but these quickly became infested with cinquefoil and bindweed, requiring more work, pain, *paracétamol,* and Pouilly-Fumé. Still, the new flower beds gave Mary moments of such intense pride and pleasure that everyone came to regard the stubby lines of carnations and lobelia as sacred ground. With bright green gardening gloves and her box of tools, amid myriad garden creatures—worms, beetles, grubs, ants, voles, wasps, butterflies, and bees—Mary was the queen of her own creation: uprooted weeds, stacks of empty plastic plant containers, small piles of deadheaded rose blossoms.

After our terrace wedding, and with the generous services of Mary's nieces, the border garden expanded rapidly and came to include the entire perimeter of the terrace. In a garden the size of Mary's, the sections have micro-climates, depending on their exposure to the sun and their relation to different walls and trees, and therefore the compositions were unique. Each section acquired its own name. The garden of nasturtiums and poppies next to the stables became the "California garden." The garden of pinks, blues, and whites started next to our fig tree and was named the "fig garden." The reds, whites, and yellows were planted near the catalpa, which means head of wings; that was the "wing garden." The irises and cosmos formed the "bedroom garden" because of their place under our bedroom window. Finally, there was the "fountain garden," filled with camellias, rhododendrons, hortensia, lilies of the valley, and ferns. It ran the length of the tall shady wall on the church side, and at its center was a stone fountain with a carved angel.

Mary and I bought the fountain on a short trip through Alsace the summer before my mother's arrival. We had learned of a certain type of *entreprise* that recuperates materials from old demolished buildings and properties. Such businesses are relatively rare, but we sought them out, never knowing what we might find. The grounds of these businesses are like a forsaken world. There are fragments of châteaux and churches; spiral staircases winding nowhere; fireplaces standing forlornly in crabgrass; *pierre de taille*, or cut stone, piled up in mounds; old millstones set on end like Celtic monuments; wrought-iron railings rusting at the periphery of the property; and columns rising idiosyncratically over stray goats, chickens, and donkeys.

In Alsace, a proprietor, Monsieur Pflieger, had constructed several fountains using stone watering troughs for animals called *abreuvoirs*. The system was simple—a small pump circulated water from the *abreuvoir* through a garden hose around the back of a stone column, then through a copper spout that Monsieur Pflieger claimed was the nozzle from a fire hose. One *abreuvoir* was much more finely cut than the rest, and Mary and I fell for its simple charm. As we walked the yard, among cornices and pillars, we also came across a carved angel, mottled with moss and lichen, tilted back on her wings in the wreckage. She was melancholic. In one hand she held roses; with the other she pointed to the earth. She had escaped from a cemetery only to come to comfortless rest in Monsieur Pflieger's field of dead houses. The angel appeared very old, since many details of her face and wings had been worn away, but Monsieur Pflieger would only volunteer, "She is certainly older than any of us!" This meant he had no idea.

It occurred to me that we could construct a fountain with the angel on a stone column and the copper fire-hose spout mounted over the *abreuvoir*. I explained my idea to Monsieur Pflieger, who knew immediately that he could have made a killing if he had thought of it himself. Still, in good faith, he made a drawing with a stubby pencil, and the image of our fountain appeared.

Three months later Monsieur Pflieger arrived from Alsace, reversed his truck through the gate and across our terrace, and parked next to the wall on the church side. He and his son dug a hole and poured a cement foundation for the column. He then lay down *dalles,* flat rectangular pieces of stone, creating a supporting stone bed for the *abreuvoir,* which was cradled in straps and hoisted into the air at the end of a hydraulic winch. The final piece was the angel. Monsieur Pflieger had wrapped her in canvas secured with rope, a kidnap victim tossed into the back of the truck. The angel was uncovered and lifted into place on top of the column; there she would preside over the copper fire-hose spout and the church side of Mary's terrace gardens.

Immediately after the fountain was set up, Mary and I drove off to the garden store and bought a large pink water lily and a plastic sack full of goldfish, on sale, nine for fifty francs. Of course, they were small and, once released into the fountain, fled under the lily pads when anyone approached. Since there were nine, we named them after the planets. When one died, we changed their names to scientists in *The Eighth Day of Creation.* Finally, when a second fish died, the rest became the days of the week. Then we added three *comètes,* a type of fish related to goldfish but much

more silvery. We stopped calling them anything, and the ten fish
have thrived for years now, wintering in an aquarium that sits in the
library window on the place de l'Église.

The fountain added a new sensual dimension to the terrace and
Mary's gardens—the sound of a single spout of water pouring into
a basin. The fountain was near the "bedroom garden," so at night,
as we read before sleeping, we could hear it, or we could see it out
the window on starlit sleepless nights and feel it calm us. Mornings,
small birds bathed in it, and evenings, swallows swiped insects flying above it. In the winter, it sits emptied, except for captured
leaves, recalling what is given up with the seasons, reminding me of
Eliot's "Burnt Norton."

for the roses

Had the look of flowers that are looked at.
There they were as our guests, accepted and accepting.
So we moved, and they, in a formal pattern,
Along the empty alley, into the box circle,
To look down into the drained pool.

One truth about gardens is that they are never static. The borders of Mary's gardens crept out farther from the walls. Her selection of colors, forms, and varieties of foliage grew more
impressionistic in the overall effect. Spring bulbs gave way to tall
summer flowers. And a major transformation came when my
mother staked claim to her own garden. In her original letter, pro-
posing to retire in France, she had stipulated that she would require
only a room and a little space for a garden. She was happily
ensconced now, and she had set up the rest of the house to her lik-
ing; now it was time to garden.

From her teenage years in Wilton, my mother has always had gardens—organic vegetable gardens, rock gardens, sidewalk gardens, backyard city gardens, and raised gardens. As soon as she moved into the presbytery, she planned to build a raised garden out in front of the stables so that she could grow lettuces, tomatoes, peppers, beans, squash, and herbs. To accomplish this, she would have to enlist Coco's services to find large oak beams for the outer frame and to have soil delivered, which would then have to be enriched with *fumier,* fertilizer.

Coco was convinced that my mother didn't know the first thing about gardens. First of all, no one makes a garden with beams; second, no one puts a garden in the middle of a yard, particularly in front of the stables, where Coco wanted my mother to park her car since my mother continued to leave it unlocked, enticing innocent people to become thieves. Meanwhile, my mother deemed that most French country gardens, the classic *potager,* or kitchen garden, hadn't progressed beyond the Middle Ages and that Coco's garden, in particular, was bereft of imagination and beauty—a dirt patch of healthy but ungainly leeks, carrots, onions, potatoes, and parsley. My mother applied to her garden the maxim she applied to her house: "Don't let anything that isn't beautiful and useful enter it." Her gardens, whether of flowers or vegetables, have always been rich bouquets, albeit somewhat unruly ones. Still, Coco was very proud of his *potager* and often left a stack of leeks or a pail of potatoes on our windowsill as a gift.

Coco grabbed my mother by the arm, led her to the edge of the terrace next to the well, and insisted on the place she should have her garden dug. He spat out, *"Là! Là! Mettez le jardin en bas. C'est beaucoup mieux. Il y a du soleil, de l'eau, et de l'espace."* With polite imperiousness, my mother dismissed him. She already had a spot in mind. "A kitchen garden has to be outside the kitchen door." Coco had no choice but to bow to what he considered my mother's folly and arrange a delivery with his best friend, Monsieur Delapierre.

Rarely have I seen anyone more adept at operating machinery than Monsieur Delapierre. With his noble white hair and beard and dressed in khaki hunting clothes, he arrived on the place de l'Église enthroned on a green John Deere tractor with a backhoe raised over a trailer loaded with beams and soil. He wheeled the tractor around and backed the trailer into our yard while I imagined a less skilled driver knocking down the stables. The beams were lowered into place by a chain attached to the backhoe, and soon Monsieur Delapierre was scooping out soil into a rhomboid-shaped raised garden that stood between the stables and the curé's former pigsties, where my mother had already started a compost heap.

My mother couldn't have been more pleased with all the activity in the yard. Her raised garden was being installed, and a *cavalier* had appeared astride his John Deere charger. Monsieur Delapierre was not only handsome but also seemed naturally bound by the chivalric code of courtesy and generosity, something one would have thought long lost in the fumes of *pastis* and modernity. What an unlikely couple, elegant Monsieur Delapierre and feisty Coco, shoveling *fumier* into my mother's new raised garden. Once the garden had been fertilized and leveled, Coco planted a *marronnier*, hardly more than a seedling, in the middle. My mother didn't exactly appreciate the tree but accepted it as a joke with a barb. Such a small *marronnier* couldn't suck all the water out of the ground.

For Coco and my mother, the rhomboid raised garden quickly became disputed territory. For one thing, my mother arranged for the delivery of ten bales of straw from Fougère's farm. She spread newspaper around the base of her new plants and then covered it with the straw. The straw served three purposes: to smother weeds, to hold in moisture, and to rot eventually into nutritive mulch. My mother had learned this method from Ruth Stout's *How to Have a Green Thumb Without an Aching Back*. Coco, who thought from the beginning that building a raised garden in the middle of the yard was crazy, was now witness to the even greater absurdity of heaping a garden with straw. He'd never seen anything like it. He appealed to Mary: *"Dites à Madame, n'enterrez jamais un jardin de la paille."* Mary dutifully transmitted the message, not to bury the garden alive in straw, and my mother dismissed it as provincial ignorance.

Because Coco was convinced that my mother's garden was doomed, he decided to take it over. He planted tomatoes, onions, and parsley, filling up a third of her *potager* before she could stop him. My mother was particularly annoyed that Coco had planted his tomatoes instead of F1 hybrids, which she was about to put in herself. The type of tomato plant was of quintessential importance to my mother, since growers had developed tomatoes, more than most fruits and vegetables, for traits other than flavor: resistance to bruising, for instance, and uniform ripening. To make matters worse for my mother, the French have strict rules for growing tomatoes, none of which my mother followed. Coco decided that he should be the tomato-growing constable for the garden.

That first summer after my mother's arrival was unusually hot and dry, so my mother watered her garden, eliciting from Coco a scathing *"N'arrosez jamais les tomates."* According to Coco, tomatoes, like wine grapes, must concentrate their flavor, and watering makes them tasteless. In addition, my mother made tripod supports rather than staking and tying each plant. But above all other crimes, my mother failed to pinch off the lower growths of leaves. Coco was convinced, as are many country Frenchmen, that the plant puts all its energy into making leaves at the expense of good fruit. Also the leaves obscure direct sunlight, which is crucial for ripening the tomatoes. A sort of mystical ceremony for growing tomatoes is totally engrained in the French mentality and even has a name, *ébourgeonner*. I read an article in *Le Monde* thoroughly debunking country superstitions about growing tomatoes, and explaining that both the fruit and the plant itself depend on the leaves for photosynthesis, the means by which a plant produces sugar and amino acids essential for survival.

Mary grew weary of transmitting Coco's messages to "Madame," whose response was always the same: "Oh, nonsense!" Mary, impressed with the spectacular production of my mother's tomatoes, took up the argument herself.

She said, "Look, Coco," pointing to a huge tomato-laden stem. "How can you argue with that?"

Coco got down on his knees and genuflected mockingly to my mother's tomatoes, which he couldn't deny were admirable, and began pinching off leaves, claiming that there was still time to grow the tomatoes properly.

Mary explained the basic principle that plants must have chlorophyll in their leaves in order to transform carbon dioxide into nutrients necessary for producing tomatoes.

"They will never ripen!" Coco insisted, even though my mother's tomatoes had already turned bright red and in some cases had even begun to rot because they hadn't been picked. The inhabitants of the Haut-Bourg withheld water to concentrate flavor and watched their sparsely leafed plants wither. In the end, to my mother's great satisfaction, even Coco's plants shriveled up.

While Mary and my mother gardened, I generally looked after the grounds and the fruit trees. It is a cliché to say that there is something very human about old fruit trees, their bearing arthritic and stoical, their cropped branches amputated like arms, their wounds like ears and eyes. I hadn't climbed a tree since I was a kid, but I found myself climbing up into a half-dead pear tree to prune off parts that were rotting. There was no easy access, so I had to pull myself off a ladder and work my way into the limbs, none of which, all lichen-covered and mossy, I trusted to hold my weight. Swaying, if only slightly, knowing that the tree was almost dead at its core, I felt that I was held by the tree's will and that it could break my bones if it so chose.

Few places I've been are so filled with flowering trees as the Puisaye. Usually, in the spring, the countryside is a costume party of blossoms. But that year, one pear tree had been stung by frost and had no fruit and very few leaves. Sawing through the dead wood, I could see that it was pointless to try to save the tree, as pointless as trying to save a neighboring old cherry tree, whose hollow trunk had become a nesting spot for a blue tit. Still, it was hard not to think of how over the years the curés had come out and picked fruit from these trees and how children and parents had danced and played games under them at the *kermesse*. The two old trees were brooding presences that imbued the orchard with a pathos of history, and I was struck by an unexpected sense of loss when Coco came over with his chain saw and had them both cut up for firewood in less than an hour. Throughout the following winter, when I put the pear or cherry wood on the fire, it felt like a ritual, the pieces of fruit wood seemed to burn with a deliberate slowness, a lower, steady flame, as the brooding presences of the two trees conjured themselves away in a final release of ancient energy.

To ease the pain of sacrificing the old fruit trees, I planted four young cherry trees—*coeur de pigeon*, *Montmorency*, *bigarreaux Napoléon*, and a weeping ornamental. It was the first time I had planted fruit trees by myself, and the whole time I remembered helping my father with his trees when I was a kid. Planting young trees is a way of investing in the future; it is impossible not to wonder what they will look like ten or twenty years down the line, even beyond one's own lifetime. Fortunately, we still had plenty of venerable old trees, including the pear tree under which Mary and I were married by our friends and three apple trees that I liberated from an ambitious hedge of blackberry brambles. I'd had no idea that I'd find pruning and restoring old fruit trees so gratifying.

Like Mary and my mother, I decided to start my own garden, mainly because it is impossible to get fresh corn on the cob in France. I figured that while I was at it, I might as well plant other fruits and vegetables that I'm passionate about, mainly raspberries, strawberries, and green asparagus. I took Coco's advice about where to place the garden, in a sunny spot between the well and the new cherry trees. I began to dig up the sod with a fork, but while I enjoyed the exercise, the work progressed too slowly, so I asked Monsieur Marteau to help me out with his rototiller, which he was more than happy to do. In forty-five minutes, he tilled an area that would have taken me days to dig up, and in exchange for his *bon voisinage* I gave him a case of Pouilly-Fumé. As he rolled his rototiller home and I carried his case of wine, he asked, "What do you propose to plant in your garden?"

"*Maïs*," I responded honestly.

"Pour manger?" he asked, with restrained incredulousness.

"Nothing is more wonderful than sweet corn cooked minutes after it is picked. I'll give you some when it comes up. You cook it immediately. That's the secret."

"It's American, isn't it? Indians eat corn."

"Everyone eats corn," I said.

"We feed it to animals."

"That's a different kind of corn."

It was clear that Marteau wondered how different animal corn could be from human corn. I have seen some corn on the cob in grocery stores in France, but it is always wrapped in cellophane and desiccated from months of shelf death. In truth, it doesn't look fit even for animals. Sometimes in French restaurants imported canned corn is put in salads so that they can be called Mexican salads and show an international flair.

"You eat it in your hands like an animal," Marteau finally declared.

He had a point there. Still, I like eating some things with my hands, but then I'm an American, and I eat corn off the cob. Whether it works out to a strict syllogism or not, the suggestion was that I was asking Monsieur Marteau to eat animal food like an animal, which in essence was to be American. All of this resulted in his firm "It's not for me."

To soften his disdain, I declared, "I'm also going to grow green asparagus near the cherry trees."

At the time, no one grew green asparagus in their country gardens; if they grew asparagus at all, it would be white, and in the markets you could get only white asparagus, which the French consider a great delicacy. I happened to prefer green asparagus, and I ordered a special hybrid developed by the University of California, which, when I mentioned it, made no impression on Monsieur Marteau, who considered white to be the only genuine asparagus. Besides, growing asparagus takes patience, expertise, and, above all, sandy soil, but ours was dense with clay. In any case, the cornerstone of any Frenchman's garden is leeks and potatoes; but then one becomes ambitious and grows all the rest, leading up to tomatoes, which are the source of the greatest pride. Growing corn and green asparagus was an American preoccupation—our own onions, as the expression goes—and he gave me a sympathetic grin, put away his rototiller, and unburdened me of the case of wine.

Still, I was disappointed that I couldn't convince Marteau to try corn. We owed him plenty. The previous summer, he had banged on the kitchen window to deliver lettuces, carrots, tomatoes, as well as zucchinis the size of torpedoes. It was peculiar that ie had been so generous with us, since he had a reputation for miserliness.

Ariane said, "*Il est terrible*. Listen, do you know what he did? He asked Monsieur Bougé if he and some friends could hunt on his property. Monsieur Bougé said, 'But of course.' A few weeks later, Monsieur Bougé snuck up to see what Marteau was up to. You know what he saw? Well, he saw Marteau lining up *gibier* to sell in Paris."

I didn't imagine that the game one sees in Paris would come from the likes of Marteau, but then it has to come from somewhere.

My garden flourished, although the newly planted asparagus got a rough start. Madame Bourgeois's ewe and two lambs had been evicted from a nearby field, so we offered them temporary quarters in the orchard. However, they liked to trample specifically on the asparagus. To keep them and the hordes of rabbits out of my garden, I surrounded it with railings and chicken wire. There were two creatures I couldn't keep out. The first was a large green lizard, almost a foot long, who decided that the new garden was his personal kingdom. I suspected him of eating some of the strawberries, but I learned later that lizards don't ordinarily eat them. The other creature was Coco, who secretly planted some spring onions and tomatoes along the western border of the garden. What could I do but let them stay?

Soon after Madame Bourgeois brought over our new temporary guests, she told us that the ewe would give milk to only one of the lambs, and the other had to be hand-fed several times a day, a chore which Mary coveted, though she often had to relinquish it to the neighborhood kids, who had decided nothing was more fun than feeding an overeager, milk-guzzling lamb. Who would have guessed how voracious and animated a lamb could be? And this one was a runt. As soon as Madame Bourgeois found a pasture more suitable than our orchard, she roped her animals and marched them down the passage beside the church and across the *place*. We were left wondering if we shouldn't get some sort of country animals of our own. With a *pigeonnier*, pigsties, and stables, it was clear that the former inhabitants, the old curés, had kept animals, though probably not l'Abbé Camus and certainly not Père Jo. I tried to maintain a healthy skepticism about our owning farm animals for amusement, but then Mary said, "Let's get a donkey. They're very smart, you know."

And my mother, who should have been wiser after the Wilton catastrophe, countered with "Goats."

"Donkeys need a companion. They get lonely, and when they're lonely they bray all the time. The neighbors will hate it. We'll just have to get two donkeys," Mary said.

"How about a donkey and a goat?"

Mary wasn't about to give in to getting a goat, even if goats made fine donkey companions. It would be like nuking the garden. She didn't say no; she just pretended not to hear what my mother said. I thought the whole idea of acquiring farm animals was preposterous enough to merit little concern until Mary began ordering books—*The Definitive Donkey: The Textbook of the Modern Ass; The Professional Handbook of the Donkey* compiled for the Donkey Sanctuary; and *l'Âne: Sa Vie et Son Histoire.* My mother began visiting the small village animal shows and scanned *les petites annonces,* the small ads proclaiming goats for sale.

Having such animals was not unprecedented in the Haut-Bourg. Neighbors down the rue des Vignes keep a goat, a pony, and a Border collie in their yard, where even the few remaining heavily thorned roses are caged in wire mesh. Down the rue Gabriel-Landy, there are three ponies. Not far behind Coco's house are a donkey, a horse, and a peacock. There are horses and cows down the rue de la Montagne, and there are sheep everywhere.

Ariane said, "This is out of the question. An ass will drive everyone mad." Jean-Louis was delighted with the idea, having always wanted a donkey himself. He also said that some donkey breeds have a cross on their backs, making them symbolically fitting for a *jardin de curé.* Meanwhile, Marteau thought it was none of his business, and Mary was afraid to discuss it with Bougé. But Bougé had his sheep, so why shouldn't we have a donkey? Coco just stared at Mary for a moment as if she had spoken English instead of French. Then he said, holding up fingers to number the points, *"Les vétérinaires, les vaccins, fourrage, foin, l'eau, espace, et un abri."* Veterinarians, vaccines, fodder, hay, water, space, and shelter. He didn't have to add, "And for what?"

Mary phoned Madame le Docteur Vassallo for intelligence on local donkey breeders, and we soon found ourselves standing in a field on a rather shabby farm, petting massive workhorses and a small group of friendly Poitou donkeys, which are hardly dwarfs themselves. All the animals were in gorgeous shape, making a sharp contrast with the desolate, weedy pastures and collapsing outbuildings. It was as if the breeder could only occupy himself with one thing—care for the animals—while the rest of the world disintegrated. Mary actually fell in love with the workhorses, petting them and apologizing to each, "I have nothing for you." But, fortunately, she realized that a workhorse would hardly have enough room to turn around in our orchard. The Poitous were also too large, particularly if we bought two.

The breeder, an older man, seemed completely unconcerned as to whether we bought a donkey or not. He said, "You know, even after the war, donkeys like these pulled barges. Ropes tied to them, they worked hard on the *chemin de halage*. They ate poorly. *C'était dur*. Now look at them. The life of the château."

That summer a banner was hung at the entrance to the village announcing the Réunion de la Fédération Départementale des Clubs Ruraux des Ânes—a departmental meeting of rural donkey clubs. It would be held near the Stade du Cottard, the grounds of the château that was annihilated in the Revolution and where now local kids play soccer. Clearly, having a regional donkey exposition in our own village was a sign, and now Mary, who is normally our most dependable skeptic, assumed that owning donkeys was simply a matter of fate after all. My mother, however, was starting to come to her senses, suddenly wondering if her bold retirement in France might have only led her to do heavy farm work.

On one of the hottest days that summer, our village filled with old people, some of them very old. They came in cars and buses. They walked in groups of twenty or more, all entering the Stade de Cottard, as in a strange sort of dream. We were among them, those who had lived for the major part of the century. Who knew what each had experienced during the various wars, whom they lost or how they suffered, and we thought that, like us, they were all going to see the donkeys. Actually, there were no donkeys; only stalls selling cushions, watercolors, embroidery, *confiture*, painted milk cans, handmade dolls, and lace. The stalls were set up around the Stade de Cottard, each stall representing a *club d'amitié* from villages in our region, each manned by kind-looking, albeit overheated old people. They were gathering to watch the dancers from Charny and the choral groups Les Genêts and Les Éclusettes de Rogny.

Most of our neighbors were not interested enough in donkeys to go to the *réunion,* and Jean-Louis had planned to go but heat held him hostage to the garden shade. Only Jo could come up with an explanation for why the donkeys had evaporated and old people were arriving like pilgrims.

"Someone changed the word *aînés to ânes*. The *î* and the *accent aigu* were painted out." *Aîné* literally means "firstborn" and is used as a sort of euphemism for the elderly.

Jo must have seen such pranks before when working in retirement homes. What we actually attended was a regional meeting of friendship clubs for the elderly. We had been led to an odd vision in our small village, the region's elderly amassed on the lost grounds of a vanished château.

As a relief from the confusion and as a consolation, we went off to splurge on our three gardens. Since the planting of the gardens, I observed a marked change in my mother and Mary when they walked into a plant store, the Jardinerie, for example, down by the Loire. A deep earnestness seized these otherwise lighthearted beings as they scanned the bounty. It was, in fact, nothing other than pure greed. Each grabbed a *chariot* or two, and then set off in separate directions to plunder the displays: annual and perennial, weeping and climbing, shade and *plein soleil;* floppy, bold, fragrant, tall, small, and forget-me-not, all captured and wheeled toward the register after much expert advice from two spunky Frenchwomen, one blonde and one brunette, who managed somehow to keep up with the frenzy. It wasn't a matter of buying only plants but also all the rich gifts that plants require to flourish. Sacks of *fumier* and peat moss seemed fine to me, but I didn't know that plants like blood, bone, and ground-up horns.

I confess that I wasn't entirely immune to the plant-buying frenzies, but I interfered only timidly with certain preferences among flowers. However, I decided that we should definitely grow an espalier around my garden fence. Certainly the fence itself would hold the training supports, and the trees would mask the chicken wire. I acceded to Mary's insistence that the espalier be Williams pears, since they were her favorites and also seemed a fitting substitute for the old pear tree that we had cut down.

What could be more fitting for a presbytery garden than espaliers? In the evening when I have a drink and tend to the barbecue, control of the airspace passing from swallows to bats, I look out at the espaliers in full leaf around the orchard garden. How fitting a symbol of this home they are. Former curés spent their lives training the human spirit to grow on the framework of French Catholic ritual and mystery. What a shock it must have been for the farm kids of the village, after baptism, catechism, Communion, retreats, and charity fairs to find themselves in Algeria, where steeples were being knocked off Catholic churches.

An espalier is nature bent to an ordered notion of beauty, and some gardens are hardly different. In the preposterous gardens of Versailles, every flower, hedge, and tree was planted, pruned, and trained to demonstrate man's tyranny over nature. In great part, what I love about the Puisaye is its natural give-and-take; if grounds were left to themselves, blackberries and nettles would soon reclaim all lost territory. For the time being, with the espalier, we've obscured some chicken wire and the realm of a gorgeous green lizard.

Passing Through

At the presbytery, late summer can blaze; the grass burns up, and all the flower beds and young fruit trees require prodigious watering. Mary plants cosmos, cleome, dahlias, and *lavatère* so that by August her garden gains volume, height, and color. That is also when the roses begin to rally. Still, you sense the vegetable world hopelessly overextending itself, pears and apples dropping and fermenting, as they did our first summer. The water cannons irrigate the fields in great sweeping arches like the massive wings of imaginary creatures.

I like to jog to Ailliant, six kilometers to the north, past the small algae-fetid duck ponds and the cemetery and then into the rolling open fields of the plateau. The late-summer crops are mainly wheat, corn, and sunflowers, the latter growing so heavy that their heads no longer turn and the brightness burns off their faces. I run early enough so that on my return an hour later I won't be caught in the hottest part of the day. No matter which way I go, I have to pass Coco's door, and if we happen to cross paths he immediately begins to mock me, jogging briskly alongside, then staggering into a pantomimed heart attack.

Since Coco's universe is ruled by the absolutes of utility and alcoholism, he believes nothing is more foolish than jogging, and each time I jog by him I'm seized by a wave of guilt—jogging is an extravagance! When I come back, he suggests projects—clearing land, hauling wood, or building a shed. He can't figure out what I'm doing in shorts and a baseball cap, traipsing off down the hot road into the fields. His consternation over my jogging is not unlike his disdain for Mary's cosmos, cleome, dahlias, and *lavatère*. He is happy to help dig up the beds but tells her, as always, to plant vegetables.

When I passed Coco's door one August morning, maybe the hottest that year, I wondered why I do jog. My mother says that I run from devils: imagined cancer and heart attacks, old loves and embarrassments, professional failures, inevitable losses, wrongdoings, and a host of others. I contend that it's to get outdoors, to be alone with my thoughts, and to balance my immoderate love of caloric food and wine with severe punishment.

That August morning I didn't see Coco, and as I was passing the cemetery of the Harmelles, Claude Savin, the Bourgeois, and the rest of the notable and unnotable village dead, I thought there might be some substance to my mother's claim that devils were chasing me. After all, the only thing that intrudes on my thoughts, once I'm alone with them, is discomfort, and that August morning my discomfort was extreme. I knew I might end up crawling into the cemetery to look for a cool marble slab in the shade of a pine tree surrounded by funeral plaques—"Memories," "Regrets," "Sorrows." In fact, that morning I ran only three kilometers to an old farm at the edge of a copse before turning back, encouraged homeward by the steeple of our church rising out of fields of parched sunflowers.

I didn't even make it to the cemetery. I stopped in the shade of a small roadside apple tree while indisputable devils in the form of bottleflies caught up with me and exploited thoroughly their sole talent—to torment the miserable. In that one moment, all the clichés of death were gathered in one place—flies, shadows, the cemetery, the first hints of autumn in the yellowed leaves. I vowed to be more reasonable about jogging in hot weather.

After I caught my breath, I left my patch of shade before the gates of the cemetery and walked into the Haut-Bourg, my head orbited by bottleflies, and saw the flashing of two SAMU emergency medical vehicles in front of Coco's door.

All the inhabitants of the Haut-Bourg had formed a vigil on the place de l'Église. Before I could find out what had happened, Jean-Louis was already scolding me for jogging in such heat— *"C'est idiot! C'est idiot!"*—as if my jogging had somehow been responsible for the immediate emergency. A chair had been set out for Madame Briançon, who had herself recently returned from the hospital, her legs elephantine with edema from her diabetes. It was the first time we'd seen her outside her house in over a year. My mother had brought out the chair for her, and Jean-Louis placed it beside the public well in the shade of the Liberty Tree. She was wailing out, *"Exactement comme mon premier mari! Exactement!"* Just like my first husband. Then she burst into a generous fit of tears that would last the next hour, Madame Marteau, of all people, trying to console her by patting her shoulders. Madame Marteau, despite the deterioration of her mental state, had been allowed out and even seemed to understand that the situation was grave; her eyes darted about, dark and troubled, and she shook her head in shared disbelief, muttering, *"Affreux."* I looked at Mary, and I knew that this was a defining crisis in the otherwise uninterruptedly calm passage of hot summer days.

We could only watch helplessly from a distance as the medical team carried their black cases and an IV rack into Coco's house. The men gathered in a huddle—Delapierre, Jean-Louis, Marteau, and even Bougé—to reexamine the morning's events, as if they could come up with a diagnosis. The women stood silently behind the sobbing Madame Briançon.

The truth was that no one knew what was wrong with Coco, except that he had gone to bed exhausted, and that morning Marteau had heard moans filling the place de l'Église and traced them to Coco's house. He had poked his head through the door to inquire, *"Ça va?"* It was no rehearsal this time—Coco couldn't breathe. Marteau called the SAMU, who didn't know which department Rogny was in, though it is a village of some historical distinction and has been in the Yonne since the original establishment of departments. Help arrived forty-five minutes later after emergency vehicles from Gien, only twenty kilometers away, turned back because they realized that Rogny was in the Yonne, not the Loiret, and radioed Auxerre, fifty kilometers away, for help. Finally, the confusion was sorted out, and vehicles from the correct SAMU station were dispatched to our village.

As the medical team worked on Coco, everyone in the little crowd gathered on the *place* was thinking the same thing: Coco had finally had his heart attack. While Coco had declared funerals for himself all of his life, his family and the inhabitants of the Haut-Bourg had been burying him for only seven years. As soon as Coco had been diagnosed with cancer, members of his family, some of whom Coco would, in fact, outlive, came to the place de l'Église to assess whether his hovel, with only a wood stove and no hot water, had any value at all. Meanwhile, Coco's neighbors believed that, with the cancer, his smoking, and his heavy drinking, he was living on blessings.

The Haut-Bourg has been populated for millennia, but for us there was only one Coco, as for others there had been only one Père Jo. I tried to imagine the day Père Jo left the presbytery, sick as he was. His scant belongings were moved out. The heavy old furniture was moved into the attics of neighbors. The table he danced on was carted off. The only remnants of his presence were the piles of wine bottles and the *Jeu de Massacre*. The presbytery was closed up and the house slipped into a comalike sleep onto which the only light, season after season, came through the louvered shutters and the holes that opened in the roof. For the inhabitants, some genial spirit of place had evaporated and the house drifted into disrepair. How many lively spirits have come and gone? Who could replace presences like Père Jo or Coco? If we lost Coco, we'd look out on the *place* and still think it his.

I was surprised at how long the doctor and paramedics worked. The members of the vigil increased with the arrival of Véronique and Jo on their motorcycles. Also, some children from down the rue Gabriel-Landy and the rue de Dammarie assembled to inspect the emergency vehicles and hang around in case they might see Coco as a corpse. The small crowd remained mostly quiet as the sun rose directly overhead and the air grew even hotter. My mother brought out some cold drinks and said that the medics would try to stabilize Coco's breathing before moving him to the hospital. After working for thirty years at the Yale medical school, she knows more medicine than many doctors.

Madame Briançon's stormy weeping gave way to steady moaning. She rocked forward and back in her chair, leaning on the aluminum walker in front of her. Suddenly the moaning stopped, and she brightened as if she'd seen a benevolent apparition among the stainless-steel paraphernalia of life support barely visible through Coco's dark doorway. Jolting the funereal mood, she announced, "This is good for André. He's been drinking too much!"

We were all shocked. How could she make such a pronouncement? After all, Coco couldn't breathe, and we all imagined that his heart might fibrillate at any moment. Still, Madame Briançon had suddenly become angry with Coco for putting us through all this worry. "This will be a lesson to him. He's a fool, drinking the way he does." She decided it was irresponsible of Coco to have a heart attack. "He brought it on himself." Coco's critical condition had become a part of a long-running domestic squabble.

The couples of the Haut-Bourg are, at times, more like spirited adversaries, even defiant combatants, embraced in all the intimacy of an ancient, humiliating war. Ariane, more than once, has come over to the presbytery in a state somewhere between hysteria and triumph to make public the fact that she and Jean-Louis had been fighting. Their war is a good thirty-five years old now. Each time they battle, they manage to achieve a satisfactory balance of hurt. Monsieur Marteau has thrown frying pans and broken every dish in the house. The men still control the money; thus, they can dash any dreams of an indoor shower or a trip to see family. The women, on the other hand, control public opinion and recount their husbands' crimes against humanity, winning the propaganda war.

Ariane has told Mary and me that we are the only happy couple she's ever known. We think how unlikely that is. We run couples through our minds, assigning grades, and conclude that we know many couples who seem perfectly suited to each other; still, we are not really in a position to assess the quality of their happiness. Then there are couples who no one admits are couples, out of respect for their privacy, out of respect for human need and intimacy, and out of sheer incredulousness—Coco and Madame Briançon are an example.

After Madame Briançon's husband died of a heart attack, leaving her only a little money and property, she took up with Coco, who is at least ten years her junior. Clearly, they were different creatures then. Coco had both sides of his jaw and a whole tongue. Words fit comfortably in his mouth. Madame Briançon's nerves were yet to be damaged by diabetes, and her blood vessels functioned so that she still walked on human legs. But even now, Coco spends many nights with Madame Briançon. While there is no point in imagining what their intimacy is like, I am amazed by how the two, after all the wreckage of their difficult lives, look out so generously for each other. Coco attends to Madame Briançon's needs, supplying wood, watering the garden, and caring for the house when she is in the hospital. She, in turn, cooks for him and pesters him about his drinking. All this despite their leading, in some respects, very separate lives, Coco independent and Madame Briançon housebound.

Ariane contends that all the village men are brutes, and that Marteau is the worst because he is too cheap to pay for special help for his wife, which would include expenses beyond what social security provides. Madame Marteau ambushes Ariane in her garden, using her finger as a laser, or she appears in the presbytery in the middle of our dinner claiming that her visit was all her dog's idea. But we hear Marteau shouting at her when she hides his laundry in toolboxes or under furniture. Maybe he is a brute, but with the progress of his wife's illness he has lost weight and shuffles across a darkened planet.

That summer day on the place de l'Église has become what the psychologists call a flashbulb memory—a moment marked by trauma. Madame Briançon, crippled as she was, wailed her way to a sudden surge of optimism—perhaps Coco wouldn't drink so much now. The rest of us stood behind her and watched as the doctors and paramedics finally wheeled Coco out of his dingy room into the blinding sunlight. Amid glaring chrome and vinyl, on a starched sheet, Coco lay as I had never seen him, the red flush gone from his cheeks and the mischief from his eyes. His gray hair stood straight up. One of his arms was strapped down and spiked with an IV that had a confluence of tubes hanging from a hat rack of revitalizing fluids; his other hand rose in weak tribute to us. Dan was left in the house. As the SAMU drove off with Coco, the children disbanded quickly while the rest of us promised to pass on any information we received from the hospital.

My mother volunteered to take in Dan, who came over so often anyway, but Monsieur Delapierre protested, saying that he would feed and walk him a few times a day. In any case, Dan would be far more at ease in Coco's bed in his own shabby little home. Late that evening, my mother and Mary rushed out to greet Delapierre, hoping for news of Coco. The three of them stood out on the place de l'Église, the elegant Monsieur Delapierre subdued and thoughtful. The hot evening light made his white beard and hair even whiter, almost luminous. The three strolled off down the rue de Dammarie, past Marteau's gardens and a large grassless pen full of hens, roosters, and geese. Monsieur Delapierre had no news, the hospital reluctant to release information to nonfamily. We didn't know Coco's remaining family members or even if they'd trouble themselves to learn about his condition.

Dan was accustomed to sleeping alone when Coco would close his one set of shutters and cross the *place* to spend the night with Madame Briançon. Some nights we'd hear Dan's muffled howls, which were not so muffled in the adjacent household of Madame Bourgeois. Still, when I heard the dog that night, I imagined the small, deformed woodsman, his hair standing on end, passing the night in the drab remove of the hospital world. There in starched sheets above the polished floors, amid chrome bars and translucent tubes, there in the night shift, Coco was becoming no one.

When I was growing up, death seemed both terrifying and intriguing. My uncle died when I was nine, but I had never met him. He just went to bed and didn't come to dinner when he was called. My little cousins, trying to rouse him, thought he was just playing dead. He had his fatal heart attack at thirty-five, and afterward my aunt and my four cousins came all the way from Ohio to stay with us in Wilton. I had never seen children whose father was freshly dead. Also, it was the first time I'd seen true adult grief. I was fascinated, meeting family under such dark circumstances. I've never before or since seen a woman cry so thoroughly as my aunt—her dark hair dampened, her light cotton dress clinging, her clasped hands detailing and filling out a portrait of sorrow. I just sat quietly alone with her.

I was close to the epicenter of death, but it wasn't death itself. The curés who lived in our presbytery would have witnessed dozens of deaths. After all, beyond baptism, catechism, and marriage, their duty was to preside over the process of death, administer unction, and say the funeral mass. In our stables, the curés kept the horses and the funeral carriage. It was only a hundred years ago that Rogny experienced such deadly outbreaks of cholera that the curé would preside over sixty-eight deaths in two months.

I happened to be with my grandmother when she died one night in late May. It was clear that she was at the end, having suffered for years with chronic lung disease. I was visiting my mother at the time and agreed to stay and help out around the house. The night her mother died it was my turn to take over the watch in the small back room, its windows filled with dark purple hedges of lilacs. There was a black-and-white television next to her butler's tray, and I was watching Muhammad Ali sustain some of the worst damage of his late career. My grandmother actually loved boxing, which seemed unlikely for a woman of her intellect and refinement. Still, in her own life, she was a bitter combatant who mixed charm and intelligence to set up insults, many of which had a kind of delayed but powerful effect. Other times she would sit in my mother's living room just after my mother got home, exhausted from work. My grandmother would begin talking to her Pekingese, whose name was Shingfu, Chinese for "happiness."

"Oh, dear, my daughter is a slob, isn't she? Is there no cure? Look at that kitchen. One could put the butter away, and it saves so much work when one at least rinses and stacks! It is horrible, isn't it, for such a well-bred little dog to have to live here?"

My grandmother had grown up ordering maids around. Her mother, Tillie, didn't really know how to run a house, and Charlie was wheeling and dealing, selling furnaces in the steel industry. My grandmother attended finishing school, and when she married, she had her own set of household help. She was friends with Fitzgerald and Thurber and knew many of the early staff members of *The*

New Yorker. Her friends would gather in Westport and sometimes on the Thimble Islands off the shore of Stony Creek. But my grandmother became a lightning rod for tragedy. Her mother committed suicide, her husband died young, she battled abdominal cancer, and her house burned down. Left penniless, she supported two daughters to whom she was incapable of showing love or affection.

My grandmother lingered in my mother's house for four difficult years. Before her death, she had a Linde Walker, a portable air supply. It was as if for her the earth had become an alien environment. She would be toiling in the flower beds by the white fences, working slowly as if underwater. Sometimes still desperate for cigarettes, she would try to back out of the drive in her blue VW Bug, only to hit the fence and abandon the car in the roses.

My mother has very strong opinions, but she is peaceful, generous, and humane, the antithesis of my grandmother's bitterness and belligerence. Though her mother continually hurt her, my mother felt obliged to prepare a homestyle death. It had all been worked out with my grandmother's doctor. When it made little sense to drag my grandmother into the hospital for another "fluffing up," as my mother put it, we'd just keep her at home and make her as comfortable as possible.

Despite a considerable oxygen deficiency to her brain, my grandmother remained lucid and cruel to the end, complaining extravagantly to Shingfu about my mother's faults when my mother brought in her meals or arranged large vases of lilacs. Finally, the room filled up with ghosts, and she could no longer see any of us. She shuttled through layerings of time, speaking to Tillie, Charlie, or her brothers; she even mistook her Pekingese for some other dog that had danced about in the twenties.

There was no mystery when my grandmother died; she simply

stopped breathing beside me. Each organ had failed, as did her heart, and she drowned, in the end, in her own fluids. I switched off the TV, walked out, and told my mother. Some men from the funeral home wrapped my grandmother in a black blanket and wheeled her out like luggage. How different the process has been with friends and family members who have died since—the years of adjustment to mysterious disappearances.

For ten years, my grandmother's ashes remained at the funeral home until my mother felt motivated to recover them one wintry Friday afternoon. For another ten years or so, the ashes sat on a window shelf in a container that looked like a cookie tin. When my mother decided to move to France, she certainly was not going to bring my grandmother's ashes with her, so she called my brother; together they took the cookie tin, wrapped in a colorful silk scarf, to the dock at Stony Creek, the one place where my grandmother had known happiness. Their ceremony consisted of merely tossing the tin into the turbid water of Long Island Sound; however, it didn't sink. Instead, to the horror of my mother and brother standing helplessly on the dock, it simply bobbed on the surface, drifting toward the Thimble Islands, my grandmother defiant to the end, off to perplex some unsuspecting youngster poking in the seaweed for treasure.

The total body water content of a thin man is 65 percent. It is regulated by thirst, antidiuretic hormones, and the kidneys and is all held in a delicate balance of sodium, potassium, and blood urea nitrogen. Once the extracellular fluid is reduced by 5 percent, symptoms may include tachycardia, hypertension, and decreased central venous pressure. All of this is to say that Coco's heart attack turned out to be a case of severe dehydration from drinking alcohol and no other fluids while cutting wood in the sort of heat that I had jogged in.

Within a few days, he was back from the hospital and standing on our terrace. He took three large steps toward me, adjusted his cowboy hat, and drew two invisible six-shooters from invisible holsters. I couldn't believe it. Coco was utterly the same. The red flush had returned to his face, and he shouted, "Ho-kay."

How did Madame Briançon know, the moment before Coco was whisked off in the SAMU emergency vehicle, that he was simply being punished for immoderation, that he would not pass away exactly as her first husband had? Maybe it's that Coco seems indestructible in spite of all the damage he has sustained. Or, perhaps, in the country one develops an intuition for real tragedy. Still the odd combination of selfless generosity and relentless self-abuse brought him to the brink.

Living in the presbytery, I find myself dreaming often about the airspace we share with the swallows, bats, and owls; the couples, the lovers, and families of other times; the curés in their own time standing on the terrace, men of the spirit absorbed by their senses. The Abbé Jean Briffaut, in his homily at Père Jo's funeral, conceded that for all Père Jo's generosity to the poor and for all his love of children he was a man of certain fragilities. As gregarious as Père Jo must have been, a man loved by hardworking neighbors, he would also descend on private drunken nights through the gradients of self-indulgence. The paradox of those fragilities, as the abbé put it, makes Père Jo seem all the more real.

My mother made the decision to join the odd, intimate mix of village life, past and present. I had to face how vulnerable she had become, how limited physically, as she has gotten older. She became clumsy and tired quickly. She relied more and more on Jo and Coco to do small chores. The adjustment was not easy for me; my mother was, at one time, as independent and indestructible as Coco. She'd come home after a day at the laboratory and make dinner, dressed in her skimpy blue cocktail-waitress outfit before going off to the Midtown Motor Inn. She'd finish there at one in the morning, only to get up early for work again, the next night working part-time at a clinic. On weekends, she'd garden and in the evenings she'd date some stranger whom my brother and I treated with rather predictable hostility. But a friend who came to visit us in Burgundy told me that my mother was just the same as she had always been when on vacation at a small cottage by the shore. The goal for two weeks was to do absolutely nothing but swim and read during the day and watch the fireflies in the beach roses at night.

The presbytery is suffused with my mother's presence and will be as long as Mary and I are around to remember her years there. But the presbytery is the kind of building we are all just passing through. We make the renovations, we enjoy the gardens, and we do our own work. We have no kids to leave it to, and throughout its own strange history since the French Revolution, habitation has been based on charity. Who knows what will become of it?

Mary and I did not take my mother into our house because we were trying to make her last years as comfortable as possible; we took her in because of a series of miscalculations on my mother's part and confused acquiescence on ours. Certainly, we were not making plans based on the imminence of anyone's death.

For the children down the rue Gabriel-Landy, we had become familiar facts in the landscape of their young lives. Père Jo didn't exist for them, nor was the church itself much of an influence anymore. We were becoming less and less a mystery, the Americans who keep their shutters open day and night and listen to the Bach suites as if to some passionate internal argument. The children love to wave crazily to my mother, the American lady, a little hard-of-hearing and unabashed by her poor French. She passes by in her large gray Peugeot 405, a big yellow dog beside her in the front seat.

La Charmille du Presbytère

*O*ne of the most mysterious places in the village is the *charmille* of the ancient presbytery. The two rows of trees, with Monsieur Bougé's sheep pastures on either side, consist of huge hornbeams, called *charmes*, mixed with some massive oaks that have managed to survive past their time. Some of the hornbeams are half-dead giants, bark stripped in places, limbs broken off, hunting grounds for woodpeckers. Yet to our relief, when spring comes, their tops fill with gentle, pale green leaves. There are many stumps along the prayer path where some old trees had been cut down; unruly young trees vie with one another to take their place.

No one knows how old the *charmille* is. The sad, old, noble trees follow a straight line along the crest of the Haut-Bourg. Once a place where villagers played *boules* and ate at banquet tables at the *kermesse*, it is now a secret domain where ordered nature has become disordered again, where rabbits dig under the moonlit statue of Christ and hedgehogs trundle through the rot, nosing for grubs. Dozens of birds nest in hedges of wild roses or in the undergrowth, while owls on their nightly sorties use the branches as a way station. Every morning I stroll across the orchard to the two guardian hedges of lilacs at the entrance, then down the steps to the length of the *charmille*. I always discover something—old colored bottles rising from the fill, a legless lizard weaving timidly toward the nettles, the wreckage of some poor bird overtaken by a predator, snails the size of a child's fist, or a kind of mushroom I've never seen before.

I'm always on the lookout for special mushrooms, but I'm anything but an expert. The French are notoriously cagey about their secret mushrooming places. With, invariably, a smug, toothy grin, Marteau insists that he has a spot for *morilles*, and Jean-Louis hints knowingly about his spot for *girolles*. Coco, on the other hand, leaves us a little basket of *mousserons* on the windowsill: no grin, no hint, just the gift. While intrigued by the aura of a treasure hunt, I'm also terrified that I'll end up convulsing from amanita toxin. Each time I eat Coco's *mousserons*, I wonder if the rarely sober little man might have picked the wrong thing; the pleasure of eating wild mushrooms has a tinge of brinkmanship.

We bought a guide which ranked edible mushrooms by so many little blue skillets; for the inedible, there was a white circle enclosing the word *inmangeable* or, worse, a bright red skull and crossbones. Almost year-round, there is some sort of mushroom to identify in the *charmille*, but early autumn, in particular, we had a great variety. To my delight, I discovered several roundish mushrooms with spongelike undersides that I was sure were the highly sought-after *cèpes*. I immediately brought Mary down to show her my discovery, and we agreed that for the first time since acquiring the presbytery we had finally found real treasure on our property.

Cèpes are large mushrooms related to the Italian porcinis, and the French, as is their wont, invent irresistible recipes for them. Often in autumn, Mary and I stop at a little restaurant called La Terrasse for their classic *omelette aux cèpes*.

A cautious woman when it comes to self-poisoning, Mary suggested that we bring our proud harvest to the pharmacist, who is a paramedic and also the area's official expert on mushrooms, identifying them and ranking their savor or toxicity. I decided that since we were going to the pharmacist anyway we should bring four or five varieties and get an expert evaluation of our mushroom-abundant *charmille*. Mary ran to the house to get a plate, a bright hand-painted one we'd bought in Italy for picnics. We filled it with odd sizes and exotic forms of mushrooms, with our greenish *cèpes* occupying the position of honor at the center.

Our pharmacy is down the hill, across from the school on the rue du Port. It is the only modern-looking building in the village, and all its trim is painted in Howard Johnson's green. We walked in with our plate of mushrooms and confronted our pharmacist. He was a thin, balding man, without much of a chin, dressed in his starched pale green smock.

"We think we've found some special mushrooms in our garden," Mary told him. "We hoped that you could help us identify them."

The pharmacist, restocking prescription drawers at the time, looked across the room at the plate. "Madame, you have nothing of interest there."

"But are these not *cèpes*?" Mary pointed at our insulted fungi.

The pharmacist condescended to walk over and give the mushrooms a little shove with his finger. "*Des bolets,* madame, the same family, but these won't have much flavor. You can eat them if you want, but they are old. See for yourself. Slugs have been eating them."

He pointed around the plate, naming the fungi as if they were in a class of shameful students. They were not dangerous, but neither were they interesting, gastronomically speaking.

We were amazed at how quickly the pharmacist identified each mushroom, and we had nothing like Marteau's *morilles*, Jean-Louis's *girolles*, and Coco's *mousserons*. We had brought in a whole plate of mushrooms, and none was even exciting enough to be deadly.

We wouldn't learn how to identify mushrooms until Véronique came over one rainy weekend with a basket and a couple of fruit knives. She took us to her special spot, where, through the trees, you could see the still canal reflect the November gray above us. It took an hour before we started to find some *cèpes* and *pieds de mouton* along odd, tree-filled craters. Véronique pointed with her fruit knife and said, "That is from the war."

I never gave up looking for edible mushrooms on our land. I'd go down into the *charmille*, with coffee in the morning, a drink in the evening, to look at the light sifting through leaves to the damp corners between stumps: so many mushrooms appearing out of nowhere; soft brown, white, yellow, and dark red; all their intriguing forms, so many umbrellas, rings, clouds, and phalluses; all composed of such vulnerable flesh; and all the earthy odors, beneath the ferns, and bursts of applause, the wind in the leaves of the old trees.

The *charmille* required attention. Many of the trees were being strangled by ivy vines thick as small trees. They root at the base of the massive oaks and hornbeams and climb high into the branches, where they leaf in an evergreen cascade. Though the effect is beautiful, the process is parasitic. I cut the vines at their base and cleared underbrush and low-hanging branches, but we hired Coco to bring down the dead trees and cut them up for firewood. He had so keen a sense of the architecture of trees that he could angle a cut in such a way that a ninety-foot tree fell precisely down a stretch of the prayer path and did not come down on top of Bougé's fences. Bougé was, nonetheless, convinced that when Coco set large fires to dispose of unwanted branches, he would burn down Bougé's shed across the pasture. When we saw the blaze in the middle of the prayer path, we were more concerned that Coco might burn down the entire Haut-Bourg. But if nothing else, Coco was a master woodsman, and his fires would harmlessly burn themselves out.

That damp, mushroomy autumn, Mary and I first considered making a living space for ourselves in the *grenier,* the large open space under the roof. My mother had decided to live year-round in the country, and for so unknown a part of France, we had more friends and family coming to stay with us than we'd ever imagined. The presbytery was no longer the private country playground and retreat that we intended. Now Mary wanted a place to herself where she could take up the cello, and I wanted a study, off-limits to all but Mary and Christabel. The space in the *grenier,* with its eighteenth-century oak beam structure, is the most attractive in the house. If we installed dormers on the back, we'd have views not only over the garden, the orchard, and the *charmille* but also over the Loing Valley and the Briare Canal. With dormers in the front, we'd have views over the place de l'Église and over Monsieur Marteau's house to pastures and wheat fields in the far distance.

True to our natures, we grew passionate about the idea of constructing a home inside of a home. We began studying country houses wherever we went, gathering ideas for cutaway terraces, large shed dormers with a wall of windows, charming doghouse dormers, and economical Velux skylights. We consulted with Deluche and Nottin about the feasibility and costs of such a large project. Deluche even prepared an estimate for building standard doghouse dormers and installing a few Velux windows, but Nottin advised us to consult an architect, since we would be obliged, in any case, to submit an application to the Bureau des Monuments Historiques for a construction permit. He knew an architect, curiously named James P. Hargrove, who lived in an old château in the Loiret. Nottin said, "One hears that he is very good."

Mary and I drove to the château to introduce ourselves and perhaps engage the services of the architect. We were astonished when, after we addressed the man who opened the door as Monsieur Hargrove, he replied politely, "Pardon, Jim will do." He had the strange accent that Americans acquire after living a long time abroad, particularly in Britain. Jim was originally from the Northwest, but after military service in Germany and marriage to a Frenchwoman, he spent most of the following years in Scotland and France. He lives now at the château, which had been converted into a hotel. His wife, Catherine, who looked like a bohemian scat singer, dressed in skintight black turtleneck and stretch pants, was the hotel manager. Jim supervised ongoing renovations and the care of the grounds. When clients disrupted his hotel routine, he transformed his wife's business office into a makeshift *cabinet d'architecture*. In spite of this odd arrangement, the château provided an impressive environment for our consultations.

Well into his fifties, Jim was a charming, slightly overweight man, with a Dutch-boy haircut and dark, neatly trimmed beard. He seemed to smoke constantly. His French was not strong, relying mainly on ruthless attempts at a language he thought resembled it. He was able to communicate through earnestness, "ay"-sound endings, and a handful of technical nouns. I knew his difficulties all too intimately, trying to acquire a new language late in life. Jim collaborated with Monsieur Loiseau, a Paris-based architect whom we saw just once on the first site visit at the presbytery. Loiseau, a small, expressive man, spoke with his head slightly tilted, trying unsuccessfully to keep his own smoke out of his eyes. Though it seemed hardly possible, Monsieur Loiseau smoked even more than Jim.

I suspect that flattery is a standard sales ploy of all architects, but I also think that the beauty and potential of our pre-Revolutionary building genuinely intrigued Jim and Monsieur Loiseau. They saw the grandeur and the detail that bespoke the original curé's ambitions. Monsieur Loiseau switched eloquently between French and English, explaining to us how the house had been built, how fine the woodwork was, and how unusually large the windows were. Meanwhile, Jim barked ideas in his made-up French, which no one really understood until he translated them into English. His convivial colleague listened to him while carefully inspecting the *grenier*. They both characterized our highly esteemed Deluche as a criminal for installing large supporting beams along the length of the house. The beams were unnecessary and would interfere with the lines of Sheetrock if the roof was insulated and finished off. "Oh, no, no, no, this is dreadful. What a shame." We were stung by such comments because of our strong sense of loyalty to the man who had rescued us during our *polyplaque* crises and seemed so capable in his restoration of the roof.

The tour finished on the terrace, where my mother had put out salted nuts and a cold bottle of Pouilly-Fumé. Jim thought we should install three dormers overlooking the place de l'Église and two large *portes-fenêtres,* window doors, on the garden side. On the north facade, in the small room over the kitchen, we could install a large window where there had originally been an opening for storing grain. Jim refused even to discuss Velux or a shed dormer, dismissing the former as hideous, the latter as nontraditional.

"And at the end of the day"—one of Jim's favorite expressions—"an application including Velux or a shed dormer would be refused out of hand by the Office of Historical Monuments."

Monsieur Loiseau, his cigarette a permanent fixture in his mouth, nodded in agreement. Their respect for the presbytery and their commitment to maintaining the integrity of old buildings won over all of us, though my mother thought the presbytery fine just as it was.

Jim promised to have drawings by the following weekend. I told him that was great for me because I was leaving for the States in two weeks. At the same time, I confessed a half-crazy conviction that the plane would crash just when I was beginning to really enjoy life. Ordinarily, I expect people to laugh at such silliness, but James P. Hargrove launched into a description of a 707 crash he'd survived in Alaska and how he had heroically dragged passengers out of the wreckage in twenty-below-zero weather.

A 707 crash. In Alaska. At twenty below. I had never met an aircrash survivor before, and here was one, all in one piece, as if nothing had ever happened, a man who clearly smoked, ate, and drank too much, a man who practiced the profession of architecture in France even though he couldn't speak French well. He had chutzpah. It was impossible not to like him, an architect who had saved people's lives. I took him once again around the grounds for a series of Polaroid shots.

The next weekend we met at the château to look at Jim's drawings. Instead of meeting in the manager's office, we were led to the hotel bar, where we were served wine by Catherine, as always in her beatnik outfit. She confessed that she was suffering through a hangover after celebrating her fiftieth birthday into the morning hours. The room was eccentrically decorated, with Asian paneling around the bar while, in the center, a large glass table was supported on the wings of a massive brass eagle. We were in the lounge area, where the couches were black leather. Jim showed us his drawings of the presbytery, first the facades east and west as they existed and then as he envisioned them with dormers and *portes-fenêtres*. Next he showed us details of the dormers, with three-sided capucine roofs, a front surface of tiles following the slope of the roof. The detailing around the windows resembled the cut-stone blocks on the corners of the house and the church. The dormers with *portes-fenêtres* in back ennobled the long, low facade. Undeniably, Jim presented us with a marvelous plan, its elements entirely in harmony with the spirit of the house.

"We can't afford it!" Mary blurted out in a rush of sensible panic. "Maybe we could just have a few dormers built and put the rest off for a year or two. Or maybe we could just submit a dossier for a *permis de construire*. Maybe we just need to think about it."

I could see that Jim was unprepared for such a setback. He dropped his head a bit, narrowed his eyes slightly, and spoke as if Mary were a foolish little girl, hysterical over nothing.

"Look, the longer you wait, the more it will cost you. Hence, at the end of the day, it is better to absorb the cost now and enjoy the space now rather than to wait and pay more. What can you do with a few dormers?"

"Maybe we should just put in the window in the study."

Jim shook his head and said, "Fine, but at the end of the day, you want to keep the larger goal in mind. Each time you bring in workers for a job, it costs you. Materials, workers, time, my time. Hence, you lose in the long run."

How strange to hear those transitional words and phrases. I kept seeing "at the end of the day" on our terrace, the sun burning through the treetops in the *charmille*. Like my mother, I have an unruly mind. The larger goal has always managed to escape me.

I said, "I'll be leaving in a few days. Why don't we just submit the *dossier* to the *mairie* for the construction permit? That'll give us time to think."

I could see that Mary was relieved. "At the end of the day," a country house is no investment. Hence, we'd never get the money back out of it in the event of disaster. Jim had clearly been prepared to bring in contractors, plumbers, and electricians to give estimates. If nothing else, he knew that his design was beautiful and that, when executed, it would serve him well in getting other jobs. Still, we were committed at least to having the *dossier* accepted, and then we'd have two years to begin the work.

The next day Mary and I walked down the rue de la Montagne to visit the *mairie* and see what was involved in making an application for a *permis de construire*. Jim had informed us that we would need a map of the Haut-Bourg showing our property and the *cadastre* (land-survey register) numbers for our land parcels.

We were greeted by the efficient and friendly Madame Bernard, the mayor's secretary, who had taken it upon herself to be my mother's conscience when it came to French administrative matters: namely, acquiring a *carte de séjour*, legal permission to stay in the country. After two years of missing this or that document from a bank, insurance company, retirement fund, or official translator, my mother would say, "Screw them!" Madame Bernard would call Mary at work, exasperated with my mother, since she hadn't picked up her *récépissé*, which gives her temporary permission to stay in the country while she awaits her official permission, a one-year *carte de séjour*. Invariably, the *carte de séjour* arrives one month before the process must be reinitiated, and meanwhile the *préfecture de police* adds to the list of requirements a few more obscure documents, eliciting another "Screw them!" and another concerned call to the Pasteur Institute from Madame Bernard.

Our visit was, of course, for a different matter, and we explained to the helpful Madame Bernard that we needed all the materials to apply for a *permis de construire* from the Bureau of Historical Monuments. Madame Bernard, a tall, handsome woman, with dark hair cut shoulder length, moved knowingly about the office collecting various forms, telling us exactly how to compile the materials, with drawings, photographs, maps, and verbal descriptions. She then took us into a larger adjacent room, one where small meetings are held and the large *registre de cadastre* kept. The *cadastre* was a meter-square bound assemblage of documents defining property and tax responsibilities. Madame Bernard wrote down, from an index, that we owned parcel *374*, which included the house, the stables, and the *pigeonnier*, and parcel *373*, the orchard.

When she opened to the maps, Mary said, "We also own the *charmille*. This piece here. Three seventy-eight." She ran her finger down the odd, narrow strip of land between two featureless blocks of white representing Bougé's pastures.

"I'm afraid three seventy-eight is not listed in your name."

"No, our property goes like this, in an L," Mary asserted. "It's enclosed in fences and there is a staircase, right here, at the end of the orchard."

We were all looking down at the map, with blocks that were buildings, blocks that were fields, and blocks that were communal roads.

"I'm sure there is some mistake," Mary said.

After double-checking the register for *propriété foncière*, taxable land, Madame Bernard said, "Parcel three seventy-eight belongs to the *famille* d'Harmelle."

Mary protested, "But it's the *charmille du presbytère*, enclosed by fences. It's of no use to the Harmelles. No one can get in."

Madame Bernard, kind as always, advised us to look over the *promesse de vente* and the *acte de vente* to see if there had been an oversight and said we should contact the *notaires* involved in the sale. She assured us that this sort of confusion is not unheard of. But I remembered when the neatly dressed Madame Brissot, our clever real estate agent, took us through the presbytery and across the grounds to the *charmille*. The strange and beautiful path had been presented as the final enticement. What place could have been more appropriate, for our verbal offer to buy, than the presbytery's half-wild *charmille*? Madame Malaud, who had bought the presbytery from the Harmelles, had never owned the *charmille* and must have known it. In the *acte de vente*, the whole property was described as a *jardin clos*, a fenced garden that would include the *charmille*. But nowhere is parcel 378 listed in the legal documents. We were left with no more than our word.

We immediately asked advice from our French friends, who echoed Madame Bernard's qualification that these things are not unheard of. In French villages, parcels of land have a disturbing propensity for scattering themselves, and one of the abundant sources of local antipathy is the sorting out of ownership and access rights. These sorts of problems are handled by the *notaires*, the lawyers in the French legal system who occupy themselves exclusively with property transactions, either through sales or inheritance. Our French friends advised us to forget that the issue had ever come to our attention and enjoy the *charmille* as before. Certainly, the Harmelle family, mainly Paris bankers and huge landowners, wouldn't bother themselves over such a small parcel. It was incomprehensible that the *charmille du presbytère* had become marooned at the edge of the Haut-Bourg. We understood that Madame Malaud and l'Immoblière Continentale had acted in bad faith, but we were laughably naive, itself a crime in France, where wiliness is widely considered a virtue. We got what we deserved. While Mary seemed willing to take the advice of our friends, I felt that we had to have a legal right to use and maintain the property. What would happen if Coco were injured or if one of his fires spread or if a tree fell on Bougé's fence in a storm? I hadn't overcome my American paranoia over liabilities. Besides, I adored the *charmille*.

We began our campaign to recover the *charmille* by getting advice from a friend's sister who happened to be a *notaire*. She exclaimed on hearing our story, *"C'est classique."* It happens all the time. "Surely the *notaires* can sort it out among themselves." We were advised to contact our *notaire;* in turn, our *notaire* would contact the *notaires* of Madame Malaud and the Harmelles. We felt a great sense of relief—the whole matter was a mere technicality among *notaires*. We called Madame Jacquin of Régnier, Régnier, Hervet, Bricard and Associates and sent her a formal letter along with all the materials necessary to proceed with the matter of the lost *charmille*. Madame Jacquin researched the sale and confirmed that the *charmille* was indeed the property of the Harmelles. She then sent formal letters to the other *notaires*, Maître DeJean de la Batie representing the Malauds, and Maître Savy representing the Harmelles. These formal letters concerning our lost *charmille* were ignored, requiring us to impose on Madame Jacquin each month to send follow-up letters. The other *notaires* appeared to have calculated that there was no money to be made; thus the affair could only be a terrible nuisance—better just to ignore it. Finally, after six months, Maître Dejean de la Batie was moved to write a formal letter informing Madame Jacquin that the *parcelle* in question had never been acquired by Madame Malaud and it would be worthwhile for Madame Jacquin to make herself known to Maître Savy, *notaire* of the Harmelles. He would remain at her disposal to supply any relevant information. Signed, "Your Very Devoted Colleague."

Even after a year, Maître Savy still hadn't responded. Mary thought that maybe he'd died or retired, but we looked him up in Bonny-sur-Loire, and he was still listed. The truth was that he couldn't care less about our case. After all, the Harmelles didn't retain his services to have him give away their land. Mary and I decided that our only hope was to write directly to the Marquis Jacques d'Harmelle, the one family member who was still living *en permanence* at their château. But first I thought that we should talk to the mayor and get his advice on the whole matter. We assumed that he knew the marquis personally and that, in the best scenario, he would intercede on our behalf, recognizing the injustice done us, the Americans who brought the decaying presbytery back to life.

We called Madame Bernard to make a Saturday appointment

with the mayor concerning the ownership of *la charmille du presbytère*. Even a year later Madame Bernard remembered the misunderstanding. She gladly wrote us in for 10:00 A.M. and took the opportunity to complain about my mother's neglecting to pick up her latest temporary permission to stay in the country. "It is a required legal document. Please make her understand the importance." When we dutifully delivered the message, my mother, as was her habit, said, "Nonsense. They aren't going to drive a fat old lady to the border."

Mary and I showed up on the dot with our stack of letters and documents, carefully ordered to reveal a tragic conspiracy of indifference on the part of the various *notaires* and possible misrepresentation by Madame Malaud and l'Immoblière Continentale. Mary had duplicated all the documents, including the relevant pages of the forty-page-long *acte de vente*, should the mayor wish to have copies to study. Madame Bernard was saved the trouble of announcing us; Monsieur le Maire graciously came out of his office to greet us himself. In truth, he didn't seem at all busy.

The mayor was a large man in his sixties with a well-groomed mustache. His hair was combed straight back, though he was partly bald, and he wore large wire-rimmed glasses, which tended to magnify his sensible-looking blue eyes. Above all, he seemed relaxed and convivial as Mary retold, in detail, how the poor *charmille* had become disenfranchised. Mary then handed him the *acte de vente* and confessed that we hadn't demanded that a surveyor verify the land described in the deed. The mayor offered a sympathetic half smile and several thoughtful nods, meaning, on the surface, yes, these things can happen, but his inner voice was saying that we were poor naïfs who had been *roulés*.

He proceeded to read through the *acte de vente*, arriving at the page that contained the list of previous owners. He read out each name, which actually was a composite of up to four names that ended often with "Comte d'Harmelle" and "Marquis d'Harmelle." With some of the names, he related anecdotes. One married unhappily, the divorce causing a family scandal. Another died years back, meaning that the property passed to her children. The count could be difficult, as we had already heard. The Harmelles still possessed a considerable fortune and thus had family squabbles. *C'est typique!*

Finally, we asked the mayor if, in his opinion, it would be a good idea to write directly to the Marquis Jacques d'Harmelle and explain our situation. Mildly encouraging, the mayor responded that the marquis was generally a reasonable man, but we should take care to be diplomatic and use the accepted forms, showing respect for the marquis's position. Since we were Americans, the mayor assumed that such behavior would be alien to us, that we would not know how to pay proper homage in addressing Monsieur le Marquis.

In the end, while Monsieur le Maire was more than amiable, it was clear that he couldn't help us in the matter, and the conversation drifted to village affairs and his own miseries in dealing with property issues and the regional administration. The *boucher* had gone bankrupt, and an *entrepreneur* wanted to buy his shop to set up a high-class, prepared-foods and catering business for the tourists. But in bankruptcy cases, all property rights become tied up in the courts for years. Despite all his years in administration, the mayor still became exasperated by the inefficiency of the courts. In addition, the town wanted to purchase Monsieur Guillon's *épicerie* to use as a tourist center, but he was asking too much. The Guillons had abruptly left Rogny after Monsieur Guillon, the Richard Gere look-alike, had an ill-advised romantic adventure in the village.

The mayor made it clear to us that he was retired, and having been a French *fonctionnaire*, he was not being paid for all the headaches he endured on behalf of the village. His grandchildren had asked him, "You've worked so hard all your life. Haven't you earned your repose?" But the mayor confessed that he wouldn't know what to do with himself. At that point, we rose from our chairs and thanked the good man.

Late that afternoon, Mary sat at the table in the *salle de séjour* composing a letter to Monsieur le Marquis d'Harmelle. The letter was polite but earnest in tone, urging the modern-day nobleman to take notice of our predicament, the likes of which have afflicted villages for centuries. In the first two paragraphs, Mary, with appropriate economy, named the principals and related the critical events involved in our misunderstanding. The letter ends with a strong logical appeal:

> *We want to move this situation forward as quickly as possible because we are conserving the trees in the* charmille, *which is not our property. It is a delicate situation. We are entirely at your disposition should you believe that we can help resolve this problem.*
>
> *I thank you for your attention and ask you to believe, Monsieur le Marquis, the expression of my sincere esteem.*

Mary had her French carefully checked by Jean-Louis, who had been a proofreader all his life, and the letter was sent to the Harmelles' château on Monday. On Friday, we received a letter from the marquis. It consisted of three sentences that confirmed that the Harmelles possessed the parcel of land in question. Since the land was jointly owned, it would be necessary to consult the rest of the family. The letter finished with "While awaiting a response, I beg of you, madame, to accept the expression of my sincerest best wishes."

Our hearts dropped with the final sentence full of formulaic French politeness. To reach a consensus on what to do about the *charmille* ensconced behind the ancient presbytery, the marquis was obliged to contact each member of the family. Was there any chance that they were even on speaking terms? When, years earlier, there had been buyers interested in the ancient presbytery, the Harmelles hadn't been able to agree on selling it, and so it fell into disrepair. We suddenly understood that we were entering a land dispute with a famous and noble French family, a dispute that might go unsettled in our lifetimes. Polluche, the first curé, battled with the wood merchants over leasing church property for storing logs, and he felt compelled to reconfirm church holdings to assert his legal control. And now, appealing to the Marquis d'Harmelle, we sensed the intricacies of the old social order still infused in the life of our village. Abbé Camus wrote that, once a year, the Harmelles invited the entire parish to the château for a picnic. The Harmelles provided the château grounds, the food, and a generous supply of wine. During the event, the marquis and marquise would appear on a balcony and offer a toast to the villagers, then withdraw from the festivities. That was back in the fifties. Now the property is strictly off-limits.

In Rogny, the notion of ownership is an odd one for us. The presbytery is a principal house in the village, both historically and in appearance. We still say, from time to time, that it belongs to

Coco, as do the church and the place de l'Église. He is the provincial of a forsaken order. In the same sense, the *charmille* belongs to us. It is difficult to imagine the count, the marquis, and the sixteenth-*arrondissement* bankers gathering in the *charmille* to enjoy its sad old trees and rather worthless mushrooms.

The Last Curé

In the midst of our property dispute, as if to underline how transitory ownership or occupancy is, or even our stay on earth, we learned that Père Jo had died. We had made numerous imaginary visits with him but hadn't arranged actually to see him during his convalescence outside Avallon. I believe he would have welcomed us with real joy. We missed that blessing.

Père Jo had two funerals, one in l'Église de Joux-la-Ville and the other in l'Église de Saint-Loup, both overflowing with colleagues, parishioners, and friends. The first was the more formal, with thirty priests gathered before the simple wooden *cercueil* that stood near the altar, while Monseigneur François Tricard, *vicaire général*, presided over the mass and the Abbé Jean Briffaut delivered the homily. I read the homily, which was reprinted in a local paper.

L'abbé begins, "Père Jo summons us this last time to be with him for his departure. His little silhouette has softened to make a place with another presence." L'abbé calls on the congregation to reflect on the Christian name Joseph and compares Père Jo, in his evangelical simplicity, stoicism, and generosity, to Saint Joseph, the head of the sacred family. Anyone familiar with Père Jo when he was younger probably envisioned Saint Joseph, in a soccer jersey, leading the Holy Family into a bar.

Ariane told my mother that Père Jo asked to be buried in the cemetery of Rogny, the village to which he had remained most attached. Everyone in the Haut-Bourg planned to attend the funeral celebration, and my mother decided that she should go as well. After all, she was one of the first full-time residents in the presbytery since Père Jo, and she felt that her attendance was a fitting tribute to his legacy. Besides, she was curious. I asked her to describe the funeral to me; I was curious, too.

She reported that she had been caught up in a crowd of people who came from all over the region. She had never seen so many people at l'Église de Saint-Loup, which had been filled with donated flowers. There were five priests, including the curé from Bléneau, each one giving a short eulogy and participating in the celebration of the mass. The mayor sat in front, as did Madame Bernard. Père Jo was at rest inside his *cercueil,* just off to the right of the altar where he himself had spoken the last words for so many grandparents, parents, husbands, and wives.

My mother said that from where she was sitting far back on the right, she could look out into the bright August light and see Coco in the crowd outside the Romanesque portal. The church couldn't accommodate everyone; besides, Coco was antireligious and would never enter the church during mass. Still, for his friend Père Jo, Coco put on his black cowboy hat and stood for a couple of minutes, peering through the portal, his face lit up as always. Finally, though, the only funeral that interested Coco was his own, so back he went to his house to stack wood for the coming autumn.

I often wonder what sorts of neighbors they made, the blasphemer and the priest, drinking together and exchanging friendly insults, both living on small means in single rooms. I'm sure that Père Jo had depended on Coco, as he did on the community itself, for a thousand favors to keep the presbytery and the church going. Coco liked to make himself useful. His charity was not of a religious sort. I'm sure that Père Jo, a friend to believers and nonbelievers alike, would not pass harsh judgment on his irreverent friend.

When Père Jo still inhabited the presbytery, the two-story house across the *place* had been a bar. The owners have since converted it into a residence and put it on the market for a fortune, so it sits unlived in, year after year. Monsieur Marteau has the keys and once gave us a tour of the renovated bar. Forever amused by the wayward curé, Marteau said, "Père Jo was a rebel. After he finished mass, he and everyone else would file over here for *un verre*."

Through the windows of the former bar, you can see the presbytery, the long stone building with white shutters wide open. How convenient for Père Jo to walk across the *place* and join his *copains*, drinking in the evening. The *place* must have been lively in those days. No doubt the wobbly curé, making his way to the garden gate at the end of the evening, cut a familiar figure in it.

The same curé was loaded into the back of a black station wagon, and the funeral party shuffled past our *pigeonnier*, along the garden wall, and around the Liberty Tree to the rue Gabriel-Landy, passing the former bar. It was a walk that during his twenty years as the curé de Rogny, Père Jo made hundreds of times, burying a neighbor, parishioner, or friend. My mother did not follow the crowd to the cemetery but instead watched from the kitchen window as the last stragglers in the funeral party disappeared into the midday heat.

Six months later Ariane complained, "It's a disgrace! He doesn't even have a marker. Just dirt, *c'est tout*. He didn't get a proper burial."

It was true. I went to the cemetery several times that winter, looking for Père Jo's grave. The village was honored to have Père Jo in the cemetery, but no one wanted to pay for a stone with his name on it. He became one of Rogny's unmarked dead, like those evicted from the original church graveyard in 1828. Unless you had followed the black station wagon down the rue du Haut-Bois and watched as the *cercueil* was lowered, you wouldn't know where to pay tribute. Numerous unnamed patches of ground had funeral plaques, but no "Memories," "Regrets," or "Sorrows" betrayed the whereabouts of Rogny's notorious last curé.

Polluche lived for ten years in the presbytery that he had fought so hard to have constructed in 1754. No doubt the ambitious Polluche was eventually named curé of a more substantial parish, and chances are he didn't live to see the entire social structure of France implode, sending the likes of the Harmelles into hiding to emerge much later, clinging pridefully to their inherited titles. The clergy themselves were guillotined or turned into outcasts if they did not vow their allegiance to the Civil Constitution. Now France has a social system that empowers the likes of Coco, who in Polluche's time, a time of witch burnings and other persecution, would have been a pariah.

Through these vicissitudes of French history and society, the presbytery has remained basically unchanged, from the time of Polluche's original design until the death of the last curé. That winter, however, Mary and I decided to change it. We wanted our own space in the *grenier,* and true to our impulses, which had led us to buy the presbytery in the first place, we called Jim Hargrove to tell him we were ready to go ahead with the installation of dormers and insulation of the roof.

Jim was more than a little surprised to hear from us; we had bailed out so abruptly, Mary panicking over the expense, and more than a year had passed. We hadn't bothered to file for a *permis de construire,* simply paying Jim for his services and telling him we'd call when we were prepared to go through with the project. On a Saturday afternoon, we drove up the hill to the château, to find Catherine furious and Jim perplexed over the negligence of a villager they'd hired to tend the sheep. We all stood at the edge of a rampart with a view over the valley and the lower pasture hundreds of feet below.

"Is that a dead sheep?" Mary asked.

Catherine couldn't control herself. *"C'est exact!"* That's the problem. "That sheep has been dead for two weeks, lying there just as you see it. We pay a man to look after those sheep. And where is he? He is nowhere! Drunk. You can be sure of it! I'm going to call the *gendarmes.*"

Jim offered to go into town and look for the delinquent shepherd after our meeting.

Mary and I were arrested by the view. The winter grass was deep green in the shadows from the leafless trees, but the sun stayed low and cast a sad yellow finish over the landscape as a whole. In the center of the view was the dead sheep, as if it were an emblem of the dormant world.

Throughout our meeting with Jim, Catherine kept muttering to herself, "The sheep has been dead for two weeks. Two weeks. *Mon Dieu.*"

We were once again in the manager's office of the château, and Jim plunged into the details of the work. He had received only one estimate for the construction, including digging up the old floor of broken tiles and pouring a level surface. Monsieur Boisgibault, whose *entreprise* was in neighboring Dammarie-sur-Loing, had submitted the bid. Our hearts dropped. Deluche was his neighbor, and they were probably bitter rivals.

Mary protested, "Shouldn't we compare *entreprises*? If they compete, we could get a lower estimate."

Jim answered stubbornly, "I've worked with most of the *entrepreneurs* in the area, and I always choose according to the job. At the end of the day, you don't want to undermine trust by forcing competition. Take my word. Monsieur Boisgibault is ideal. He is eager for the job, and he's the mayor's friend. Hence, he can speed up the application for a *permis*."

We still felt uneasy and asked to see examples of Monsieur Boisgibault's work. Jim explained that this would be difficult to arrange because it meant setting up appointments and intruding on people's lives. He provided us with some photographs of gates, walls, and small buildings that Boisgibault's *entreprise* had constructed, but nothing that involved an old structure or dormers. Still, we couldn't deny that it was clean, reputable-looking work. We told Jim we'd go ahead with the project and Monsieur Boisgibault as long as we could set an absolute ceiling for the total cost; we wanted none of the unanticipated expenses that typically crop up each week in big projects, doubling the original estimate. We were guarding our cash reserves to install central heating, and we made the blunder of asking Jim's opinion on whether gas or oil would be better.

"For an old house, like the presbytery, oil is better. The heat is more ambient," Jim asserted.

"More what?" asked Mary.

"More ambient. Gas works better for new houses because they are better insulated. But old houses are drafty and the rooms tend to heat unevenly, so oil is better." Jim held his hands out level, trying to show uniform ambient heat.

"Wait a minute. The water circulates through the same pipes and radiators, right? So it's just a matter of how the water is heated, gas or oil," Mary said incredulously.

When Jim shifted to problems of condensation from gas heat, we shifted to "whatever." Catherine continued to curse the hired drunk for leaving the dead sheep in the pasture. Mary and I left the château with our confidence shaken and an appointment to meet Monsieur Boisgibault to sign a final contract for the work. We asked Jean-Louis if he knew who Monsieur Boisgibault was and if we could trust him; we learned that Boisgibault was president of the hunting association for the entire department of the Loiret and had a reputation for being a brute with his workers and for not finishing work on time. He advised us to insist on a strict schedule for completion. We'd also learned from Catherine that Boisgibault was a womanizer; she said, in a sort of flattering way, "Oh, he's not so bad."

The following Saturday Mary and I prepared ourselves for a meeting with Satan himself. We wrote down a list of questions to clarify points in the estimate along with a few additional requests. We picked up Jim at the château at a quarter to ten and drove to Dammarie, only sixteen kilometers away, on roads winding through the winter fields with their remnant stalks of corn and sunflowers. We pulled up to a small warehouse with an office attached and were greeted by Monsieur Boisgibault, a bald, husky man, who looked as if he suffered from hyperthyroidism, since his eyes bulged slightly, giving him a bit of a bulldog look. Over fifty, he wore a tight leather jacket and blue jeans, and his hands and complexion testified to decades of hard labor in the roofing and masonry business.

We walked into his office past a billboard full of tacked-up photographs of men holding large dead fish, mainly pike and *sandre,* both of which are plentiful in the local rivers and lakes. We were all offered seats around Boisgibault's desk, and his blond secretary, wearing her winter coat, quickly distributed contracts for the work. No one bothered to turn on the heat or lights in the office, and Jim opened the proceedings in French, which meant that no one understood him. Finally, forced into English, he said, "These are the terms that everyone has agreed to in principle. Hence, we need only to go through them and sign."

Mary turned to Boisgibault and said in French, "My husband and I have made this list of points that we want clarified." Boisgibault put his hands together and nodded tolerantly. This was not what he wanted to hear. His secretary, who turned out to be his wife, had a stew on the stove, undoubtedly of some unfortunate creature whose days on earth had been ended by Monsieur Boisgibault himself.

We went through the list: Would there be insulation along the eaves? Would the north wall be polyplaqued? Would the roof tiles be cleaned and treated? Could he use angled tiles instead of cement for the peaks and corners of the capucine dormers? Would he take special care to place the scaffolding so as not to destroy the garden? Would he adhere to a strict time schedule?

Boisgibault, persevering through our long list, agreed to each request, *"Pas de problème, madame."* At each item, Mary turned to me and asked, *"D'accord?"* to which I nodded yes. Mary was playing the tough negotiator and growing more confident with each capitulation. She didn't mind making Boisgibault squirm a little bit. Jim was caught off guard. He was still on flooring material while we were talking about antimoss products. Boisgibault's wife was quick with figures, her stew no doubt burning, and adjustments were made to our satisfaction. We were assured that we'd all celebrate the completion of the work with a Fourth of July barbecue.

Mary looked Boisgibault straight in the eyes: "You are sure that you won't hurt my flowers." After Mary extracted *"pas de problème, madame"* several times on this score, pens were passed around, and we surrendered the first check. We walked out past the glossy photos of dead fish, and in the parking lot Boisgibault asked if we'd *prendre un pot,* which we declined, appreciatively. We have not succumbed to the country tradition of drinking on weekend mornings. Jim, however, accepted graciously.

The next day Jim's nose was out of joint. The signing was supposed to have been a formality, and the details should have been sorted out with him in advance. Also, in such business dealings, one is expected to accept a drink as a gesture of goodwill and cheer all around. Perhaps we had been naughty children, but at the meeting we had realized that we could work directly with Boisgibault, who had gained our respect. He had made a number of large concessions that we might not have achieved by relying on Jim, and he was eager to have the job and was certain that it could be done well.

The application for a *permis de construire* sailed through the *mairie* and the Office of Historical Monuments. The mayor lent it full support. In the letter of approval, the only stipulation was that we use no material brighter than *blanc cassé*, off-white, so that new elements would harmonize with the old. The work was scheduled for early spring, when the large hawks return to Eastern Europe and the cranes and songbirds come back from their exotic travels.

The work began in mid-April, as did the worst rains we'd had in years. The workers arrived at 8:30 sharp each morning, in a cacophony of hammering, power saws, and cement mixers, all of which meant that my mother would suffer sleep deficit. Boisgibault's crew, who resembled a sodden, but energetic, band of Wild West desperadoes in the cold drenching rain, had invaded her life. The men, all different ages and sizes, looked hard—they smoked, barely talked, focused only on the miserable job at hand. They rarely took a break, except to piss on the side of the church. They erected scaffolding across both the front and back facades, with large tents of clear plastic over the holes cut through the roof. Remarkably, they were able to position the legs of the scaffolding so that they landed between a clematis and a peony or between a camellia and a tree rose. Mary's stern look into Monsieur Boisgibault's eyes had achieved its intended results. The desperadoes treated her defenseless flowers as if they were land mines.

Most of the inhabitants of the place de l'Église had no idea that such a large construction project had been planned for the presbytery, and nothing since Coco's brush with death aroused such intense interest. The three new front dormers would change the whole aspect of the *place*, and the inhabitants were wondering, as were we, if the project would turn out dreadfully. Whenever the rain let up at all, a symposium including Jean-Louis, Marteau, and Bougé would form to discuss the skills of Boisgibault and his men and the amazing speed with which the dormers appeared. Our neighbors watched the large red forklift that had taken up residence on the *place* haul up bricks and vats of cement. They would point and judge, squabbling among themselves about whether the dormers should have visible brick or corners that looked like the cut stone around the windows and on the corners of the rest of the house. The rain would start again, dispersing the symposium, but Boisgibault's men worked on through the soaking rain until 5:30, when they vanished, leaving the forklift huddled beside the church and large sheets of plastic flapping in the wind.

After the first week, Mary and I arrived to find the cement forms of two dormers already in place and the third bricked in and well under way. Boisgibault arrived in his small Renault truck with a springer spaniel in the passenger seat, certainly his hunting accomplice in the field. Greeting him in the unrelenting rain, Mary and I made no secret of how impressed we were with his work. Our estimation of the heavy, bald man with bulging eyes had changed completely, and each week we would follow him to the *grenier,* to make an inspection of the work together. He complained fiercely about the heavy April rains and cursed the four holidays coming up in May. He went out on the scaffolding and pushed over the great pillows of rainwater that had gathered in the plastic, and there were five buckets to be emptied where water was collected from various leaks. We got the impression that we were on an inverted ship; somehow the captain managed to keep it from sinking into the sky.

We pitied Boisgibault's men for having to work in such conditions, and we told Boisgibault that my mother had offered to let the men warm up downstairs or use the toilet anytime. She'd make coffee or give them lunch, whatever they'd like.

Boisgibault responded bluntly, "They are accustomed to the

hard life." We took this to mean that they would just as soon piss on the church.

True to her nature, my mother was not easily deterred. One way or another, she was going to be hospitable; she bought several cases of beer and parked in front of Coco's house, then rapped on the door to ask Coco to give the beer to the workmen. Coco couldn't have been more delighted, so during the following weeks the men would come and go from his house, picking up a beer. Because they wouldn't stop the construction, except to piss on the church, the upstairs would fill up with beer bottles. When the rains stopped, they couldn't complain much about the conditions, except for the times when Christabel, in an explosion of snarls, managed to corner a desperado and we'd have to come apologetically to his rescue. The skies turned blue and sunny, Mary's garden flourished under the scaffolding, and the desperadoes remained grim but busy.

Mary and I were so encouraged by the work that we decided to go to a local *ferronnerie d'art* to have wrought-iron balustrades made for the *portes-fenêtres*. We walked into a large, dark shed where an enormous iron staircase loomed over muscular men hammering glowing metal bars. The whole space was carbonized, including the men, sweating and streaked with oil as they reheated a bar in charcoal pits. I wondered what level of hell this was, with pornographic centerfolds hung at each station. The photos were not art prints but hard-core porn. The poses of the models were designed to torment. Like Dante's victims, the men would never achieve gratification as they pounded the hot, softened metal, their faces grim.

Mary didn't even notice them. *"On voudrait parler avec quelqu'un pour faire faire des balustrades."*

One of the poor inmates shrugged, offering only, *"Le patron n'est pas là."* The boss isn't here. It seemed no one wanted to help us. The idea was not to sell ironwork but just to suffer the charcoal pits and the select group of pornographic tormentors.

We left a number but never received a call. We visited several other *ferronneries d'art,* each one with pornography covering the walls, all the rest carbonized. We were asked to come back, or it turned out that the prices were out of the question. We finally drove fifty kilometers to Dordive and found Monsieur Robert. His shed had only calendars with nudes, each worker keeping track of his own days and weeks. Monsieur Robert pulled down a book full of classic patterns and said, "Take your time. Let me know what you choose." He went off for coffee.

Amid the clatter, grinding, and hammering of metal, we found a simple, though attractive, pattern that cost a fortune and was clearly not what one might expect on an ancient presbytery; nevertheless, it was what we wanted. When Monsieur Robert learned we were Americans, he proudly announced that his son had been away for six months in the States, doing ironwork renovation on New York's City Hall. We wondered which was more incredible—that Monsieur Robert's son was renovating New York's City Hall or that we were being deafened in a forge in a French village no one had ever heard of.

The front dormers were finally finished, with capucine roofs of high-quality carpentry. When the symposium gathered, there were no longer arguments or criticisms. All the members agreed that the work was *très, très bien fait.* Monsieur Bougé called the presbytery a *colonie de vacances* because he imagined that each of the five dormers represented a separate room where kids could stay for a country vacation. Jean-Louis thought of it as a large American loft because we had mentioned to him that we wanted one room with vast open space. Coco would stand in front of the house and intone proudly, *"Mon château! Mon petit Versailles!"* Then he rubbed his fingers together, meaning "big expense." We realized that, because the presbytery was such a prominent building in the village, Boisgibault and Jim were using it as a showcase.

On that third Sunday, a terrible wave of guilt washed over me when I went upstairs and watched through one of the new dormers as the parishioners arrived for their eleven-o'clock mass. They were taken unawares by the changes in the historic old building, and each one stopped to read Boisgibault's large plaque in front of the house displaying our names, the *permis* number, and a brief description of the work to be done.

For a moment, I felt that I had trespassed onto their personal landscape, that I had violated a fixture of their past and present. I thought for a moment: This is the sort of thing Americans do to another culture. They do what they want, and the presbytery is no longer a presbytery, the house where a curé once lived and still might, if interest in the church hadn't all but evaporated. It seemed selfish to want so much space for oneself, to make a religious building into something it wasn't intended to be, something more elegant, although in truth there is no shortage of elegant presbyteries in France. But ours is in a small village, and I watched the elderly parishioners try to make out our names and give the building a good look-over before heading in for mass to repeat prayers and sing hymns under the great fissures in the plaster. Perhaps we should have spent our days researching the architecture of old presbyteries and restored the building as authentically as possible.

When Boisgibault finished the dormers with *portes-fenêtres* in the back, we had two extraordinary views, the more dramatic one looking out over Mary's border garden, the orchard, and the valley.

The other, more intimate, gave a view over the fountain garden, the *pigeonnier*, and the alley along the church. It also provided an angle from which to see across Bougé's pasture and the length of the disputed *charmille*. We might have changed the presbytery, but the building had come to new, full life, after suffering centuries of impoverishment. It now ennobled the place de l'Église.

As once Coco had abruptly taken me up into the bell tower, Mary and I brought him to the *grenier* one late afternoon to see the nearly finished work. We were sure he would be impressed by the quality of the construction, the different views, the large clean space so well lit. We wanted to include him in our projects, but, in fact, he seemed strange in the new space, as if he had been invited for a moment into a future where the old, dusty, leaky, spider-filled spaces of the past had been buried in Sheetrock and cement. He went to the *porte-fenêtre* with a view over the orchard and the valley and played sniper, picking off rabbits, Germans, and curés.

It was decided that we would have the Fourth of July barbecue to celebrate completion of the work. My mother invited Boisgibault and his desperadoes for a traditional American Independence Day meal. Meanwhile, Jim, on his own initiative, brought a grizzled, good-natured old painter around to give an estimate for finishing the work. Jim was afraid that I would do sloppy work and mar his masterpiece. In spite of all the times Mary and I were left shaking our heads in doubt, Jim had come through for us—creating a fine design, engaging the incomparable Boisgibault gang, and coming in under the cost cap. We couldn't have been happier with Jim and his work.

Some evenings I've walked upstairs and looked out the dormer with a view of the rue Gabriel-Landy. Once, some girls had put a radio in their window, had NRJ or FUN radio blaring, and were showing off moves they had seen on MTV's *Brooklyn Grind*. They were only nine or ten but had the moves down, as if they had been abducted into the heat and strut of Brooklyn—hip, gyrate, hop, step—bare, childish midriffs exposed in the evening light. How adapted to change they seemed. They'd saunter provocatively to the sidewalk when a car or motorcycle zipped past.

The same girls, along with the children from the rue des Hirondelles and the allée des Fauvettes, came knocking on the door to sell us lottery tickets. They were raising funds for school activities. Word must have circulated that the Americans were saps; we filled a drawer with slips of green and yellow paper, hoping that we wouldn't win the Ping-Pong table or ice bucket on offer. Half the fun for them was to pet Zouzou, who basked in any form of attention.

If Polluche could see his presbytery now, I'm sure he would approve of its stately presence on the *place*. After all, such architectural statements were a sign of power in the eighteenth century. Still, he would have to traverse centuries of improbable change, both technological and social, to a world of satellite dishes, John Deere combines, French rap, bare-midriffed girls dancing on the pavement, low-flying Mirages roaring by a church collapsing on its south side, a presbytery where the last curé drank and slept in the last usable room, the kitchen. The power of the Catholic religion in France has declined, but it is refreshing to think of an individual, flawed but spiritual, like Père Jo, for whom possessions were meant to be shared with the needy. I'm sure that for him the changes in the presbytery would be hardly more than a curiosity.

My mother finally got her large house, one with gardens, comfort, and beauty all around. In a sense, she had recovered the large childhood home that burned, the squirrel chewing on the wires, harbinger of unhappy early years. The paintings and furniture that survived the fire fill the *salle de séjour,* the library, and her bedroom. Mary likes to call my mother "the lady of the manor." Coco calls her *mémé,* granny. My mother fights back, inflicting filial guilt by calling herself *la bonne,* the housemaid. After three years, her friends in the States have grown frustrated. Surely this extended vacation abroad has gone on long enough. What kind of life could she possibly have, out in the unmapped French sticks?

While the workers pounded away upstairs, laying down conduits for electricity, water, and heating before pouring light cement for a level new floor, my mother teased Zouzou, the big, gentle golden retriever, commanding her to "stay" and then sneaking off and hiding in one of the rooms of the presbytery. Zouzou always broke down and searched for her. Zouzou usually found her quickly behind a door or armoire. Usually—but sometimes it seemed to her that my mother just disappeared.

The Cherry Tree

$\mathcal{M}$ore than three years before the work on the *grenier,* in the winter before my mother's arrival, we spent New Year's Eve in the cold, unfinished rooms of the presbytery. Mary's stepdaughter, Anne, and her Icelandic husband Halldor joined us for a country feast. Anne was three months pregnant, so we all felt that this New Year's Eve was more special than most. Mary isn't literally Anne's stepmother. Anne's mother had died young, and when her father died, too, she asked Mary to be her immediate family. Given a baby on the way and my mother's France-or-bust plan, the presbytery was prospectively a family place in a rural, foreign landscape. At the time, Anne thought Mary and me foolish to acquire a presbytery in a peculiar part of France. She found the house, and the region, sad. It would take several years for her to reverse her opinion.

The richly laden table seemed all the more festive juxtaposed with the unpainted walls with their tall pale crosses of taping compound. The windows were stark black with early nightfall, the glass reflecting the candles, the firelight, and a few childish strands of tinsel. For the main course, we would have pheasant from Coco: two dead birds had appeared on our sill. The hunters, already sick of eating them, were giving them away as fast as they could shoot them. With his deformed jaw, Coco himself found pheasant too much of a bother to eat. Mary went directly across the street and rapped on his door to express our gratitude—and to confess that none of us knew the first thing about plucking or cleaning pheasants.

"Ça ne fait rien. Je les préparerai. Attendez." Mary was greatly relieved when Coco took the two dead birds out of her hands and put them in the sink. His room was lit, like an office, with two white tubes of dull fluorescence. For me, he poured a *pastis* in a dirty glass that had already been sitting on the table. I figured that half the town had already stopped in for a holiday drink from the communal glass. But Coco took a clean wineglass from his cupboard and poured Mary *gros rouge*, proving himself a genteel host after all. Then, with a cheerful "ho-kay," he attacked one of the birds, vigorously ripping out feathers and making one hell of a mess in his austere, all-purpose *cuisine–salle de séjour–chambre*. Even Dan was alarmed by the down floating copiously about his nose.

Within twenty minutes, we had two cleaned pheasants. Mary blurted out apologetically, "Please, Coco, no heads!" He held one head between his fingers and pointed the beak toward himself: *"Ah, le pauvre!"* He then happily deferred, with a double beheading, to Mary's squeamishness.

As though he hadn't already been generous enough, Coco gave us a gift for the holidays, a calendar that he pulled out of a stack of *Petites Annonces,* a local advertising publication that anyone can pick up free. He was giving calendars to all his friends.

Despite the rickety old stove my mother had battled with during our wedding, we began preparing an ambitious New Year's Eve feast. Mary stuffed the birds with wild rice, walnuts, and currants and covered their skin in herb butter; Halldor peeled a pile of shallots for *confit d'échalottes*—a dish of sautéed shallots cooked in reducing vinegar and then lightly sugared. Anne and I, between sips of champagne, began opening *Fines de Claire* no. 2, the perfect size; I find nos. 1 and 00 to be *trop gourmand*. Each oyster had outer petals rimmed in black and inner ones the color of jade. The sink filled with the odor of the fresh Breton seaside. Mary set out eggs to reach room temperature and prepared the double boiler for a Grand Marnier soufflé.

Although it was inadvisable for Anne to eat raw oysters, or drink, for that matter, she couldn't possibly resist. At the end of the first course, we each had a considerable pile of shells, and there was an emptied bottle of Chassagne-Montrachet, Grandes-Ruchottes, from our producer in the Côte d'Or. We honored Coco's birds with two venerable bottles of '78 Santenay, which lasted through the course of Époisse and goat cheese, and then Mary took on the ultimate challenge of making a soufflé. Her effort, although noble, rose only to the lip of the soufflé dish. Still, Halldor flattered her: "It's like clouds of Grand Marnier." The feast was completed with some of Jean-Louis's pear *eau-de-vie*, which came in a glass jug corked with a rag so that it resembled a Molotov cocktail rather than fine country moonshine.

None of us was immune to so much wine and spirits, and for our midnight celebration, Halldor had brought skyrockets, of all things. He said that at New Year's midnight in his hometown of Reykjavík, the whole sky is a fountain of incendiary light. Halldor, professor of social anthropology and so a student of customs, is one of the most superstitious people I've ever met. In his mind, skyrockets at midnight were essential for good luck in the coming year. There was no escape; Icelandic rockets would hit Rogny on New Year's Eve.

Halldor armed himself with his formidable-looking skyrockets, and all of us, including Christabel, set off down the hill into the Bas-Bourg, four grown-up professionals out to make a public nuisance of ourselves. The village in winter is shuttered by seven in the evening. Even the town Christmas lights, in the shape of little comets over the street lamps, go off by eleven. The air that night was typically cold and misty. We passed the *mairie*, the pharmacy, and the school, with stenciled snowflakes visible in all its windows. We walked up the rue du Pont past the blacked-out Bar de Saint-Mathurin, the *boulangerie, la poste*, and the *coiffeur*. Finally, beyond the Quai Sully, we stood on the bridge over Henry IV's canal, where you can see the whole layout of the village—its island, bridges, locks, waterfalls. You can look up and see the shadowy childlike church on the hilltop.

On the bridge rebuilt after the German bombs, Halldor intently prepared his skyrocket barrage. I picked up Christabel and held her head against my chest, a hand over her ear. With a loud *phhht*, the first rocket shot up in a thin orange beam and popped into a globe of green-white light. Off went another and another, all of them greenish white. Then he set off a few innocuous Roman candles—red, white, green balls arcing off the bridge into the dark steamy water. The only other sound came from the waterfall under the Bridge of Donkeys, where Phyllis had taken a dozen photographs, always in the same pose, of Mary's father, that large man with the dragon-headed cane.

We returned to the presbytery, but Halldor hadn't finished

ensuring his good luck for the New Year. He set up more rockets on the terrace while Anne and Mary tried to stay warm with a blanket over their shoulders. Long ready for bed, they lingered on the stone steps of the garden door and watched Halldor explode the country silence. I worried that we'd end up setting Bougé's childhood home on fire since the rockets were reliably unpredictable. Sure enough, one went up only twenty feet before turning sideways, passing over the terrace wall, and exploding into one of our fruit trees. It was the old diseased cherry, with black peeling bark covered in moss. We'd watched a blue tit vanish last spring into the hollow heartwood, a nest inside. With a loud bang that echoed off the church, the tree was showered in green-white light, as if hit by a weapon in a cheap sci-fi film. Then the dark returned, and Burgundian winter mist, and the cold mossy odors of winter. A few dogs barked in the distance; Dan gave several muffled howls. I remember thinking that nothing would wake our village.